Reproduced on the front cover of this distinguished art book is an outstanding example of a style of painting called Abstract Expressionism. It was painted by Jackson Pollock, an American, who has had as much influence in the post-World War II international art world as did the French Impressionists in their day.

Abstract Expressionism is only one of the American schools analyzed by Mr. Hunter. And Pollock is only one of over thirty artists whose works are described. They include:

Sloan	Dove	Hopper
Henri	Marin	Shahn
Weber	Demuth	Gorky
Hartley	Burchfield	Motherwell

SAM HUNTER is Acting Director of The Minneapolis Institute of Arts. He is the author of books on Pollock, Miró, Mondrian, Picasso, and the sculptor David Smith. In the recent past he has lectured on art history at Barnard College and the University of California in Los Angeles. He was formerly an art critic for *The New York Times* as well as Associate Curator of Painting and Sculpture at the Museum of Modern Art in New York.

Modern American
Painting and Sculpture

by Sam Hunter

Acting Director,

The Minneapolis Institute of Arts

Laurel Edition

Published by
DELL PUBLISHING CO., INC.
750 Third Avenue
New York 17, N.Y.

© Copyright, 1959, by Sam Hunter

Laurel ® TM 674623, Dell Publishing Co., Inc.

Acknowledgments for the use of paintings
and sculpture, photographs of which are
incorporated in this volume, appear with
the respective pictures.

Cover paintings by Jackson Pollock and John Sloan

First printing—November, 1959
Second printing—November, 1960
Third printing—May, 1962
Fourth printing—September, 1963

Printed in U.S.A.

Dedication

For Emily Cara Hunter, age four

Acknowledgments

The author wishes to express his appreciation to the many collectors, museums and private galleries that have permitted him to reproduce their paintings and sculptures. To Bernard Karpel of the Museum of Modern Art library and to Charles McCurdy of the Pratt Institute library he owes a special debt for their bibliography and artists' biographies respectively.

Originally the author planned a book of wider scope, but with even greater emphasis on contemporary abstraction where his strongest sympathies perhaps obviously lie. Limitations in space, and the need to strike a workable balance between the past and the present, however, led him to reduce the contemporary section. For an expansion of the subject matter treated in the last three chapters the reader is referred to the author's section on American painting in *Art Since 1945;* the manuscript for that book was begun some time after the present text reached completion, but there were unavoidable delays in the publication of *Modern American Painting and Sculpture*.

With the permission of the publisher and author, chapter II appeared in essentially the same form as "The Eight—Insurgent Realists," *Art in America,* Fall, 1956; and chapter VII was published with minor modifications under the title "Jackson Pollock: The Maze and the Minotaur," *New World Writing,* 9th Mentor Selection, 1956.

Contents

Illustrations

Plate 36. Lassaw. *Monoceros*. 1952. Bronze, steel and chromium. Collection Mrs. Albert H. Newman, Chicago

Plate 37. Lipton. *The Cloak*. 1951. Bronze and steel. Private Collection, New York

Plate 38. Rothko. *Earth and Green*. 1956. Oil. Collection Mr. and Mrs. Ben Heller, New York

Plate 39. Guston. *The Clock*. 1957. Oil. The Museum of Modern Art, New York

Plate 40. Baziotes. *Red Landscape*. 1957. Oil. The Minneapolis Institute of Arts

Plate 41. Hare. *Sunset II*. 1953. Bronze and steel. Courtesy Samuel M. Koòtz Gallery, New York

Plate 42. Still. *Number 2*. 1949. Oil. Collection Mr. and Mrs. Ben Heller, New York

Plate 43. Tworkov. *Pink Mississippi*. 1954. Oil. Courtesy Stable Gallery, New York

Plate 44. Gottlieb. *Frozen Sounds II*. 1952. Oil. Albright Art Gallery, Buffalo

Plate 45. Brooks. *Gordian 1957*. 1957. Oil. Courtesy Stable Gallery, New York

Plate 46. Frankenthaler. *Eden*. 1956. Oil. Courtesy Tibor De Nagy Gallery, New York

Plate 47. Hartigan. *Billboard*. 1957. Oil. The Minneapolis Institute of Arts

Plate 48. Cornell. *Pavilion*. 1953. Painted wood, pasted paper, glass. Collection Mr. and Mrs. Herbert Ferber, New York

ERRATA

Plate 3: The year of Maurice Prendergast's death should be 1924 rather than 1923.

Plate 3: *Acadia* should read *Arcadia*.

Plate 8: Stanton MacDonald-Wright should be Stanton Macdonald-Wright.

Plate 11: The year of John Marin's death should be 1953 rather than 1955.

Plate 39: For "Sidney Janis Gallery" read "The Museum of Modern Art."

Plate 42: Clifford Still should be Clyfford Still.

1

The Usable Past

"We are at that dramatic moment in our national life wherein we tremble evenly between decay and evolution, . . . That the forces of decadence predominate in quantity there can be no doubt. . . . That there is in our national life, in the genius of our people, a fruitful germ, and that there are a handful who perceive this, is likewise beyond question."

—Louis Sullivan, *Kindergarten Chats,* 1901

It is a measure of the powerful pressures of American provincialism that the story of the modern spirit in art in the nineteenth century was a chronicle of lonely and defeated ventures against academic orthodoxy, Puritan prohibitions and the timid proprieties of the "genteel tradition" by a few unusual and courageous artists. Our great triad of native painters near the close of the century, Thomas Eakins, Albert Ryder and Winslow Homer, stand out distinctly from the art scene by reason of their proud, stern independence. In their separate and distinguished styles these men found viable native idioms. Homer created an epic of the American out-of-doors; Eakins pursued an unpopular naturalism; Ryder, a contemplative, visionary art. They created no movements or schools, and more often than not public hostility or indifference rewarded their efforts to delineate truthfully the American experience as they felt it. Homer and Eakins stood apart, too, in that they had followed the course of European art, and arrived independently at a form of *plein air* painting. But America was not ready for even such elementary affirmations, which it regarded with the suspicion usually reserved in that period for political radicalism. Only in the twentieth century did these struggles produce a sustained, collective artistic effort which could meet the challenge of modern life and bring American culture into the international mainstream.

In the interval, the sequence of our art was highly individualistic and erratic. Strange hiatuses appeared within the body of progressive painting; Impressionism and Post-Impressionism were only superficially explored, long after the mood that helped produce them in Europe had passed. Eakins's personal campaign for naturalism enlisted virtually no critical or artistic support at home, although by European standards the style was no longer revolutionary, and continental painters were preoccupied with more complex pictorial problems. How could one expect Eakins, who had spent four years in Paris during the great formative years of early Impressionism, to welcome and investigate the most advanced styles of his time when his attempts to establish first principles of candor and seriousness even under the banner of naturalism were to meet violent opposition?

Realism did not arrive officially until the early twentieth century, on the wings of political progressivism and with the awakening on a national scale of the reform spirit. The new dispensation was short-lived, however, and the realists were soon briskly dispatched to the American attic of obsolescence by a more radical modernism. The realist discoverers of the American scene themselves scarcely had the opportunity to enjoy their victory before abstract painting styles made their innovations as outmoded as last year's Ford. The reasons for the skittish evolution of our art, which moved from a state of uncritical provincialism to a self-conscious, contemporary sophistication in a few brief years, must be sought in the changing character of American life. The modern spirit advanced and retreated with the mood of the times. It was precipitated finally in significant artistic productions by our rapid industrial expansion, and by the same economic and social forces which so profoundly transformed American life, thought and manners after the Civil War.

In 1900 America could look back on an amazing half-century of progress during which the nation had been capitalized on an unprecedented scale, vast fortunes amassed, and a whole new urban, industrial population created. In a very short time, the conflicts and inequities brought by our heady industrial growth were to be expressed in an art and literature of protest, under the aegis of naturalism. But as the country stood poised uncertainly between the old order and a new emerging metropolitan culture, and as the contradictions in American life deepened, the whole motive for the new era—a growing sentiment for radical reform—was momentarily lost in a wave of renewed business confidence. The boundless and infectious self-assurance of a prospering business community seemed to have closed the gate firmly on social change and on the stirrings of agrarian protest that had been set off by the depression of the mid-nineties. Populism and agrarian grievance, which had inspired the first primitive realism of Hamlin Garland and other western writers, were deflated as issues by the Alaskan gold rush and the disappearance of the free silver issue. Bryan's defeat in 1896, and then the fulfillment of American imperialist ambitions in Cuba, cut away the underpinnings of Populist dissent and converted an emerging literature of protest from a utopianism which questioned the fundamental economic relationships of American society, to a more pragmatic social criticism which was at the same time more effective and less basic. Since a consciousness of vital social issues had anyway never deeply penetrated art, painting merely prolonged its provincial idyl as a relaxed America contemplated the green and lovely prospects of endless prosperity and unlimited opportunity. The irrepressible Age of Confidence had reached full tide.

"I find America so cheerful, and so full of swagger and self-satisfaction, that I hardly know it," Henry Adams marveled and complained in a letter of 1900. "The change since 1893 is startling. . . ." In its leading editorial on the first day of the new century, *The New York Times* reflected the national mood of complacent optimism, describing the year past as an *annus mirabilis* in business and production, and anticipating even more remarkable performances in the one ahead. That same year some sort of apogee was reached when J. P. Morgan and Andrew Carnegie (the multimillionaire who began life as a $1.20-a-week bobbin boy) began negotiations for the formation of the world's biggest corporation, United States Steel.

In a country where the worship of bigness was deep in the temper of the time, art objects were being accumulated on the same colossal scale as the new fortunes. The business plutocrats continued that wholesale appropriation of European art which was eventually to flood the country with truckloads of horrible bric-a-brac and ornament, and, almost incidentally, to enrich our national museums with old masters. For their homes, in keeping with their public eminence, the *nouveau riche* chose expensive vulgar imitations of grand European residences: the *schloss, château* and *palazzo*. It was the time of the craze for the emblems of European magnificence and power. According to one critic, the most fashionable architect of the Gilded Age, Richard Morris Hunt, was kept busy building Fifth Avenue French *châteaux* on the order of the resplendent Vanderbilt home at the corner of Fifty-Second Street, "while less eminent rivals were designing Rhine castles for brewers, or weird combinations of architectural souvenirs—an eclecticism that reached its climax in a brilliant design, unfortunately not executed, for a building exhibiting a different historical style on every story."

One of the few who dared question the prevailing tastes which so transparently reflected the yearning for showy, *nouveau-riche* trappings was the architect, Louis Sullivan: "Must I show you," he wrote mockingly, "this French *château*, this little *Château de Blois,* on this street corner here in New York, and still you do not laugh? Must you wait until you see a *gentleman* in a silk hat come out of it before you laugh? Have you no sense of humor, no sense of pathos? Must I tell you that while the man may live in the house physically (for a man may live in any kind of house, physically), that he cannot possibly live in it morally, mentally, or spiritually, that he and his home are a paradox, a contradiction, an absurdity, a characteristically New York absurdity; that he is no part of the house, and his house is no part of him?"

The more fanciful forms of private bad taste had their counterpart in the general stylistic anarchy and indifferent standards of public decoration. In words that were to remain unhappily apropos for the next half-century, a sensitive critic, James Jackson Jarves, wrote in 1864: "In America, the present is an epoch of monstrous plaster figures, daubed with crazy paint; of mammoth cast-iron washbasins called fountains; of cast-iron architecture and clumsy gateways to public parks; of shoddy portrait statues and inane ideal ones; of ornaments, pictures and sculptures made to gull and sell."

The decades after the Civil War, indeed, were the dark ages of American taste, a period during which resistance to the gathering forces of modernism was expressed both by its ostentatious vulgarizations and by its shy withdrawals into a negative estheticism and refinement. The Gilded Age's uninhibited extravagance at least caught something of the energy of the times, but the other side of the coin was a spirit of esthetic discouragement. It was reflected in the stubborn adherence to dead traditional forms in architecture when a robust, native style of building had emerged and its much maligned champions were crying to be heard, and hired. Characteristic, too, was the vogue for painters like Sargent and Whistler whose styles, whatever their other merits, were unvital, aristocratic, European in the fashionable sense—another symptom of the flight from the vulgar American present. Collectors and patrons also joined the conspiracy of fashion against a distressing, problematic present by concentrating their purchases in the old masters, whose values were certified and sure.

Many of the most discerning and cultivated critics were ultimately impotent before their prejudice against their own times. They were "apostles" of old world culture in the New World. Charles Eliot Norton, the last of the Boston Brahmins; art critic and collector James Jackson Jarves who formed the famous group of Italian primitives now at Yale University; and the painters William Morris Hunt and John La Farge had dedicated themselves in their varied ways to the task of broadening American civilization by making intelligible and accessible great areas of the European and

Oriental artistic past. In the living American present, however, they could discern only the negative aspects of democratic vulgarity and anarchy. They expressed their fear of modern life, of a present and future in which Norton, for one, could only envision "outbreak after outbreak of passion and violence," by taking refuge in a refined estheticism and cultivating a new traditionalism. Their writings and art re-established contact with the Renaissance, the late medieval and Oriental past, as if they hoped to exorcise the noisy age of progress and the irrevocably changed conditions of modern life. Such nostalgia put our spokesmen for sensibility and esthetic values as much out of touch with the vital elements in American life as did the pretentious taste of the *nouveau-riche* vulgarians.

Lewis Mumford has described the post-bellum years as "The Brown Decades," delineating an era that began in mourning at Lincoln's funeral and took its general coloration from "the smut of industrialism." To extend his figure, "brown" was also the deepening hue of discouragement and defeatism in the genteel tradition, was reflected in the décor of both fashionable and popular life, and was repeated, too, in the palette of American art. After the fifties brownstone caught the public fancy in New York building; and brown, or dark, lugubrious interiors were characteristic—interiors that denied light with their window hangings of double thickness, maroon wallpapers and massive walnut suites upholstered in red plush. How remote from the fresh and intense colors of French Impressionism which accorded with a modern spirit of hopefulness and freedom, was the sober palette of the period's significant American art! A Rembrandtesque gloom, half pensiveness, half resignation, darkens the atmosphere of Thomas Eakins's forthright realism. The golden dreams of Ryder, Inness and Blakelock are fogged by rich brown varnishes, and a crepuscular and elegaic mood steals over romantic painting of the period. The morning freshness of Winslow Homer's first significant style of outdoor painting, around 1866, emerged from a duskier academicism. But in later years he returned to a more sober, autumnal palette. In its first flush of youth, modern American painting managed to look prematurely mellow and time-worn.

The prevailing murkiness and obscurities of American art after the Civil War, and its romantic introspections, were in part the result of a creative tradition dominated by transcendental and subjective elements, mistrustful of any hedonism. But the romantic resignation of our art, so out of tune with the blatant energies of a growing, prosperous land, also registered an esthetic uncertainty. The critic Frank Jewett Mather held the times responsible for the mood of doubt he saw mirrored in Eakins's art. It was a moment, he wrote, "of hesitation. Darwin, Huxley, Herbert, Spencer, and Matthew Arnold were novelties, presenting urgent problems, which thinking people had to cope with. Everything in belief, and much in practice, had to be radically reconstructed, with a dire off-chance that only destruction was possible. There had been no time to think it through, nor yet to adopt the defeatist policy of letting it alone. . . . His gift was to understand a generation, seeking grimly to find itself, and saddened by an uncertain quest." That same "uncertain quest," however, produced quite positive liberations in continental painting which somehow were stifled or distorted into egocentric dreams and romantic fancies during the same period in America. The heightened sensations of French Impressionist painting dramatize by contrast the sobriety of contemporary artistic modes in America. The best American art did not offend so flagrantly as those earlier landscape schools on the continent which Ruskin had censured for seeming "to look at nature through a black looking glass." But the dark cast of romantic sentiment and yearnings was not to be dislodged readily from American painting in the last decades of the century.

It was perhaps only fitting that the modern spirit should most vigorously proclaim itself first in Chicago, and not in painting or sculpture, but in architecture. Advances in technology brought the possibility of the steel-frame skyscraper and with it, new constructional problems and solutions. Indeed, brutal industrial necessity was the mother of radical engineering techniques and esthetic invention.

These in turn bore directly on the great revolution in taste which America was soon to experience. That these solutions, and the new sense of building for human needs and comforts they embodied, emerged in Chicago, the symbolic industrial and metropolitan center of the nineties, was also appropriate. The dynamic growth of that city and the social evils attendant on its rapid industrialization called forth new critical and creative energies. "Chicago," wrote Louis Sullivan in *Kindergarten Chats* in 1901, "is young, clumsy, foolish; its architectural sins are unstable, captious and fleeting; it can pull itself down and rebuild itself in a generation, if it will. It has done and can do great things when the mood is on. There can be no new New York, but there may be a new Chicago."

Around Chicago formed the "modern movement" in architecture. The ground had been prepared by Henry Hobson Richardson in the East, where after 1880 and until his death six years later he achieved a plain severity of style that was the parallel in architecture of the stern realism of Thomas Eakins. Richardson's expression, its sobriety notwithstanding, had distinct romantic overtones evoked by his heavy courses of rough-finished stone, and a certain medievalism in idiom. He died as the transition from masonry to steel-and-glass was being made. Despite its refreshing simplicity, his style still preserved the load-bearing wall which disguises rather than clarifies the functional aspects of the building and its frame. The plainness of his neo-Romanesque forms and the coherence of his style, however, paved the way for a new mood of independence in American building. Like Eakins's efforts at an objective realism, Richardson's structures were the first indication of a new spirit of objectivity in the arts.

In the late eighties and nineties, the office buildings and department stores of LeBaron Jenney, Holabird and Roche, Burnham and Root, and of the Richardson disciple, Louis Sullivan, gave the middle west a "functionalist" renaissance in building. Chicago became the birthplace of the steel-skeleton skyscraper and of the wholly original modern idiom developed first by Sullivan and then by his pupil, Frank Lloyd Wright. The pioneers of the modern movement unfortunately also received their first severe setback on native ground at the Chicago World's Fair of 1893. That fair was dominated by the suave Beaux-Arts classicism of McKim, Mead and White and the revivalist idioms of other fashionable, shallow eclectics of the period. "[The Exposition of 1893] condemned American architecture to the imitative and the derivative for another generation," Henry Steele Commager wrote recently in *The American Mind*. Only Sullivan's Transportation Building with its daring Golden Portal gave any indication of vital new directions in American architecture at the celebrated and influential exposition.

With the more enterprising pioneers like Richardson and Root dead, Sullivan and his pupil Wright almost single-handedly carried the burden of the new spirit in the decade after the Chicago Exposition. Sullivan had a Whitman-esque devotion to democracy and identified its ideals of freedom with modernism; he was an eloquent, if solitary, spokesman for the new principles of building which he formulated around the hard core of functionalism. His forceful and eloquent writing place him as America's first apostle of a revolutionary modernism. Where other sensitive men had shrunk from the materialism and technological realities of the age of progress, Sullivan embraced them in the belief that the new social conditions thus produced deserved a new and challenging artistic style, a creative expression that would fulfill the needs of a period of drastic change. Sullivan's theorizing, poetizing and, best of all, his actual building, represented the same search for some new esthetic fundamentalism that animated the art of the French Post-Impressionist painters in the same epoch; it was opposed to the retrospective, romantic mood of the more popular turn-of-the-century styles in art and architecture. American painting or sculpture of the period offers no esthetic radicalism comparable to Louis Sullivan's.

In the "tall office building" Sullivan found an exalted symbol of the modern spirit. "It must be," he wrote, "every inch a proud and soaring thing, rising in [such] sheer exultation that from bottom to top it is a unit without a single dissenting line—that is the new, the unexpected, the eloquent peroration of the most bald, most sinister, most forbidding conditions." And by the character of its buildings, he warned, posterity would judge society's creative health and its happiness: "What people are within, the buildings express without; and inversely, what the buildings are objectively is a sure index of what the people are subjectively. In the light of this dictum, the unhappy, irrational, heedless, pessimistic, unlovely, distracted and decadent structures which make up the great bulk of our contemporaneous architecture point with infallible accuracy to qualities in the heart and mind and soul of the American people that are unhappy." Five years later, in 1901, Sullivan's estimate of the situation in architecture perfectly summed up the crisis in the fine arts. "We are at that dramatic moment in our national life," he wrote, "wherein we tremble between decay and evolution, and our architecture, with strange fidelity, reflects this equipoise. That the forces of decadence predominate in quantity there can be no doubt. . . . That there is in our national life, in the genius of our people, a fruitful germ, and that there are a handful who perceive this, is likewise beyond question."

The forms of literature and art responded less readily to the pressures of technology than those of architecture; and changes in artistic methods faced perhaps even stronger resistance than Sullivan encountered after the Chicago Fair. During the interregnum of conservatism which lasted from Bryan's defeat in 1896 to the emergence of muckraking agitation under Theodore Roosevelt, the nation was in a complacent and self-congratulatory mood. It was the era of the Gibson Girl, of Richard Harding Davis, and of adventure fiction and historical confectionery in the novel. As the human distress produced by an unrestrained industrial colossus became more acute and began to press on the American consciousness, art and literature became more frivolous and vacant of serious content. The crudest fantasies of immaturity were given credence in writing that glorified success, romantic exploits in far-off places and a state of eternal innocence and youth. The very real and present terrors of the economic struggle—those conditions that

Louis Sullivan described as "most bald, most sinister, most forbidding"—would soon be uncovered in the realist novels of Frank Norris, Stephen Crane and Theodore Dreiser. But they were brushed aside for the moment, as the century of hope breathed its last and the Gilded Age enjoyed a final flourish.

Dreiser's *Sister Carrie* was published in 1900, and immediately suppressed as too sordid and "pornographic" because it honestly described the compromising relationships into which a member of the new urban proletariat was compelled by economic circumstances beyond her control. Dreiser's treatment was straightforward and objective without any touch of sensationalism or grossness, but his revelation of some bitter truths of the battle for survival was unacceptable to Americans who preferred the lie of the Age of Innocence. When Dreiser was being spurned and attacked, popular reading consisted of Horatio Alger's success stories and such romantic delectations as Charles Major's *When Knighthood Was in Flower*. The more literate turned to *The Century* and similar strongholds of gentility whose editors took care never to sully their pages with the more unpleasant facts of contemporary existence. In the hands of *The Century's* long-time editor, Richard Watson Gilder, the genteel tradition was safe. Gilder had the dubious distinction of rejecting Stephen Crane's early venture in realism, *Maggie;* he once confessed, too, that he had edited the indelicacies out of *Huckleberry Finn;* and at another time he refused to receive Robert Louis Stevenson in the magazine's offices on the strength of rumors questioning the author's respectability.

In painting such exaggerated prudishness was equally insidious. It was Eakins's candor and scientific objectivity that led to his dismissal from a teaching post at the powerful Pennsylvania Academy in 1886, after he defied local taboos by posing nude male and female models together in an anatomy demonstration. Walt Whitman, a close friend of the painter, once said of Eakins: "I never knew of but one artist, and that's Tom Eakins, who could resist the temptation to see what they think they ought to rather than what is." Eakins's naturalism had posed a threat to decorum, as it was understood in polite Philadelphia art circles, ever since 1875 when he dared paint objectively a surgical operation, accurate even to the surgeon's bloody hands. *The Gross Clinic,* masterpiece of Eakins's youth, was howled down in the press as a "degradation of art." One critic savagely attacked the artist because he succeeded in his intention of creating a convincing impression of actuality: ". . . as for people with nerves and stomachs, the scene is so real that they might as well go to a dissecting room and have done with it."

The fear that truth to life threatened the traditional dignity of painting was in the background of much nineteenth-century criticism. Such views stemmed from the position of privilege given by official art to the ideal stereotypes of an outworn classicism. A cosier expression of the same prejudice was the Victorian concept that art consisted of "beautiful things seen beautifully." As a consequence, art in America revolved around a sterile vogue for sugary anecdote; picturesque landscape, grandiose in dimension and elevated in sentiment; or a spurious classicism based on French Academy prototypes. Paintings in these categories could be counted on to receive the most flattering wall positions and took all the prizes at the various Academy annuals. When Eakins proposed to paint what he actually knew and what could be verified by the senses, he violated the most sacrosanct canons of contemporary art. "The business of art," a critic of the period had rather pompously intoned, in defense of the genteel taste, "is to afford joyance . . . what a shame it is the great gifts of expression should ever be wasted on heinous and joyless subjects."

That such a feeble idealism did not altogether dominate our culture was due to the persistence of a more vigorous and hardheaded tradition of empirical thought whose forms were being extended and infused with new content appropriate to the times by such pioneering spirits as Louis Sullivan, and indeed, Thomas Eakins. The need to relate art to actual American life had already been recognized and eloquently expressed as early as mid-century by Emerson when he wrote: "We do not with sufficient plainness or sufficient profoundness address ourselves to life, nor dare we chant our times and social circumstances. . . . Banks and tariffs, the newspaper and the caucus, Methodism and Unitarianism, are flat and dull to dull people, but rest on the same foundations of wonder, as the town of Troy, and the temple of Delphos, and are as swiftly passing away." By 1880 the critic W. Mackay Laffan could rather more irreverently express the growing sense of the validity of the commonplace American reality: "There be more joy over one honest and sincere American horse pond, over one truthful and dirty tenement, over one unaffected sugar refinery, over one vulgar but unostentatious coal wharf than there shall be over ninety and nine mosques of St. Sophia, Golden Horns, Normandy cathedrals, and all the rest of the holy conventionalities and orthodox bosh." Its downright, colloquial language and preference for the humble, unvarnished American thing over the grandest European artifact give this statement an authentic Whitman ring. Behind it were new but as yet unfocused artistic attitudes: an affirmation of the American experience, accepted in all its rawness; and the rejection of European authority. It was not until the next century, however, that there appeared an entire school of artists dedicated to the ideal that the artist must paint the life he knew best if a genuine American art were to develop.

In the intervening years the impact of American thought and American life on art was less important than the awakening among artists of a new interest in European painting. Quickened by contacts with Rome, Düsseldorf, Munich and Paris during the last three decades of the century, a number of American painters besides Homer and Eakins had begun to seek more sophisticated viewpoints and techniques. In the seventies William Chase, Frank Duveneck and Abbott Thayer were linked with Eakins in a loose association known as "The New Movement." For a time Düsseldorf and then Munich, with its more sentimental adaptions of French naturalist styles, became the fashionable foreign center for American art pilgrims. Frank Duveneck established a school in Munich in 1878 and many young Americans, later known as "the Duveneck boys," came to study. Duveneck based his style on the bravura brushwork and dark palette of the Bavarian painter, Wilhelm Liebl, who in turn had been influenced by Hals and the early Manet. Despite the obvious appeal of the Munich style to shallow technicians, the new manner nonetheless embodied a more liberal spirit than much of the art current in America. One of "the Duveneck boys" was John Twachtman who later turned to Impressionism after the Munich style had been discredited for its "brown sauce" and emphasis on "technique for technique's sake." Twachtman joined Childe Hassam, J. Alden Weir and other artists in 1898 to form an Impressionist group called "The Ten"; and Ernest Lawson, a Twachtman pupil, later became a charter member of the twentieth century's first band of rebel realists, "The Eight."

The protest against current academic practices by the Munich-trained painters and then by "The Ten" had been rare instances of organized American protest in the latter half of the nineteenth century, a period that in France had been rich in examples of artistic truancy. In this country, the problem of re-creating those successive phases of revolution which punctuated modern European art was a difficult one. During the Brown Decades, provincial tastes and prevailing academic styles presented serious obstacles to the artist who wished to experiment with new and progressive ideas. The absence of continuous and profound visual traditions was equally discouraging. Hypothetically, the artist in America had greater freedom of choice than the European, but actually he found it more difficult to forge new idioms, there being so few examples of high creativeness in his own past to support original ventures. While the academic caste in America was relatively new and far less powerful than its French counterpart, our visual traditions as a whole were impoverished; provincial eccentricity in an art of little consequence, or a shallow imitation of the more conventional European modes were the usual results of our illusory condition of freedom.

Everything conspired, it seems, to give America a minor role in the fine arts during the late nineteenth century. Even the independent position of Eakins, Ryder and Homer was somewhat compromised at the end of their careers when they accepted membership in the most august, official art body, the National Academy of Design. Revolutions in art were absorbed or deflected before they had had the opportunity to gather momentum, in part because the division between "official" art and advanced art was never altogether clear. Advanced art, as the Duveneck boys practiced it in the eighties, was woefully backward in relation to contemporary France, and it had only an academic interest in America by the following decade. At that, the new generation of American realists relied heavily on the Duveneck pictorial formula, a style which originated with the French *avant-garde* back in the 1860s.

Our history of organized artistic protest had not been an inspiring one. Sometimes it seemed indeed that revolts were made only to provide new opportunities for defections. An excellent example was William Merritt Chase. He had been associated with Eakins in "The New Movement" of the seventies, and a leading spirit in the formation of the Society of American Artists in 1877, which set out to free painters from the stuffy attitudes and restrictive exhibition policies of the powerful National Academy. But by 1892 the Society had also become parochial, when it forced Eakins's resignation by refusing to exhibit his *Agnew Clinic* on the grounds of "his neglect of the beauties and graces of painting." Chase himself later became the prime apostle of *le morçeau bien fait*, or the well-turned detail, and, from an exalted teaching post at the Art Students League, one of the main custodians of a conservative traditionalism. In time he would be the very symbol of artistic reaction against which the new generation of realists made their revolt. The Society of American Artists, in which Chase played the dominating role, closed the final chapter of progressive nineteenth-century art by disbanding and merging with the National Academy in 1906. It was left to a group of young insurgents to revive the moribund spirit of rebellion and give new substance to a neglected ideal of independents exhibitions.

2

Insurgent Realists

"It is not necessary to paint the American flag to be an American painter. As if you didn't see the American scene every time you opened your eyes."

—John Sloan

The elements of progressivism in art, which had repeatedly been underground or converted to a genteel academicism by the pressures of provincialism and Victorian prudishness in the decades after the Civil War, erupted after 1904. In Theodore Roosevelt's second term a new spirit of insurgence seized the American imagination, as national interest was focused on reform. Writers and artists suddenly came out into the open to take up the cause of the common man against organized corporate power and abuses of privilege. Painters awoke to the teeming life of the streets and found a new sympathy for the oppressed humanity of our industrial centers. It was characteristic that in the period of "exposé" journalism and the "exposé" fiction of the naturalists, progressive painting should be in the hands of a group of newspaper-trained, artist-journalists. There was a certain naïve romanticism and boyish opportunism in the manner in which these new painters, and even such new writers as Jack London, assumed reformist attitudes. The Rooseveltian appetite for life, which helped free them from a stagnant past, was refreshing and salutary. But it was shallow, too; sheer gusto did not promise to be the most durable basis for art.

The new movement in painting was not, however, so directly concerned with radical politics or the class struggle as was literature, and on the whole substituted a spirit of irony or humor for the moral indignation and reforming zeal of the naturalist writers. Mainly, it was an expression of an awakened sense of life and of the need to be more direct and open-hearted. Although later identified with the New York scene, it first centered around Philadelphia, and many of its participants had studied at the Pennsylvania Academy with Thomas Anschutz, the pupil of Thomas Eakins.

Spokesman and champion of the group of rebels was Robert Henri, perhaps the most vital and influential artistic personality of his day. In the words of John Sloan, who later acknowledged Henri as his "father in art," his message was "making pictures from life." For Henri, "life" became the operative word in his vocabulary; it referred not so much to the artist's objective recording of something in the external world as the inward sensation of "being alive," achieved through the exercise of the craft of painting. Henri pleaded for the viability of the emotions, and his appeal was in line with a growing sentiment of freedom which was rapidly undercutting the stuffy Victorian outlook. "Because we are saturated with life, because we are human," he wrote later in *The Art Spirit,* "our strongest motive is life, humanity; and the stronger the motive back of a line, the stronger, and therefore more beautiful, the line will be. . . . It isn't the subject that counts but what you feel about it."

Henri had studied two years at the Pennsylvania Academy under Anschutz, and then repaired to Paris where in 1888 he entered a conventional Beaux-Arts studio of the Academy. The academic productions of Paris seemed sterile and unpromising, and he, like most Frenchmen, was at a loss before late Impressionism and unfamiliar with Post-Impressionist painting. In the late eighties and in the nineties, the Post-Impressionism of Cézanne, Van Gogh and Gauguin was known by a very small, select circle in Paris. Only with the great private and salon retrospectives of Van Gogh in 1901 and 1905, of Gauguin in 1903 and 1906, and of Cézanne in 1906 and 1907, did the new generation in Paris experience at first hand those major innovations in color and form which were to be the direct inspiration of Fauvism and Cubism.

In the early "Spanish" Manet, in Hals and in Velásquez, Henri found both a simple pictorial formula and, in the first two artists, a sympathetic taste for picturesque subject matter. There was often a certain gypsy quality about Henri's choice of subjects. The formula Henri finally arrived at was no more or less daring than Duveneck's, although his themes were less conventional. Like so many late-nineteenth-century painters he worked in the vein of what Frank Jewett Mather has called Manet's "dark Impressionism." Naturalism with vivacity of surface execution would be a more exact description of the manner for it involved little of the Impressionists' analytical methods or their spirit of objectivity. It was pre-Impressionist painting; the expression of the artist's interest in subject matter bulked larger than any objective technical system. In Henri's art there was little hint of those optical and plastic "sensations" that were at the core of French Impressionism. Nor was he aware of the most dynamic elements in the art of Manet or the radical painters of the decades of the sixties and seventies. Their focus on artistic method at the expense of representation, their atomization of the world of appearances—the rude beginnings of "the recollection by painting of its own particular means," that generic characteristic of all "modern" art—were to result in the denial of naturalistic illusion altogether in the twentieth century, a tendency Henri could not understand and later bitterly opposed.

Still, it isn't quite just to isolate the backwardness of Henri's methods as a phenomenon peculiar to America. Even in France around the turn of the century and until 1905 there was a relaxation in styles and painting was ridden by archaisms. Matisse around 1901 repudiated the bright colors of Neo-Impressionism and returned to a "dark" manner based on Courbet and early Manet. In the first years of the new century Picasso painted in dark tonalities and then in pervasive blues a depressed subject matter of fringe bohemian life. Not until Fauvist painting erupted in 1905, with its brilliant, fresh color, heightened sensations and expressive freedom of handling was there any painting that corresponded to twentieth-century man's new sense of liberation and optimism. Once the Fauves had emancipated painting, however, contemporary American techniques seemed woefully retarded and obsolete.

The methods and styles of the realists could not be regarded as innovations, in any case. Their spirit of insurgence and desire to address art to life was the real substance of their radicalism. That in itself was enough to assure them a tortuous, uphill climb to recognition.

On that ascent Henri kept the younger painters' morale up and acted as a living catalyst for their art, encouraging them to paint seriously and keeping them abreast of at least the more conservative European tendencies. In 1891 Henri returned from abroad to teach at the Pennsylvania Academy. It was then that he met the group of young artist-illustrators who had been working for Edward Davis, the father of Stuart Davis and art director on the *Philadelphia Press*. These were William Glackens, George Luks, Everett Shinn and John Sloan. Henri imparted to his young disciples a new cosmopolitan spirit, urged them to travel abroad and to choose the medium of oil painting over illustration, or at least to combine the two vocations. In 1904 he set up a school of his own in New York City's Lincoln Arcade, a Latin Quarter district on upper Broadway. There gathered all the rebels against the American genteel tradition, the Philadelphia artists who had followed Henri to New York, and others like George Bellows and Glenn O. Coleman who would also associate themseves with the new realism.

The Philadelphia group were highly varied in individual temperament and even in their styles. Glackens and Shinn were the worldings, naturally drawn to society and the life of fashion which they nevertheless rendered in their early work with an abundance of life and zest. After a year in Paris in the mid-nineties Glackens had worked in a muted, Whistlerian landscape idiom. And then, with the examples of Henri and of Parisian painting of the sixties in mind, he had begun to paint in a dark, robust manner that suggests Daumier, the early Manet and the romantic Cézanne. *On the Quai,* in the collection of the Kraushaar Gallery, New York, is the promising if rudimentary beginning, not

so much of realism, curiously enough, but of an assimilation of the more vital continental painting modes of the
previous generation. There was, however, too much ground
for Glackens to retrace and in too short a space of time;
and there were many distractions and pressures in the
American social scene. As a result he made do with an
elementary, reportorial realism rather than probe the medium of painting more deeply, in the analytical European
spirit.

After Glackens had served his apprenticeship with the
Philadelphia Press, and following his Paris sojourn, he went
to Cuba, in 1898, along with George Luks, to cover the
Spanish-American War. Upon his return to New York, he
began drawing its street scenes with more directness, finding
the pushcarts, crowds and tenements a stimulating new
source of subject matter. He became most celebrated for his
festive paintings of human groups in a holiday mood, and
for such scenes of fashionable life as *Chez Mouquin* (Plate
4). Around 1910 the tempo of the realists' response to life
slackened, and they began to strain after "style" and a more
authoritative pictorialism. Glackens succumbed to a sac-
charine formula derived from Renoir that in time approached commercial magazine illustration.

Something of the same pattern may be discerned in the
evolution of Shinn's art. He submitted to European modes
of the past, applying them in a lively if somewhat derivative
fashion to the American scene. Degas was his greatest inspiration, and like the French master, Shinn found his most
sympathetic subject matter in the theater's world of illusion.
He showed performers caught in a moment of action under
the lights, or fashionable theater-goers descending from
their carriages beside a bright marquee, often with an ash
can or disheveled looking passers-by in the background. His
themes seemed to exhaust themselves with repetition, and
in later years he devoted himself doggedly to re-creating his
early subjects in pastel. These sadly lacked fresh observation and were little better than pedestrian illustration.

Everett Shinn was the dandy of the realists, with many
friends in the theater and in society. Perhaps it was his taste
for luxury in conjunction with the realism of his art that

attracted Theodore Dreiser, for he was said to be the model
for the painter Eugene Witla in Dreiser's novel about a
realist artist, *The Genius*. In that novel the painter is remarkable, but still credible, realizing both his "artistic
ambition to create truthful images of the world about him,
and his vainest dreams of power in the commercial world as
a celebrated publishing potentate. Witla is finally corrupted
by power and all but destroyed by ruthless commercialism.
After a number of bitter experiences, he recovers his first
moment of truth by returning successfully to painting, producing works that seem to shout: "I'm dirty, I'm commonplace, I am grim, I am shabby, but I am life." Dreiser's
novel interests us now not so much for its inexorable demonstration of the destructiveness of the American success-wor-
ship but because he could conceive of an artist equally com-
fortable and equally effective in the studio and at the reins
of a powerful business establishment. Eugene Witla embodies a certain romanticism about the possible social role
of the artist which in an oblique way must explain the
realist painters' failure to reach more radical pictorial solutions. With so much of their artistic personalities absorbed
by life, they were unable to proceed to a serious investigation of the more demanding formal problems of art.

Famous for his tall tales and bombast, George Luks was
the most colorful figure among the new realists, and perhaps
best projected the boyish romanticism of the Roosevelt era.
He was trained in Düsseldorf where he joined the cult of the
slashing brush, studied at the Pennsylvania Academy, served
as a war correspondent in Cuba and did a prodigious
amount of newspaper illustration before his paintings began
to sell. Technically, Luks, like Henri, found his inspiration
in the direct painting tradition of Manet, Hals, and Velásquez. Hals' earthy themes, good humor and animal spirits
especially appealed to Luks, but he applied Hals to the
American scene with a curiously anachronistic effect. For
despite the Dutch master's sympathies for common people,
his art always retains the stamp of aristocratic style. When
Hals was circumspect or impressionistic to a degree in his
handling and registered his subjects broadly as merry types,
he was expressing the prerogative of his patron class. He

was responsible to the ruling burghers of Holland and reproduced, in a sense, their pleasure in the spectacle of common life. His art implies an hierarchical social order, and his more raffish tavern scenes, like Shakespeare's low-comedy incidents, are designed as relief to the procession of upper-class life. Life presented itself to Luks, on the other hand, in less schematized fashion, and he necessarily identified himself with his dirty street gamins, athletes in violent action, scenes of the Gansevoort Docks in winter, or drew on his childhood in the Pennsylvania mining country for subject matter. In the circumstances of contemporary painting, this work achieved a fresh impact; yet, like Henri's, his rather dashing style always seemed superimposed on its content and was never free of artificiality.

In the search for viable styles, the realists had little enough in their own past to consult. Even those artists whom they had come to recognize for their distinct American qualities were of no immediate use to them. The tradition of popular illustration and genre painting, given a variety of individual inflections by Caleb Bingham, William Sidney Mount and Winslow Homer, was hopelessly dated; Eakins's realism with its passionate scientific concern for form seemed pedantic; and the crude artisanship and contemplative strain of Ryder's painting scarcely suited the new age of energy. Drawing on the European past instead, Luks, Henri and other realists apparently fixed on painting idioms of maximum informality to convey in the most direct, elementary way their pleasure in everyday reality. Yet they strained, too, for authority of style, in a hallowed European sense. Despite their insistent talk that art should be informal, democratic and viable in human terms, they were extremely conscious of their artistic posture, and perhaps unwittingly invested their ideal of the artist with attributes of the superman. Henri spoke of the vocation of art as fit only for "commanding" and "energetic" personalities; Luks was a supreme egoist. Such behavior was perhaps a backhanded admission of the high seriousness of the life of art, of what Henry James called its "sacred office."

While the emulation of obsolete European styles was a move in the direction of re-educating and internationalizing

American painting, the realists were unable to square life and art, and wished for the best of both possible worlds. With the sublime arrogance of the provincial, Luks characteristically begged the question, admitting his roots in European tradition and in the same breath denying any artistic authority or esthetic values. "The world has but two artists," he would boast, "Frans Hals and little old George Luks." And he would fume when people spoke of painting as an end in itself: "Art—my slats! Guts! Guts! Life! Life! I can paint with a shoe string dipped in pitch and lard."

Of all the artists who felt Henri's influence, John Sloan was on the most intimate personal terms and perhaps owed most to the older artist. He began to paint seriously in 1897 when he shared a studio with Henri; later he followed Henri to New York and acquired most of his education in modern art through him. Until Henri had introduced him to Forain, Daumier and Goya, Sloan had been doing intricate illustration inspired by the decorative style of *Art Nouveau*. From these new and more vital esthetic hints, and from Henri's own "dark Impressionism," Sloan evolved the pictorial formula of his realism. It mixed elements of illustration and caricature with a sensitive feeling for paint quality. Like that of so many of the other newspaper-trained artists, his work is a curious mixture of hackwork and sensibility.

Sloan came to New York permanently in 1904, continuing his career as illustrator for magazines and newspapers but finding more time to paint. He had begun to establish his link with the new American realists as early as 1900 with paintings of Philadelphia city life. These still retained a certain nineteenth-century flavor of picturesque genre, however, and only after 1904 did he begin systematically to observe the life of the streets in New York from a fresh and less sentimental point of view, seeking a more robust, meaningful realism. A tireless stroller and "incorrigible window watcher," in his own words, Sloan came to see the New York slums as a kind of stage set where all sorts of lively, unexpected business was in progress; and he became indefatigable in his search for human drama, recording little vignettes of urban life in a diary as well as in his paintings. The lower East Side, the West Side below Fourteenth Street, the Bowery, which he described as "a maze of living incident," were some of his favorite haunts. The fact that he found vitality and human interest in the seamier pockets of the big city was quite in tune with the spirit of the new realism, as was his tendency to give human squalor the touch of romance.

It was a period when Theodore Roosevelt was reprimanding American writers for being less interested in the Fulton Market than they were in the picturesque marketplaces of Europe. In his essay, *Dante in the Bowery*, Roosevelt proclaimed: "The Bowery is one of the great highways of humanity, a highway of seething life, of varied interest, of fun, of work, of sordid and terrible tragedy; and it is haunted by demons as evil as any that stalk through the pages of *The Inferno*." The literature and art of the Gilded Age had either sentimentalized "the poor" and the derelict as harmless, lovable ruffians or ignored them altogether. Under the new dispensation of social reform, they became real and present problems, enlisting the passionate interest not only of social workers but of artists and writers as well. Stephen Crane stood on his feet most of one night in a blizzard down on the Bowery, observing a breadline for his story, "The Men in the Storm," one of the first primitive ventures in naturalism. In his own way, John Sloan was as conscientious about immersing himself in the raw American experience and painting lower-class life.

Sloan's naturalism was not so coarse-grained as Luks's, nor as superficial in its investigation of natural appearances as Shinn's or Glackens's. He was more the careful craftsman, and though a less fluent stylist, achieved an art of greater sincerity and depth. His foreground was the unpromising commonplace: the sidewalks of New York, a gloomy downtown barroom, a woman wearily hanging out wash from a tenement fire escape. But his background was often mysterious, and he invested the dreary prose of everyday life with the touch of romantic lavishness. That he managed to do this even within the atmosphere of his "small" style was something of a triumph. He is remembered as an American Hogarth for his ability to catch common people in gross character, or he is singled out for his profound hu-

man sympathies. Actually, despite a certain humor and
energy in handling, Sloan's people are neither very deeply
felt nor are they remarkable comic inventions. The artist's
rather crude caricatures represented a struggle to conquer
his ineptness at vital characterization; at best, his figuration
goes just beyond the clichés of popular illustration. Sloan
did have something urgent to communicate about life, but
with pictorial means that were not altogether adequate for
the job. He than compensated, however, by evoking
romantic atmosphere and mood, and by conveying his own
innocence and sense of wonder before "the lure of the great
cities."

Dreiser's novels, Crane's New York sketches and Sloan's
city painting are of a period, and all have about them the
atmosphere of the American dream. They express a wish
for some larger individual fulfillment, for a more splendid
existence than the crushing real world offers. Like Dreiser
in his ponderous, labored technique, and Crane in his pat-
ently artificial reproductions of lower-class speech, Sloan
reveals the strain of forging a romantic idiom around the re-
fractory materials of the new naturalism. He was not sufficiently sophisticated or detached to be able to subdue the
grosser aspects of experience within a framework of esthetic
hedonism, as the continental realists Degas and Lautrec had
done. His message was that of a wayward, romantic sensibility: if he was to fail ultimately at fitting life into a substantial artistic system, Sloan seems to have decided, then he
would remove his art to a different atmosphere altogether.
This he did by means of a certain richness of chiaroscuro
and the suggestive play of his lighting.

A nocturnal scene like *The Haymarket* (1907) (Plate 2)
achieves a mystery which blurs and enlarges its literal meaning as a transcription of fact. In one of the city's disreputa-
ble districts, three dressy ladies emerge from a rich, mahog-
any darkness into the luminous doorway of a rooming
house, under the appreciative eye of a sidewalk Lothario;
to one side a child rolls a hoop; a mother, carrying wash,
tries to distract her little daughter from taking an interest in
the scene. One is reminded that Sloan on one of his many
walks noted a streetwalker gaudily arrayed in a great

plumed hat that made her look like "some wild creature of the night"; and one remembers that Daumier's treatment of lower-class life was also compounded of sentimentalism, energy and mystery. Even in daylight Sloan preferred gray weather as a shield against a too stark and bald reality. *The Wake of the Ferry* (1907), painted on such a day, merely frames a blank expanse of gleaming water against the dark silhouettes of boat struts, gate and a huddled figure. The rich shadows and the scintillation of light create an intense, lyric impression. J. B. Yeats, the father of the poet William Butler Yeats and an intimate of Sloan, liked to speak of the artist's "mountain gloom." One could "never be tired of peering into that gloom," he wrote in *Harper's Weekly* of Sloan's painting, *McSorley's Back Room*. Sloan's darkling romanticism brings the Brown Decades full circle; when in later years, he pursued a more brilliant, objective color scheme in the effort to meet the challenge of the School of Paris and of an ultra-modernism that bewildered him, his art lost all its savor.

The realist group's new departures in mood, subject matter and social attitude, if not in technique, very soon aroused the open hostility of the official art world. The challenge of Henri, Luks, Sloan, Glackens and Shinn to contemporary authority met with increasing rejections of their work by the National Academy and the Society of American Artists. Suppression by these institutions was tantamount to being denied a public viewing since private art galleries—the alternative exhibiting opportunities for the artist as we now know them—were virtually nonexistent. When in 1907 the jury for the National Academy annual, on which Henri ironically enough served, voted to limit the number of entries by Sloan and reserved judgment on Henri's work, the two artists withdrew from the exhibition in protest. With Glackens, Sloan and Henri laid plans for a counter-exhibition in a private gallery, and thus was born the germ of the first large "independents" show of the new century.

The show took place at the Macbeth Gallery in New York in 1908. Henri, Sloan, Luks, Glackens and Shinn, the original Philadelphia rebels, were joined by Maurice Prendergast, Ernest Lawson, and Arthur B. Davies; the group became known in the newspapers as the "Eight Independent Painters" or simply "The Eight." Prendergast was an Impressionist who was aware of Cézanne; Lawson also worked in an Impressionist style; and Davies painted allegorical landscape in a dreaming Pre-Raphaelite manner. The realists were central to the group, but the other painters, whose work seemed more conservative, shared with them a spirit of rebellion against the parochial policies of the Academies.

The Eight almost immediately scored a success of notoriety; but to everyone's surprise, the financial results of their demonstration were also extremely gratifying. In the press their efforts were greeted with the same vindictive glee that artistic innovation in Europe had aroused; and such epithets were produced, then and subsequently, as "the apostles of ugliness," "the revolutionary gang," "the black gang," and—the most popular—"ash-can school." Even so generally perceptive a critic as James Huneker of the *New York Sun* described their canvases disapprovingly as "darkest Henri." Despite, or possibly because, of the sniping of journalists, the public came in droves. The new insurgent spirit could no longer be either contained or denied and, with so much to support it in the atmosphere of political progressivism, encountered less actual resistance than had been anticipated. "We've made a success," Sloan wrote in elation after the first sales returns were in, "—Davies says as *epoch*. The sales at the exhibition amount to near $4000. Macbeth is pleased as 'Punch'!" Even the Pennsylvania Academy soon jumped on the bandwagon, asking for the show and circulating it to eight cities after the New York exhibition closed.

The amorphous program and heterogeneous styles of the Eight did not promise a long collective life, and the 1908 grouping was never repeated. As James Thrall Soby has observed, it "consisted of artists who, finding themselves more closely allied in friendship than in belief, formed their title by the anti-doctrinal expedient of counting noses." Perhaps the most salutary results of their loose association was the revival of a languishing tradition of artistic protest. Organized dissent had died with the decay of the Society of American Artists. Now the insurgents laid elaborate plans for bringing new currents of art to the American public.

"Eventually the 'men of the rebellion' expect to have a gallery of their own," the *New York Herald* reported in 1907, "where they and those who may be added to them can show two or three hundred works of art. It is likely, too, that they may ask several English artists to send over their paintings from London to be exhibited with the American group. The whole collection may be shown in turn in several large cities in the United States."

This statement proved ominously prophetic and actually spelled the decline of realism. It did anticipate the huge "Exhibition of Independent Artists" organized in 1910 by the original members of the Eight and such camp-followers as George Bellows and Glenn Coleman. But more importantly, it foreshadowed New York's great international show of modernism at the Twenty-Sixth Street Armory in 1913, which put the new realism quite in the shade.

With the Armory Show, and with the concurrent exhibitions of the more radical European and American moderns that Alfred Stieglitz had begun to stage in 1908, New York was swept by the excitement of the experimental and experienced a dramatic reversal in fashions and tastes. The relaxed, slightly old-fashioned atmosphere of Pepitas on Twenty-third Street where Sloan, Henri, J. B. Yeats and other progressive artists had forgathered gave way to a more knowing and perhaps more anxiously *au courant* Greenwich Village Bohemia. Mabel Dodge Luhan, who played hostess to the artist evangelists of the New Freedom from her lower Fifth Avenue salon, announced later: ". . . it seems as though everywhere, in that year of 1913, barriers went down and people reached each other who had never been in touch before; there were all sorts of new ways to communicate, as well as new communications. The new spirit was abroad and swept us all together." It also gave short shrift to the Eight and to their realism and somewhat obscured their accomplishment—for they were first to revive an insurgent mood, to attack ugliness and provincialism, and to venture, albeit timidly and with outmoded pictorial means, into the modern mainstream.

3

The New Spirit

If anything is done and something is done then
somebody has to do it.
Or somebody has to have done it.
That is Stieglitz's way.
He has done it.

—*Stieglitz,* by Gertrude Stein

With you, I feel free.
—Constantin Brancusi to Alfred Stieglitz, in conversation

The year 1908 saw the real-
ism of the Eight established and also inaugurated Alfred
Stieglitz's exhibitions of the radical European moderns. It
was a year in which the representatives of the official art
world were suddenly awakened to the threat to traditional
values in the new art. The growing misgiving with which
contemporary authority faced the future was candidly expressed, if inadvertently, by Sir Purdon Clarke, director of
the august Metropolitan Museum. In an interview which,
like so many of the more painful dodo observations deliv-
ered by conservative opinion, was reprinted and embalmed
for posterity in the pages of Stieglitz's magazine, *Camera
Work,* he solemnly warned: "There is a state of unrest all
over the world in art as in all other things. It is the same in
literature, as in music, in painting and in sculpture. And I
dislike unrest."

Sir Purdon could not have chosen a more apt word to
describe that new mood which was to produce so stimulating
and fertile an episode in the saga of American creative life.
Out of the ferment of the Progressive period, out of its
challenge to stagnant conventions in painting, and drawing
on the example of the advanced art of Europe, a new gen-

eration had come forward to claim its liberation. Between 1908 and the war a group of young artists emerged who were newly oriented to contemporary European art and felt little or no inhibition about testing modern idioms. While the Henri group were seeking a way through realism, these young artists for the most part had been biding their time, studying or working in Paris, and there they had begun to establish direct contact with the most emancipated expressions of the time. Max Weber and Arthur Burdett Frost, Jr., were among the first foreigners to join Matisse's new painting class which started in 1907; they were followed in later years by Arthur B. Carles, Morgan Russell and Patrick Henry Bruce. At about the same time Alfred Maurer, who had come to Paris in 1900 and whose distinction it was to be the first American expatriate painter of the new generation, felt the influence of Matisse and Fauve painting. By 1908 there were enough young American artists of progressive tendency in France, including Weber, Maurer, Bruce, Edward Steichen and others, to form a New Society of American Artists in Paris, supplanting a more conservative parent organization which had been in existence for some years.

Between 1904 and 1912, Charles Demuth, John Marin, Stanton Macdonald-Wright, Arthur Dove, Andrew Dasburg, William and Marguerite Zorach, Abraham Walkowitz, Thomas Benton, Morton Schamberg, Charles Sheeler, Joseph Stella, Marsden Hartley, Oscar Bluemner and John Covert also lived and studied in Europe, and felt the influence at first hand of such new movements as Fauvism, Cubism, Futurism, *Der Blaue Reiter*, Orphism and abstract art. As they began to drift back to America in the years preceding the first World War and exhibited paintings showing distinct continental derivations, the whole center of gravity of the American art milieu shifted. The insurgent spirit of the realists survived, but their forms became outmoded by the time war overtook Europe. It seemed, indeed, that New York was about to become an esthetic outpost of Paris, and that abstract idioms might work some permanent transformation on the American art scene.

Borrowing its militancy from the Progressive era, the

modern spirit arrived in America aggressively and confidently, generating among its adherents rapt and messianic feelings. It fitted suddenly, and all too neatly, into the evolving pattern of the American's mobility of feeling and his enthusiasm for novelty and change. If America had not invented "modernism," for a time we made it our own. How profoundly or superficially its conventions in art were understood only became clear in the following decade. In the meantime, between 1908 and 1920, the spirit of intellectual adventure was abroad in the land and nothing seemed able to stem its advance. Everything seemed possible to the human spirit through art, and such nineteenth-century prophecies of the American promise as Walt Whitman's appeared to be on the verge of fulfillment.

Exciting new beginnings could be seen everywhere, from the fantastic growth of the "little" magazines to the new ventures in experimental theater; from the poetry renaissance in Chicago to the emergence of a wonderful new crop of writers and their dedicated patrons and literary hostesses who conducted salons on both sides of the Atlantic. The "new," whether poetry, prose, the theater, painting or enlightened politics, found widespread support from America's best critical and creative minds. For a number of years members of the intellectual community, reaching out to refresh and sustain each other in such distinguished new publications as *Seven Arts, Dial, The New Republic, The Little Review, Smart Set* and *Camera Work,* demonstrated the solidarity of a community of related and responsive spirits unique in our modern cultural life. To the eager champions of the new spirit who wrote for these magazines modernism became all things: an esthetic proclamation of the spirit, a social gambit and even a principle of national regeneration.

Many of the sponsors of the "new" art spoke the vitalist language of Robert Henri and shared his humanist aims. They were, however, far more receptive to European standards and more anxious to attain a contemporary sophistication. They extended a welcome to Parisian esthetic principles which the Henri group had withheld. Unlike the generation of realist painters and naturalist writers, these artistic missionaries focused on the individual rather than on social forces as the key to realizing the American promise. The social equation of the reform movement was reversed: instead of trying to make group life more equable in order to free creative forces in the individual, the new enlightenment was now seen to emanate from the liberated modern individual who was expected to transform the group. James Oppenheim, founder of *Seven Arts*, which like so many of the brightest hopes and expectations of modernism was to expire with the war, anticipated a time when "the lost soul among nations, America, could be regenerated by art." Writing and painting were envisioned as part of one great advancing cause whose aim was nothing less than the reconstruction of modern man, and therefore of society. Such brilliant, young, social-minded critics as Van Wyck Brooks, Randolph Bourne, Lewis Mumford, Paul Rosenfeld and Waldo Frank, who wrote for *Seven Arts,* proselytized for the new movement as a way of binding men together in fraternal fellowship, and directed a withering fire against entrenched powers in both the art world and the social scene. They dreamed of an "organic" art that would lead to a potent renewal of modern life. A spirit of enlightenment, verbalized in an impressionistic language of utopian yearning, invaded criticism. Painting suddenly stood for an entirely new kind of aspiration. Writing of Post-Impressionism, Hutchins Hapgood of the *New York Globe* declared significantly: "It shakes the old foundations and leads to a new life, whether the programs and ideas have permanent validity or not."

Out of this atmosphere of high hopes emerged Alfred Stieglitz, an artist with the camera in his own right, a dealer, and first impresario of modernism in America. It is customary to date the arrival of modern art from the dramatic Armory Show of 1913, an event certainly of the utmost significance in the history of American taste. The Armory Show was our first introduction to the strong medicine of European artistic innovation on a wide, popular basis. Stieglitz, however, had been administering small doses over the five years preceding it, and his bold maneuvers prepared the ground for the triumphal entry of modernism. He also supplied American artists with a whole new set of esthetic criteria. Stieglitz not only played a sheltering, patriarchal role for painters at a time when they desperately needed guidance and support, but gave them a sense of belonging to an active, cosmopolitan art life of exacting standards, comparable to the highest in Europe. For the first time in our modern history, we could point without apology to our artistic community. Thanks largely to the Stieglitz protectorate, the American artist was freed of his provincial diffidence and crushing sense of isolation. Arthur Dove, like many other Stieglitz painters, was later to acknowledge the dealer's critical role. "I do not think," he wrote, "I could have existed as a painter without that super-encouragement and the battle he has fought day by day for twenty-five years. He is without a doubt the one who has done the most for art in America."

Stieglitz himself was a new type of personality in the arts. He was a second-generation American of Jewish-German descent whose parents emigrated at the time of the Civil War. After 1900 the massive waves of immigration began to exert their pressures on the art scene, giving it a more international character and making the port of New York a more cosmopolitan cultural center. In Stieglitz's generation there were a number of other significant artistic personalities of foreign descent who also contributed to the intermingling of racial and national strains: the painters Joseph Stella, Abraham Walkowitz, Max Weber; the sculptors Jacob Epstein, Gaston Lachaise. Like Paris with the advent of Picasso, Miró, Gris, Modigliani, Soutine, Chagall and others, the mainstream of art in twentieth-century New York was fed by many currents. The mixing of different peoples and backgrounds also gave new fluidity to the social structure and created a freer and more tolerant intellectual atmosphere in which the new could be eagerly received.

After settling in America and establishing a successful business, the elder Stieglitz returned to Germany in 1881 with his family to give his children a continental education. Alfred took up the study of engineering at the Berlin Polytechnic but his imagination was soon captured by the new science of photography, whose mechanics he pursued in the academic laboratories of Berlin. By 1887 he had won a first prize in the London *Amateur Photographer*, and when he returned to New York in 1890, he had acquired a small reputation in his chosen medium. In the next two decades he became celebrated for his photographs of New York life; the impressionistic realism of his photographs corresponded to the painting of the Eight. Later, Stieglitz began to isolate his subject matter, and often to abstract it, and his own art became more formal and symbolic. He also became active in local photography groups, reorganizing the languishing Society of American Photographers and editing its official organ, *Camera Notes*. In 1903 he founded his own magazine, *Camera Work*, which in its fourteen years of existence became equally famous for its handsome, meticulously accurate gravure reproductions and its many important articles on photography and art. These were written specially for it by Bernard Shaw, Maurice Maeterlinck, Gertrude Stein (in her first appearance in an American publication), Francis Picabia, Charles Caffin, Willard Huntington Wright, Marius de Zayas and Benjamin de Casseres.

In 1906 Stieglitz and his friend, Edward Steichen, a young painter and photographer, opened the Little Gallery of the Photo-Secession in the three-room attic of a brownstone at 291 Fifth Avenue. The next year Stieglitz began to exhibit art as well as photographs, commencing with the drawings of Pamela Colman-Smith. "The Secession Idea," he explained in *Camera Work*, "is neither the servant nor the product of a medium. It is a spirit." And Stieglitz promised that his little gallery would remain hospitable to artistic effort in any medium so long as it showed "honesty of aim, honesty of self-expression, honesty of revolt against the autocracy of convention."

Soon the Photo-Secession Gallery was functioning only marginally as a show place for the new photography, and its exhibitions were dominated by advanced painting and sculpture emanating from Paris. Steichen, who spent his summers in France and was on familiar terms with many of the new French artists, served as an enthusiastic liaison. It was apparently Steichen who proposed the first two exhibitions of European moderns, a show of Rodin's water colors in January 1908, followed four months later by Matisse drawings. Between exhibitions he wrote to Stieglitz: "I have another cracker-jack exhibition for you that is going to be as fine in its way as the Rodins are.

"Drawings by Henri Matisse, the most modern of the moderns—his drawings are the same to him and his paintings as Rodin's are to his sculpture. . . . Some are more finished than Rodin's, more of a *study* of form than movement —*abstract* to the limit."

Stieglitz's first two exhibitions of European moderns encountered in the press a stony indifference that should have dampened even the most ardent spirit. The dean of American newspaper critics, Royal Cortissoz of the *New York Herald,* described the Rodin water colors as "studio driftwood." The Matisse exhibition, his first in America, excited even more of the pointed patronizing derision which soon became the customary press response to Stieglitz's shows. J. Edgar Chamberlain of the *New York Evening Mail* declared Matisse's female figures were "of an ugliness that is most appalling and haunting, and that seems to condemn this man's brain to the limbo of artistic degeneration." The same old tired epithets that had been used to discredit Eakins and progressive art of the past, revealing again the intellectual and emotional impoverishment of American art criticism at its popular level, were dusted off and pressed into service to ridicule the new and unaccustomed in art. In a moment of levity Chamberlain mockingly asked forbearance for the outlandish Matisse show. "This sort of thing," he wrote, "should be treated with respect, just as adventism, Eddyism, spiritualism, Doukhobor outbreaks, and other forms of religious fanaticism are. One never knows when a new revolution is going to get started." In point of fact, Mr. Chamberlain was more of a prophet than he could have imagined. With Stieglitz's introduction of Rodin and Matisse, and with the quickening tempo of his subsequent shows, modernism for the first time began to gain a foothold in American taste. Perhaps even more significantly, the returning expatriate painters were encouraged to go on with the bold experiments they had tentatively begun in Paris.

After the Matisse show, the Photo-Secession Gallery found itself in financial difficulties and was forced to abandon its quarters. But Stieglitz found additional outside support and in the fall of 1908 reopened his gallery in different rooms at the same address, 291 Fifth Avenue. The historic new quarters of "291," as the gallery came to be known, inaugurated a new and more intensive phase of exhibiting activities. The vital statistics of Stieglitz's shows, which took place at a time when advanced painters and sculptors had virtually no alternative opportunity for exhibiting, make a most imposing and complete survey of early modernism; they show, too, the growing participation of Americans in the new movements. In 1909 he gave Alfred Maurer, Marsden Hartley and John Marin their first one-man shows in this country. The following year when a large independents' show was organized by the New York realists with none of the Stieglitz artists participating, 291 showed a group, "Younger American Painters," which included Maurer, Hartley, Marin, Dove, Steichen, Weber and Arthur Carles. In a sense this exhibition challenged the realists' claim as representatives of progressive tendencies, and made the growing distinction between American scene painting and abstract or semi-abstract modes clear for the first time.

From 1910 until 1917, when the war temporarily closed his gallery, Stieglitz scored an impressive number of American firsts: Cézanne's water colors; Picasso's water colors and drawings; Matisse's sculpture; Henri Rousseau's paintings; Manolo's and Matisse's sculpture. Stieglitz also in this period gave Francis Picabia, Constantin Brancusi and the Americans Abraham Walkowitz, Oscar Bluemner, Elie Nadelman, Georgia O'Keeffe and Stanton Macdonald-Wright their first exhibitions in this country, and presented the first serious exhibition of children's drawings and of Negro sculpture anywhere in the world. In his succeeding galleries, The Intimate Gallery (1925-1929) and An American Place (1929-1946), Stieglitz showed the sculpture of Gaston Lachaise, Charles Demuth's paintings, and staged regular exhibitions of Marin, O'Keeffe, Hartley and Dove. No dealer in America, and few in Europe, had launched so much significant new painting and sculpture in so short a period.

Indeed Stieglitz was a good deal more than a dealer as

we understand the term today; he was a creative person in his own right, and his relations to his American artists were to say the least unconventional, with commercial considerations refreshingly absent. He saw himself and his artists as workers in the cause of creative freedom, and 291 took on a symbolic character, often encouraging among its admirers a spirit of mystical reverence. Stieglitz's incorruptibility became a legend, and many casual visitors were put off by his apparent indifference to them, and by his unwillingness either to promote or even to make the simple effort to explain the puzzling new shapes and forms inhabiting the spanking white walls of his gallery. In a foreword to the Forum Exhibition of Modern American Painters in 1916 Stieglitz bluntly expressed his views of the gallery system and hinted at his own objectives in showing art. "I feel," he wrote, "that the system now in vogue of bringing the public into contact with the painting of today is basically wrong. The usual exhibition is nothing but a noise maker. It does not do what it is professedly to do: To bring about a closer Life between Expression and Individual."

291 was in effect an experimental station for a group of free souls, united by common creative and social aims. The general public was admitted, but only initiates were entirely welcome and made to feel at home. To the naïve or bewildered who sought an explanation of the new art, Stieglitz turned a deaf ear, saying, "You will find as you go through life that if you ask what a thing means, a picture, or music, or whatever, you may learn something about the people you ask, but as for learning *about* the thing you seek to *know*, you will have to sense it in the end through your own experience, so that you had better save your energy and not go through the world asking what cannot be communicated in words. If the artist could describe in words what he does, then he would never have created it."

Stieglitz's Olympian manner intimidated more than one collector who could never be sure that their own esthetic attitudes might not suddenly offend and alienate the dealer, denying them a purchase. Despite his apparent detachment from the motives of the marketplace and his somewhat off-hand methods of dealing with the public, he consciously played for his intimates the role of educator and teacher. The degree to which he did so, and the intensity of feeling his presence generated, are reflected in the memorial volume published in 1934, *America and Alfred Stieglitz*. Many of the foremost intellectuals of his day sought stimulation and refreshment in Stieglitz's company, and he was universally known and admired by creative people, a number of whom contributed to his memorial book. In addition to the artists and art critics directly associated with his gallery or magazine, there were many others for whom 291 or the Stieglitz apartment provided a refuge and source of stimulating conversation, among them Sherwood Anderson, Carl Sandburg, the composed Ernest Bloch, Walter Lipmann, Lewis Mumford and Waldo Frank. Stieglitz, however, was also subject to a kind of adulation best compared in modern times with the group of intense, female worshipers of D. H. Lawrence. An English novelist appropriately characterized Lawrence's fanatical disciples in a book title as *The League of Impassioned Pigmies*. Stieglitz posthumously suffered such rapturous appreciations as the remarks of one female admirer who described 291, or "The Room," as "an Immaculate Conception," "the Song of Songs," and who saw Stieglitz's life as one dedicated "to the beauty of all life, derived and springing out of the love-life." There is no reason to assume that Stieglitz enjoyed or encouraged such craven worship; however, one suspects that his sense of mission may have blinded him to his own electrifying impact on his entourage.

In Stieglitz's period the self-realization of the individual was also allied with the strivings of women for place and independence; more generally, it was part of the effort to reinstate feeling and instinct as important human forces. Modern utilitarian society was served warning by the new art expressions that the life of the emotions had been unwisely neglected. Personalities like Stieglitz and Lawrence assumed the roles of faith-healers and life-givers in a period reacting violently to Victorian repressions. They supplied something that was missing in modern life, just as the radical simplifications, the joyous, intense colors, and the new primitivism of modern art had done. The novelist, Edna Bryner, found in the Stieglitz milieu a profound emotional satisfaction, based on "a remembrance back to a very ancient life when participation was common and completely satisfying." In the face of modern life, with its dominating materialist values, the creative artist sought refuge in some ideal community of like-minded spirits, or simply in his own creative powers. Stieglitz, like D. H. Lawrence, almost compulsively exaggerated the potencies of the individual creative spirit and made the most exacting demands imaginable on himself. He wished that he might have "the physical strength of a scale that can weigh a thousand tons of coal, plus a psychic sensitivity of the scale that can weigh a ray of light."

In such statements and attitudes one feels something of the unstable hopefulness that surrounded European art, not so much in the twentieth century as in the last years of the preceding century at a time when modernism on the continent was more directly identified with social aspirations and with a critical, reforming spirit. There was something of William Morris's social idealism in Stieglitz's outlook, mingled with distinctly American romantic attitudes. However, unlike the *fin-de-siècle* movements which were tied to a return to some nostalgic, neo-traditional community, Stieglitz's brave new world was forward-looking. As Waldo Frank envisioned it, 291 embodied the annunciation of a new order. It stood as a symbol of the birth of a new world where "myriad creative men and women, teachers, workers, artists, scientists toil together . . . in ways as variedly profound as must be the world in which the newborn Man— the true person—with his exquisite sensibilities and enormous powers, may prosper."

Since the new art was so mystically dedicated to the evolution of "the true person," and the ideal hopes for fundamental social-spiritual change were suddenly shattered by the war, it was to be expected that the modern art which identified itself with a discredited idealism would also suffer an enormous decline in prestige. That is precisely what happened after the war. The fact that the decline of modernism took more drastic form in America, that the movement was riddled with more damaging defections here than in Europe, is in part explained by the fact that so much Utopian sentiment which had been supporting it was suddenly cut away by the disillusioned mood of the postwar period. Perhaps even more important, however, was the fact that American artists had after all only made a superficial alliance with the new European modes, and in the absence of strong visual traditions of their own were not yet ready to surrender provincial attitudes. In any case it is unlikely that modernism as expressed by the artist members of the 291 milieu would have been even as successful as it was without Stieglitz's faith and ardent support.

In the decade of the twenties American art experienced a relaxation in abstract styles, and there was a limited reaction to the excesses of the early modern movements. European art also went through a period of cautious consolidation and returned to naturalism in some degree, but soon erupted with new assertions of independence embodied in Surrealism. Despite its sometimes academic practices and diversionary polemics, Surrealism was a genuine effort to resuscitate an important principle of creative liberty. The Surrealist revolution, or insurrection as it might better be described, was scarcely felt in America until the forties. Instead, naturalism, Expressionism and American scene painting acquired ever more tenacious holds on our art. Modernism became a series of individual directions and lost its broad, collective character, despite its manifold early promise.

From the beginning modernism had been conceived as an "interpretation" of American life and became a vehicle for the expression of certain general, shared feelings about life and the individual's aspiration. The American's view of modern art was at once both more idealized and more instrumental than the European's. Andrew Dasburg, one of the first American abstract artists, suggested in 1920 why one of the central impulses of modern art, Cubism, hadn't deeply penetrated native consciousness. "One cannot write of 'actual' Cubism in America," he declared, "but only of the effort. We lack the intellectual integrity to work logically within the limitations inherent in an idea. We want instead to gather the best from many sources. . . . This idea of combining a variety of forms of perfection into one complete ideal realization prevents any creative work being done which possesses the contagious force of Cubism." Dasburg suggests the disparity between American eclecticism and the more profound European ability continually to create something new within an established style. Perhaps our early modernism was encumbered by too much ideological baggage, diverting it from essential esthetic and formalistic considerations necessary to sustain a style. But that, too, was in the American grain and in the spirit of the time, as was Stieglitz's effort to make something high-minded and essentially moral of the artistic effort.

After two wars and a long hiatus that saw most of the initial hopes of modernism dismantled, it is inevitable that we should look back on the exalted mood of the decade between 1910 and 1920 as an age of innocence. Today, however, Stieglitz's example may be regarded as a corrective to the contemporary abstract artist's gnawing sense of isolation, for he embodied a general cultural ambition that few of our artists today permit themselves to feel. He once said to a friend, as they stood observing the New York skyline from within 291: "If what is in here cannot stand up against what is out there, then what is in here has no right to exist. But if what is out there can stand up against what is in here, then what is in here does not need to exist." Stieglitz was prepared to give way before the millennium, but in the meantime he would fight for quality in art as a noble and elevated cause. Stieglitz created a fascinating community of like-minded spirits with himself at its center, and for his ultimate goal he desired a better world. But he nurtured few illusions that it could materialize of its own accord. If his enthusiasm for the modern at times seemed undiscriminating and was obscured by a somewhat muzzy idealism, he nevertheless profoundly understood the terms of his own struggle and lived by his high principles with an altogether admirable singleness of purpose.

Stieglitz was of even more importance as a catalyst of new pictorial and sculptural ideas, than as a theorist or evangelist. 291 became the first important American center of the radical new forms of modern art, which achieved national publicity with the celebrated Armory Show of 1913. Part of the legacy of 291 was the formation of the

Société Anonyme in 1920 by Katherine Dreier, Marcel Duchamp and Man Ray. An itinerant museum and collection
of modern painting and sculpture, the *Société*, or the Museum of Modern Art as it was also known, bought and cir-
culated the new art, with the emphasis on non-objective
styles. Its guiding spirit, Katherine Dreier, an amateur
painter, also wrote, lectured extensively and arranged
lectures by such artists and critics as Walter Pach, Joseph Stella, Henry McBride and Christian Brinton in
an effort to promote the understanding of modern art in
America. Among the many important artists that the *Société* presented in their first American exhibitions were
Schwitters, Campendonk, Klee, Malevich, Miró, Baumeister
and Vantongerloo. The bulk of the Society's fine collection
was given to the Yale University Art Gallery in 1941. Here
one may still see the paintings by some of the neglected and
interesting early American moderns: Patrick Henry Bruce,
Morton Schamberg, John Covert and Joseph Stella. It is also
not too farfetched to consider the opening of the Museum
of Modern Art in New York in 1929 as another outgrowth
of the pioneering Stieglitz activity, and the prosyletizing
spirit of 291 has been passed on to other public collections
of modern art such as the Solomon R. Guggenheim Museum.

One other aspect of Stieglitz's impresarioship deserves attention: his publication *Camera Work*. In this magazine was
printed perhaps the first sustained, serious criticism of
American artistic life and culture, and the first tentative
"modern" art criticism. Many of the articles, and especially
those written by the brilliant Benjamin de Casseres and the
Mexican caricaturist and critic, Marius de Zayas, may now
seem dated. The writings of Casseres and De Zayas represent the apprenticeship of the modern spirit in America,
even though their prose reflects a turn-of-the-century literary impressionism, and their esthetic is conditioned by
the romantic decadence. It is curious to note that when
Stieglitz was showing the radical simplifications and powerful forms of the Fauve Matisse, and of Picasso during his
"Negro" period, Benjamin de Casseres could summon up
the waning epicurean glow of the nineties, of a world in

dissolution. In his essay, "Modernity and the Decadence," he wrote: "I desire a world without a center. I seek the Ultima Thule of each sensation. I love the dispersed and muffled sonorities of weakened forces. I desire as many personalities as I have moods." To Casseres the modern meant the last hot-house refinements of the romantic spirit. "Beyond Verlaine, Debussy, Picasso, Arthur Symons, Maurice Materlinck, Lafcadio Hearn, Stéphane Mallarmé, Rémy de Gourmont, Anatole France, there is nothing," he declared. Such writing and attitudes were quite in contrast to those of other early critics of modern art like Roger Fry or Clive Bell in England, whose criticism sternly avoided the purple passage and limited itself to formal analysis.

Yet the romantic writing of Casseres belongs to an important current of modern criticism, for there is a clear line of evolution from the romantic decadence of the symbolist poets and late-nineteenth-century painters like the fanciful Redon, to the dream-world and fantasies of the modern Surrealists and their champions in criticism. Casseres anticipated the Surrealists when, in a more fantastical mood, he wrote: "I desire to be ephemeral, protean, and to chase butterflies of my fancy across abyss and meadowland and even into those fatal caves in the moon where the Goddess of Lunacy spins her cataleptic dreams." And like the poet-seer Rimbaud, he relied upon disorder and unreason to free artistic intuition from the suffocating limitations of logical thought and modern civilized life. In such formulations the modern spirit of revolt and the romantic decadence join forces: they both aim to liberate the life of pure instinct. Casseres's apparently anarchic scheme of values were part of an effort to reinstate the artist's world of imagination, even at the cost of discrediting conventional reality. "Sanity and simplicity," he wrote in 1913, "are the prime curses of civilization. . . . We should mock existence at each moment, mock ourselves, mock others, mock everything by the perpetual creation of fantastic and grotesque attitudes, gestures and direct attributes."

Dated though such statements may now seem, they were important in creating a receptive atmosphere for the emergence of more vital forms of modern art. In flavor they also anticipate the war with American culture waged in the twenties by such elaborate ironists as James Branch Cabell or that more robust debunker, H. L. Mencken. The postwar debunking journalism was, as Alfred Kazin has pointed out in *On Native Grounds,* the American version of Dada. When Marius de Zayas declared in *Camera Work* in 1916, "America waits inertly for its own potentiality to be expressed in art," he expressed a sentiment, from the point of view of a profound skepticism, that became the substance of the indictment of American life in the next decade. (Holding up the American "booboisie" to ridicule, H. L. Mencken was later to suggest that the "Anglo-Saxon of the great herd is . . . the least civilized of men and the least capable of true civilization. . . . He is almost wholly devoid of aesthetic feeling.") The opening salvo in the attack on American provincialism and insensitivity to art came from Stieglitz's critics. "In all times," De Zayas wrote darkly, "art has been the synthesis of the beliefs of peoples. In America this synthesis is an impossibility, because all beliefs exist here together. One lives here in a continuous change which makes impossible the perpetuation and the universality of an idea. . . . Each individual remains isolated, struggling for his own physical and intellectual existence. In the United States there is no general sentiment in any sphere of thought."

De Zayas carried his attack on American culture over into an assault on modern art itself, however, thus anticipating the more systematic and all-encompassing negations of the Dadaists. It is a measure of Stieglitz's tolerance that he would sponsor a point of view so at variance with his own more sanguine outlook. In an essay published in *Camera Work* in 1913, "The Sun Has Set," De Zayas found that "unconsciousness" in art was "the sign of creation, while consciousness at best that of manufacture." Proceeding from this definition, which was in a sense the *reductio ad absurdum* of the revolt against reason, he described the modern artist as "an eclectic in spirit and an iconoclast in action," and took exception to his willful distortions and self-conscious primitivism. For him such strategies suggested that modern art was willed and contrived. As the Dadaists were to ask a few years later, he posed the question whether the modern artists were not "an anachronism," "a logical absurdity." He concluded that they were rather the impotent slaves of their own time, reflecting in their derivative styles the last nervous convulsions of a period that was "chaotic, neurotic, inconsequent and out of equilibrium." De Zayas terminated his argument with the statement: "Art is dead." Although he was thereby expressing the negativism of Dada, he wasn't prepared to push his view further and adopt a counter-esthetic, nor did he explore the liberating and fruitful possibilities of anti-art attitudes as the Dadaists later did with such resourcefulness and ingenuity.

For a moment, however, Dada did enjoy a certain fashionable success in America. In 1921 Marcel Duchamp and Man Ray published one issue of *New York Dada*. Picabia had come to America in 1913, and Duchamp in 1915; they soon became closely associated with the Stieglitz group. With Stieglitz, Picabia helped found a new proto-Dada publication, *291*, in 1915. For this magazine he did characteristic mechanical drawings of machine forms, to which were appended such unrelated titles as *Portrait of Alfred Stieglitz*, or *A Young American Girl in a State of Nudity*. Visual puns vied with *ideogrammes* by Guillaume Apollinaire, typographical experiments, fantastic prose-poem fragments by Stieglitz himself, and other inspirational contributions in free verse to make *291* in its brief year of existence a most exotic and interesting venture in American publishing. Like the criticism of Casseres and De Zayas, however, *291* exercised a certain restraint in stating the case for the disenchanted modern.

American artists of the period never assumed the extreme positions of the European Dadaists in their rebellion against modern society and the machine. The machine forms which Picabia and Duchamp used to deprecate and to exorcise the mechanistic environment of modern life, and also to challenge the "noble" conventions of the figurative styles of the past, did not achieve a significant influence among American artists. Perhaps the sentimental attachment of the American to the machine as a creator of material comfort, and his basic optimism about the future, did not permit him to view technology critically. There was a social violence in Dada's feigned madness and anarchism that was antipathetic to the milder, reformist American spirit. Nor were Americans capable of the kind of ingenuity and wit which animated the zany spirit of play so integral to the inventions of Dada art.

Morton Schamberg emulated Picabia for a time but died in 1918 before he had fulfilled his early promise. Charles Sheeler was in the beginning influenced by Schamberg. Demuth credited Duchamp with a significant role in the evolution of his early style. Yet neither Sheeler nor Demuth permitted himself the total defiance of either Duchamp or Picabia, or of the official Dadaists. Rather, their mature pictures were bland, diagrammatic interpretations of the new industrial landscape, objective and, with some notable exceptions, noncommittal in their observation. The American artist could not achieve the European's esthetic detachment, and he felt no deep sense of alienation from his own crude industrial environment. John Marin's exulting cry of identification before the Manhattan skyline was the classic early reaction of the American artist to the new landscape of power: "I see great forces at work, great movements; the large buildings and the small buildings; the warring of the great and the small. . . . While these powers are at work pushing, pulling, sideways, downwards, upwards, I can hear the sound of their strife and there is great music being played." Here was an echo of the affirmations of Whitman and Louis Sullivan, of Henri and of Stieglitz, up a few decibels, but still ringing hopefully with the wonder of the American promise.

In a more agitated and romantic mood, the American Futurist, Joseph Stella, registered the fresh impact on his senses of the new American dynamism. Speaking of his painting, *Brooklyn Bridge* (1918), he wrote: "To realize this towering imperative vision, I lived days of anxiety, torture and delight alike, trembling all over with emotion. . . . Upon the swarming darkness of the night, I rung all the bells of alarm with the blaze of electricity scattered in lightnings down the oblique cables, the dynamic pillars of my composition, and to render more pungent the mystery of my metallic apparition, through the green and red glare of the signals I excavated here and there caves as subterranean passages to infernal recesses."

A decade after Stella had celebrated the Brooklyn Bridge in paint, a poet, Hart Crane, used it as an imaginative symbol of technology triumphant and as a myth for moderns. Invoking the spirit of Walt Whitman, he described the bridge as the "terrific threshold of the prophet's pledge." His brilliant, packed imagery re-creates the bedazzled excitement and even the locale of Stella's painting and word-picture:

> Again the traffic light that skim thy swift
> Unfractioned idiom, immaculate sigh of stars,
> Beading thy path—condense eternity:
> And we have seen night lifted in thine arms.

For the American artist and poet, Roebling's engineering feat, the beautiful suspension bridge, became a symbol of energy and spiritual aspiration. Another manifestation of the American sensibility which shows respect for the machine may be found in Ernest Hemingway. In *A Farewell to Arms* during the retreat from Caporetto the hero finds comfort and distinct personal satisfaction in the existence of the oiled barrels of guns and of cannon simply as pure physical sensation, in the way one would find security and warmth in the presence of some reliable old friend. The Dadaists twitted the machine as a threat to civilized values or enlisted it as an accomplice to discredit traditional values in art. Only the American felt the machine as an intimate, physical presence and romantically identified his personal destiny with it. It became part of his scheme of values; he wasn't prepared to reject it so unthinkingly. Stella contemplated the "mystery" of his "metallic apparition," Brooklyn Bridge; Hart Crane made it a symbol of grace and sublime freedom. Marin, like many other contemporary artists, found release and artistic satisfaction in the dynamism of America.

America's modernist moods were on the whole romantic and idealistic. Despair was given a halfway and inconclusive formulation, as demonstrated by the writing of Casseres and

De Zayas in *Camera Work*. For the American artist modernism became identified in the decade 1910 to 1920 with the American promise. Just as John Sloan and his friends had used realism to project the quality of the American dream, so our first modern artists approached the formal discipline of modern styles in a mood of romantic excitement. They could not brook the limits imposed by Cubism, or impose on themselves the conditions of working "logically within the limitations inherent in an idea." Nor did Dada have any real success in this country. And futurism which canonized the machine and exalted modern life in a programmatic art was given a far more subjective, unsystematized accent in Joseph Stella's painting and verbal utterance, as an example.

It is remarkable that Alfred Stieglitz could have held in balance the conflicting claims of native romanticism and the new European esthetic. His great contribution, indeed, was to relate the European sense of art to his own romantic individualism and to that of his artists. He understood the experimental as part of the American's inalienable right to seek new expressions of creative liberty, and he gave this search moral and philosophic overtones. He himself, for example, once referred to a sequence of his cloud photographs as an effort "to put down my philosophy of life—to show that my photographs are not due to subject matter— not to special trees, or faces, or interiors, to special privileges, clouds were there for everyone—no tax as yet on them—free."

The painters that Stieglitz showed worked out from accepted visual facts to some subjective or interpretative statement. Even the work of the most abstract of his artists, Arthur Dove, was nature-saturated and poetic in mood. An uncompromising rejection of naturalist illusion and its replacement by some system of quite independent plastic signs—the core of European modernism—was never realized as a collective effort in America. Despite the "organic" character of Stieglitz's thought and his aim to bring about "a closer Life between Expression and the Individual," he could not take the radical step of entirely dissociating art from natural appearances. His artists perhaps *wanted* to conceive of art as a necessary, organic and independent structure, but in the end they all were forced to make conciliatory gestures toward tradition. The gap between abstraction and painting that clung to naturalist illusion was as great and crucial, to paraphrase a critic of American art, as that in the evolutionary order between the crustaceans and the vertebrates. With few exceptions, the gap in art was not decisively closed in the first period of American modernism.

Yet, if American painting could not establish itself within the more exacting continental disciplines, Stieglitz was wise enough to teach us to measure it not as a failure in terms of the European standard but as a valid local expression. It was as a projection of indigenous modes of feeling that American art in the modern period attained its first distinction and made its contribution in international art. Stieglitz's romantic individualism, his experimentalism, and his dedication to freedom made him a significant force in American art. He and 291 provided a rich soil for the new ventures; in it the modern spirit struck roots and enjoyed its first flowering.

4

Scandal on Twenty-Sixth Street

"Before it [The Armory Show], a painting truly modern
was only a rumor."

—Lee Simonson

"Our minds call for a more forceful emotion than the
simple imitation of life can give. We require problems, inspirations, incentives to thoughts. The simple melody of
many of the old masters can no longer interest us because
of its very simplicity."

—Willard H. Wright, "What Is Modern Painting,"
The Forum Exhibition of Modern American Painters, 1916

The impact of Alfred Stieg-
litz's exhibitions of new European painting and sculpture
almost immediately affected the New York art world. The
more open-minded artists were enthralled by radical European innovations and were anxious for a comprehensive
view of the world art picture, so many tantalizing glimpses
of which Stieglitz had supplied. But many of the progressive American artists, and particularly the group of realists
surrounding Henri, were thrown on the defensive; they
could not take kindly to a foreign art more revolutionary
than their own whose aims they could not share. A competi-
tive feeling arose between the two groups which later flared
into open antagonism. It emerged first at the time of the
great exhibition of "independents" in 1910. "Stieglitz,"
wrote John Sloan, one of the sponsors, "is hot under the col-
lar about our show. . . . I imagine he thinks we have stolen
his thunder in exhibiting 'independent' artists." If the independents had stolen Stieglitz's thunder, however, it was only
in the staging of their exhibition and not in its actual character. They included none of the more adventurous American

moderns such as Carles, Dove, Hartley, Marin, Maurer, Steichen, Weber, whom Stieglitz had already exhibited as a group at 291 earlier that year. The divisions among artists of progressive tendency became even more apparent the next year when Rockwell Kent proposed another independents show to Sloan, but stipulated that the exhibiting artists agree not to submit paintings to the National Academy exhibition that year. When the show was held, Sloan, Henri, Glackens, Lawson and Shinn were absent, since they refused to abide by Kent's condition. Among those that did agree and exhibited were, ironically enough, the modernists Maurer, Marin and Hartley.

In 1911 Jerome Myers, Walt Kuhn and Elmer Mac-Rae discussed a more ambitious exhibition. A committee of twenty-five, dominated by the original members of the Eight and calling itself the Association of American Painters and Sculptors, was formed to develop the idea of another comprehensive showing of independent artists. For about a year plans were discussed, and the group tried to arrange the use of an exhibition hall. Neither a location nor the money for the venture was forthcoming, and it seemed that the new independents show would have to be abandoned. At the moment of greatest discouragement, the committee approached Arthur B. Davies, who had a formidable reputation as a fund-raiser, and asked him to accept the presidency. He agreed in effect to shoulder the main responsibility for the exhibition, and immediately set about his new task with great enterprise and energy. It was Davies who almost single-handedly changed the original conception of the independents show into the great survey of modern European art now known as the Armory Show. The move did not ingratiate him with his more nationalist-minded associates, and in due time aroused their deep hostility. They were helpless to oppose him in the beginning, however, since he alone held out the promise of adequate financial backing. "Thus it was that I," wrote Jerome Myers later, describing his appeal to Davies for assistance, "an American art patriot, who painted ashcans and the little people around them, took part in inducing to become the head of our association the one American artist who had little to do with his contemporaries, who had vast influence with the wealthiest women, who painted unicorns and maidens under moonlight."

As a painter, Davies was more conservative than the realists who looked to Henri for leadership. The refined estheticism and romantic mood of his painting stemmed from the Pre-Raphaelites; one could scarcely have guessed that the bold colors of Matisse or the radical simplifications of the Cubists would engage Davies's sympathies. He was, however, an urbane man of wide artistic culture and taste, and had actually studied the new art of Europe more than most artists of his generation. Davies had shown an interest in Stieglitz's exhibitions and from them bought a Cézanne water color and a Picasso. "Davies' thorough understanding of all the new manifestations," Walt Kuhn later wrote, "was due to one thing only—his complete knowledge of the past."

There are a number of widely differing versions of the origins of the Armory Show, all of them written many years after the event by men who admitted a violent partisanship either to Davies or to the forces opposing him within the committee. From the point of view of those like Guy Pène du Bois, a fellow member and publicist for the group, who later complained of Davies as a "severe, arrogant, implacable" man, the new president robbed the show of its value as a national demonstration by showing the foreign article. It was, of course, the new European art that immediately became the public sensation of the show. Yet it is hard to believe Davies could have remained in a position of such responsibility if his behavior were as insufferable as it was later said to be, or if the majority of the committee were in open conflict with him. It was only after the exhibition was held, and public reactions were in, that the disgruntled members attacked the change in policy. In any case there seems little doubt that Davies was the guiding spirit of the show, that his ideas must have intrigued the committee to a degree since they accommodated him; it is also certain that Walt Kuhn, the secretary of the Society, and Walter Pach, a liaison in Paris, played the primary roles in making the actual European selections.

The idea of a comprehensive show of the new art currents had already occurred to many Europeans outside of France. In 1911 the critic Roger Fry staged, amid public hoots and critical protest, the first Grafton Gallery Post-Impressionist Exhibition in London. Then in 1912 a large group of Van Gogh, Gauguin, Cézanne and Munch paintings, with others by living moderns, was shown in Cologne in an exhibition called the Sonderbund. That show seems to have precipitated Davies's dream of a large European cross-section in America, for upon receiving the catalogue, he sent it to Walt Kuhn with the note: "I wish we could have a show like this." Davies's suggestion became reality when Kuhn immediately set off for Cologne and contracted to borrow a large group of paintings from the Sonderbund. Kuhn then proceeded to the Hague, where he saw pictures by Redon and borrowed a roomful for the New York exhibition. In Paris, Kuhn was suddenly overcome by "the magnitude and importance of the whole thing," and he cabled Davies, who joined him there a week later.

The next several weeks Davies and Kuhn "practically lived in taxicabs," tracking down artists and making arrangements with their dealers for loans. The American painter Alfred Maurer introduced them to Vollard, the dealer who had exhibited many of the Impressionists and Post-Impressionists. The painter Walter Pach was an invaluable contact with living French artists, among them, Marcel Duchamp, whose *Nude Descending a Staircase* became the runaway sensation of the Armory Show. In London, Davies and Kuhn went to see Roger Fry's second modern exhibition at the Grafton Gallery, and satisfied themselves that they had already selected an equally good or superior group of paintings and sculptures, though they did arrange to borrow from the show. When all arrangements had been completed, Davies and Kuhn returned to America leaving Pach to look after details of packing and shipping.

Back in New York they set about trying to arouse enthusiasm for the exciting new exhibition which was now planned for the Armory of the New York National Guard's 69th Regiment, at Twenty-Sixth Street and Lexington Avenue. Kuhn persuaded Frederick James Gregg of the *New York Sun* to take charge of publicity, and the services of Guy

Pène du Bois, editor of *Arts and Decoration,* were enlisted. At the last minute the great barracks-like hall of the Armory was softened by symbolic swags of evergreen and other decorations financed by the generous Mrs. Gertrude Vanderbilt Whitney. The exhibition opened February 17, 1913, with a band bravely playing and art students distributing catalogues and badges with the pine-tree flag of the American revolutionary period and the inscription, "The New Spirit."

The Armory Show contained about sixteen hundred pieces of sculpture, paintings, drawings and prints; it included a large American selection made by William Glackens which comprised three-quarters of the whole. Work by most of the celebrated modernists, Picasso, Matisse, Brancusi, Duchamp, Kandinsky, Picabia, Léger, Braque, Rouault, Maillol, Lehmbruck were represented as well as a large group of paintings by Cézanne, Redon, Van Gogh, and Gauguin. In fact Davies's aim was nothing less than to show the evolution of modern art from the romantic period. In order to give a proper historical perspective to the revolutionary works of the present, he set them off with pictures by Delacroix, Ingres, Corot, Courbet, as well as the Impressionists and the Post-Impressionists. Except for the absent Italian Futurists—whom Davies tended to misconstrue and overlook as "feeble realists" and who had anyway refused to show unless allowed to exhibit as a group—and despite the weak German Expressionist section, the exhibition made an impressive representation of the main modern currents. Many of the important modern works in American collections were purchased directly out of the Armory Show by such celebrated collectors as John Quinn, Dr. Albert Barnes and Arthur Jerome Eddy; Bryson Burroughs bought from the exhibition the Metropolitan Museum's first Cézanne.

With our present advantage of hindsight, we might now quarrel with certain serious omissions, and with the general tendency to group the living moderns with the dead. But whatever confusion that grouping created was more than compensated by Davies's effort to establish an historical framework for modern art. Although the Armory Show was soon to take on a carnival character so far as the press and general public were concerned, it was an admirably serious effort to present the new, and to show its logical evolution over a century of artistic effort. As Davies reasonably declared in his "Explanatory Statement": ". . . the Society has embarked on no propaganda. It proposes to enter on no controversy with an institution. Its sole object is to put the paintings, sculptures and so on, on exhibition so that the intelligent may judge for themselves, by themselves. . . ."

Overnight, however, the Armory Show became front-page news and the center of heated controversy. The press reaction ranged from mock howls of pain to threats of violent retaliation. More than one public official urged the exhibition be closed as a menace to public morality and that the activities of the Society be legally proscribed. The general public joined the chorus of jeers and catcalls, but also enjoyed the spectacle of scandal in high culture and the discomfort of the entrenched powers who were called on to defend traditional values against the new insurgents. For sheer newsprint devoted to it, the exhibition was without precedent; for the first time in American history modern art achieved national prestige, albeit a prestige of notoriety. Even such public figures as ex-President Theodore Roosevelt felt impelled to deliver an opinion in print. The result was that the Armory Show became a huge public success. In the three cities where it was shown, New York, Chicago and Boston, a quarter of a million paid admissions were registered, and it is estimated an equal number were admitted without charge.

Duchamp's *Nude Descending the Staircase* was undoubtedly the most intriguing puzzle of the show and something of a *cause célèbre*. Julian Street called it an "explosion in a shingle factory"; newspaper cartoonists had a field day lampooning it under such titles as *The Rude Descending the Staircase (Rush Hour at the Subway)*, drawing everyday American experiences in pseudo-Cubist style. Amusingly enough, the mock-Cubist styles adopted to poke fun at the new art were a good deal more lively than the intricate, *Art-Nouveau* conventions most of the newspaper illustrators normally espoused. Written criticism of the show was altogether less light-hearted; it was basically and deeply frightened, violently hostile and often unscrupulous. With the exception of the writing of the publicists hired to promote the exhibition, and apart from the enlightened Henry McBride, Harriet Monroe in Chicago, the critics who wrote for *Camera Work* and James Huneker, the reports and analyses of the exhibition were uncomprehending and unsympathetic.

The New York Times described the show as *"pathological!"*, and repeatedly accused the Cubists, and Futurists (who were, with the notable exception of Joseph Stella, not included in the exhibition) of being "cousins to the anarchists in politics." Royal Cortissoz, pundit of the *New York Herald,* fumed: "This is not a movement and a principle. It is unadulterated cheek." Banner newspaper headlines on the order of "Making Insanity Profitable," were characteristic. In an article entitled "Lawless Art," *Art and Progress,* the official magazine of the American Federation of Arts, compared the new European artists to "anarchists, bombthrowers, lunatics, depravers." And even the dignified Mr. Cortissoz indulged in the same violent jingoism, a species of criticism that has been the least creditable aspect of the puritanical, provincial outlook from the Armory Show to the period of the depression when Thomas Craven repudiated modernism as "an imported ideology." "The United States," wrote Cortissoz, "is invaded by aliens, thousands of whom constitute so many perils to the health of the body politic. Modernism is of precisely the same heterogeneous alien origin and is imperiling the republic of art in the same way."

Some years later H. L. Mencken was to discover a wonderful target for his satirical gifts in the *Homo Americanus* who could entertain such ridiculous fears and provincial prejudices. In *Prejudices: Second Series,* published in 1920, Mencken wrote: "The one permanent emotion of the inferior man, as of all the simpler mammals, is fear—fear of the unknown, the complex, the inexplicable. What he wants beyond everything else is safety. His instincts incline him toward a society so organized that it will protect him . . . against the need to grapple with unaccustomed problems, to weigh ideas, to think things out for himself, to scrutinize the platitudes upon which his everyday thinking is based." It was far more convenient, and safe, to dismiss the new artists as madmen and charlatans than seriously to examine their work on its merits.

At the Art Institute of Chicago where a selection from the Armory Show was presented after the New York closing, the exhibition also provoked incensed responses, and public disorders. The opening there coincided with an Illinois morals investigation, and the state vice commission was warned that some of the outlandish new paintings were "immoral and suggestive." The results of the commission's investigation were inconclusive and no action was taken; but according to legend the Chicago underworld, enticed by the prospect of salacious art in high places, visited the show in great numbers to see what all the fuss was about. A spokesman for the Law and Order League of that city demanded the exhibition be shut down, declaring: "The idea that people can gaze at this sort of thing without it hurting them is all bosh." And art students at the Institute were advised by their instructors to shun the show like the plague, or, alternately, were conducted through it in the spirit of "crime does not pay." The students responded enthusiastically to the moral misgivings of their seniors by burning Brancusi, Matisse and Walter Pach in effigy. To no avail were the efforts of Harriet Monroe, one of the distinguished leaders of the Chicago poetry renaissance and founder of *Poetry* magazine. As a working art critic, she patiently and reasonably tried to present the case for modern art in the press. Hers was a lonely voice; everyone could find reassurance in the statement she quoted from the European critic, Guy-Charles Cros, "The new seems absurd; it arouses not admiration but astonishment." But few were able to share Cros's further view that, "Whatever happens, these first years of our century announce an efflorescence which will be one of the richest in the history of art. And it is good to live in this time of struggle, when men are rudely fighting to capture the new beauty."

Meyer Schapiro has pointed out in a profound and, unfortunately, little-known essay on the Armory Show, "Rebellion in Art," * that the real crisis of the exhibition was not for the modernists, despite the violent attacks on them, but for the traditionalists. If the spokesmen for the status quo were correct in their repeated charges that the new art was produced by lunatics, charlatans, and political subversives, then it should have caused them little enough concern; the public were far from being taken in, or corrupted by, the new art. Yet the conservative critics and artists took it seriously enough to feel the need to justify themselves. The Armory Show was a challenge not to be ignored. The vehement rebuttals of such generally level-headed critics as Frank Jewett Mather or of the dowdier academician, Kenyon Cox, indicated that they were deeply and genuinely disturbed and thrown on the defensive. Kenyon Cox warned in a series of ponderous meditations in *The New York Times* that the "real meaning" of Cubism, Futurism and experimental art was "nothing else than the total destruction of the art of painting." Frank Jewett Mather conceded some value to the experimental mood of the new art, but then added: "Yet I feel that all such gains . . . come to very little so long as art is unguided by any sound social tradition and left the prey of boisterous and undisciplined personalities." A schism had dramatically opened between "sound" and "unsound" art values, between official and progressive painting in America. In subsequent years the enemies of the modern and those who opposed even the sentiment of modernity did not relax their attitudes of vigilance. However, they were soon unable to pose with real conviction or enthusiasm a positive alternative, since even the art they defended was becoming a retarded and diluted academic derivative of some form of modernism.

The Armory Show also represented a crisis from the liberal point of view. It created serious doubts for the realist painters and for progressive critics like Theodore Roosevelt. They were prepared to accept the spirit of change but balked at too extreme a change. Such uneasiness before the more radical appeals to freedom and modernity in art had also been characteristic in Europe, but, as Dr. Schapiro has

* *America in Crisis*, New York, 1952.

noted, it was especially "striking to observe in America where individuality and freedom are advertised as national traits." Thus, Theodore Roosevelt, in his ambiguous review of the show in *The Outlook* of March 29, 1913, conceded that at least "the note of the commonplace" was refreshingly absent from the new work. He felt his sympathies engaged, but only up to a point. He admitted, more in sorrow than in anger, that progressive movements were likely to lead to excesses, and that there was "apt to be a lunatic fringe among the votaries of any forward movement." Roosevelt concluded finally on a note of stern disapproval: "In this recent exhibition the lunatic fringe was fully in evidence, especially in the rooms devoted to the Cubists and the Futurists, or near-Impressionists."

The reaction of the American public to modern forms was perhaps no more intense than had been the inhospitable receptions of the French to advanced movements in art since Manet and the Impressionists. While we were less than prepared, at the popular level, for the impact of the Armory Show, the more sophisticated art public of France showed little more foresight or understanding before twentieth-century art forms, despite the succession of great artist-martyrs in the preceding century. Uninformed American opinion, however, was magnified by the growth of pressure groups which in the spirit of conformity and as a matter of principle opposed themselves to the more socially disturbing varieties of individualism. The values of the new art were based precisely on new expressions of individualism. They corresponded to the radical empiricism of the new science and to the adventurous spirit apparent in other areas of thought during the first two decades of the new century, conveying a new sense of enlightenment, emancipation and hope in many spheres of human endeavor. But to the group mind these values soon became a corollary of socialism, anarchism and radical politics. The division between public values and those of our best minds was more sharply accentuated as we entered upon the modern period of standardized mass culture. And the press played an aggressive role in inflaming the prejudices of the general public. It was a role shaped, as H. L. Mencken put it, by American journalism's "incurable fear of ideas, its constant effort to evade the discussion of fundamentals by translating all issues into a few elemental fears, its incessant reduction of all reflection to mere emotion."

The wider recognition accorded modernism, and its relative success here after the Armory Show, is due in great part to the efforts of a few early patrons, collectors, critics and dealers in whose activities Americans may take a justifiable pride. The Stein family in Paris had in the very first years of the century bought and encouraged Matisse and Picasso with enthusiasm and conviction, and at a time when the French were still reviling the moderns. Under the influence of the Steins, the Cone sisters of Baltimore also bought Matisse in his Fauve period, and then other modern painting. The advent of Stieglitz, and then the Armory Show, stimulated the formation of such impressive modern collections as those of John Quinn, Dr. Albert Barnes, Walter Arensberg, Arthur Jerome Eddy and Lillie P. Bliss; today they form the nucleus of our outstanding museum collections in late-nineteenth and twentieth-century art. Yet it was many years before museums, with their inevitable influence on general standards, and the public at large could accept the revolutionary art of their century.

Much of the first impact of the Armory Show on taste was felt in the field of decoration, and took the form of a transformation in the design of utilitarian objects of daily life. In the applied arts, a kind of debased currency of modernism penetrated the American environment on a grand scale and seemed to make the new forms of art familiar and welcome. It is still a question, however, whether the basic sentiment of modernity, the unceasing quest for new freedoms of expression, today disturbs the lay public any less than it did in 1913. On the basis of the shocked reactions that unfailingly greet new manifestations in contemporary painting and sculpture, one can only assume that in its more vital and still-developing contemporary formulations modern art will never be acceptable.

Whether or not the American public has yet accepted modern art in the deepest sense, the established values in the art world itself were thoroughly shaken after the Armory

Show. As an index to the change in taste, prices of the Impressionists, Post-Impressionists and twentieth-century European art jumped astoundingly after 1913, and the market for the modern boomed. Three hundred paintings were purchased directly from the Show. John Quinn spent between five and six thousand dollars to form the main body of a superb collection which was later sold at auction. After the show new galleries sympathetic to modern art such as the Daniel, the Bourgeois and the Modern Gallery, the last organized by Marius de Zayas with Walter Arensberg's financial support, sprang into existence and implemented the effort that Stieglitz had for many years carried on alone.

The "advanced" painting that no gallery other than 291 would have touched prior to the show now found its way into exhibitions. A case in point was that of the Synchromists. Late in 1913 the Carroll Gallery showed the paintings of Morgan Russell and Stanton Macdonald-Wright, co-founders of a movement which was one of the most interesting American ventures of the period. Macdonald-Wright and Russell were in Paris between 1912 and 1913 when Robert Delaunay, with Frank Kupka, had begun loosening up Cubist structure and directing it toward a free, pure-color abstraction; their brilliant chromatic experiments were allied to but independent of Kandinsky's "Improvisations" of this and the immediately preceding years. A few months after Delaunay and Kupka had made these color innovations, in a style which Guillaume Apollinaire later dubbed Orphism, Macdonald-Wright and Russell arrived at an almost indistinguishable idiom. They protested in manifestoes that they, rather than the Europeans, originated the new style. Whatever the justice of their claim, the two Americans worked with enough individuality and verve to make the problem of derivation irrelevant. They painted flowing, rhythmic abstract compositions in parallel bars and concentric arcs of intense, pure color. Later they were joined by two other Americans, Patrick Bruce and Arthur Burdett Frost, Jr. Although Synchromism petered out with the war, during its heyday it affected a number of American painters and found an articulate, influential champion in Williard Huntington Wright, the brother of one of its founders.

Another sign of the more emancipated artistic atmosphere attendant on the Armory Show was Mrs. Gertrude Vanderbilt Whitney's establishment in 1915 of the Friends of the Young Artists from which grew the Whitney Studio Club three years later. The club gave its artist members individual and group exhibitions; it was the germ of New York City's present Whitney Museum of American Art, opened in 1931. The Whitney Museum has devoted itself to encouraging contemporary American artists by purchases and exhibitions.

One of the most interesting and significant presentations of the new American art following the Armory Show was the Forum Exhibition of Modern American Painters in 1916 organized by Willard Huntington Wright. Wright had been an accomplished literary journalist and editor of *Smart Set,* thus preceding Mencken and George Jean Nathan as the director of one of the period's most sophisticated literary publications. Wright returned from Europe in 1915 to write a monthly art chronicle for the *Forum* and to contribute art criticism to *Camera Work,* and brought out his book, *Modern Painting,* a year after the publication of Arthur Jerome Eddy's *Cubists and Post-Impressionists,* the pioneering American work on modern art. Wright was a serious and discerning critic despite an extreme partisanship for Synchromism which led him to make reckless comparisons and blinded him to the far more significant contribution of Matisse, the Cubists, the Futurists, and other contemporary movements. Nevertheless, his views on modern art, in principle, were more daring than any that had been expressed, apart from contributions to *Camera Work;* the show which he induced *Forum* magazine to sponsor was one of the vital demonstrations of modern art in the period.

The Forum Exhibition was an effort to make an *authoritative show* of American moderns, the inescapable implication being that the public had been treated to a good deal of spurious art in the guise of modernism. It was also intended, as Wright declared in the foreword, "to turn attention for the moment from European art" and redirect it to native efforts, which had been obscured by the sensation made at the Armory Show by the Europeans. Wright had wisely obtained as a committee of sponsors an eclectic and prominent list of men, to certify and help explain the work in the exhibition. They were the critic Christian Brinton, an editor of *Art in America;* Robert Henri; W. H. de B. Nelson, Editor of *International Studio;* Alfred Stieglitz; and Dr. John Weichsel, President of the People's Art Guild, an organization that mixed proselytizing for advanced art with social welfare work. Seventeen artists were represented, and each wrote an explanatory note to his work. The participants were Thomas Benton, Oscar Bluemner, Andrew Dasburg, Arthur Dove, George Of, Ben Benn, Marsden Hartley, S. Macdonald-Wright, John Marin, Alfred Maurer, Henry McFee, Man Ray, Morgan Russell, Charles Sheeler, Abraham Walkowitz, Marguerite and William Zorach. All the artists but Ben Benn and George Of were working under the influence of either Cubism, Matisse, or Synchromism, and almost without exception their statements stressed the formal aspects of their art. For a number, the work they showed was to remain the most boldly experimental of their careers.

On the defensive after the nightmarish reception of the Armory Show, Wright may have protested too much in his "foreword" with the statement: "Not one man represented in this exhibition is either a charlatan or a maniac." With some impatience and in a school-masterish tone he chided the public into accepting work "vouched for by men whose integrity and knowledge of art are beyond question." He wrote: "To ridicule the pictures here on view can only be a confession of ignorance. All new excursions into the field of knowledge have been met with ridicule; but despite that ridicule, the new has persisted, in time becoming the old and the accepted." Wright's hopeful admonitions were in contrast to the Forum Exhibition statement made by Stieglitz, who answered in a decided negative the question: "Is the American really interested in . . . any form of art?" The conservative critic, Frank Jewett Mather, remained unimpressed by Wright's carefully reasoned justifications for the exhibition. "I think that the seriousness of these moderns," he wrote, "matters very little."

Yet, if there was any challenge in the criticism of the

times to the kind of smug historical point of view Mather
represented, it was Wright's. Wright was one of the first to
reverse customary critical procedures, interpreting the past
through the eyes of the present instead of stepping out of
his time and measuring the present invidiously against the
past. Following the example of Roger Fry and Clive Bell
in England, he sought in the art of the past some universal
principle of design or formal organization, of "significant
form," in Bell's apt phrase, that would provide a common
clue to all esthetic experience. In the Forum Catalogue,
Wright declared with a good deal of courage that the greatest art of the past, of El Greco, Rubens and others, moves
us for exactly the same reasons that the most experimental
art of the present does: "The truth of modern art, despite
its often formidable and bizarre appearance, is only a
striving to rehabilitate the natural and unalterable principles of rhythmic form to be found in the old masters, and
to translate them into relative and more comprehensive
terms." And he proposed the unprecedented thesis that: "A
picture to be a great work of art need not contain any recognizable objects. Provided it gives the sensations of rhythmically balanced form in three dimensions, it will have accomplished all that the greatest masters have ever striven
for."

Wright's challenging view was perhaps the most lucid
and closely argued rejection of nineteenth-century naturalism in American art criticism of his period. "Were realism
the object of art," he wrote, "painting would always be
infinitely inferior to life—a mere simulacrum of our daily
existence, ever inadequate in its illusion. . . . Our minds
call for a more forceful emotion than the simple imitation
of life can give. We require problems, inspirations, incentives to thought."

Wright's criticism corresponded in time and temper to
an heroic moment in American painting. But not long afterward, arising undoubtedly out of the cruel erosion of hope
and confidence that followed World War I, criticism retreated and so did art, seeking safer modes of thought and
feeling. Wright himself later became obsessed with color
theory and put his esthetic faith in the color organ. Then

he gave up art criticism altogether to become a famous detective-story writer under the pseudonym, S. S. Van Dine. Perhaps the radical tenor of Wright's thought might have found more to support it in the intellectual climate of England, and certainly his career as a critic could have prospered better in Paris. In provincial America he was isolated and eccentricity was his fate.

The reassertion of nationalist feeling and provincialism had come soon after the Armory Show. Even as more liberated styles received stimulation from the exhibition, there was a reaction against the domination of the Europeans. A good deal was made of the invidious comparison between the American and European art object. The publicist for the show, Frederick James Gregg, declared that "the vast mass of the American works exhibited represented simply arrested development." William Glackens was even more depressed by the American section and said: "We have no innovators here. Everything worthwhile in our art is due to the influence of French art. We have not arrived at a national art. . . . Our own art is arid and bloodless." This sense of failure, of cultural inferiority, though not universal, led in time to more aggressive attacks on internationalism. Jerome Myers complained bitterly that "Davies had unlocked the door to foreign art and thrown the key away. Our land of opportunity was thrown wide open to foreign art, unrestricted and triumphant; more than ever before, we had become provincials . . . While foreign names became familiar, un-American propaganda was ladled out wholesale."

The cross-currents and conflicts of a renewed provincialism and the rapidly growing interest in European modernism divided progressive forces in American painting. In 1917 the independents idea was revived with the founding of the Society of Independent Artists. The new officers were balanced between the moderates and radicals. William Glackens was made president; Maurice Prendergast, vice-president; Walter Pach, treasurer; John Covert, secretary; and Walter Arensberg, managing director. Taking as its motto the slogan of the celebrated French Independents of 1884, "No Jury—No Prizes," the Society held its historic first exhibition, with 2,500 works by 1,300 artists. The show was a cross-section of American art, much of it mediocre, but it also included the best moderns in this country and a number of distinguished Europeans. Among those who sent work were Schamberg, Stella, Pach, Maurer, Demuth, Bruce, Hartley, Frost, Friedman, Man Ray, O'Keeffe, Zorach, Dreier, Weber, Dove, Halpert, Hawthorne, the American realists, and the Europeans, Picasso, Gleizes, Signac, Duchamp-Villon, Vlaminck, Brancusi and Metzinger.

There was strongly divided opinion as to the importance of the show. Marcel Duchamp had withdrawn because he felt the representation was too conservative; Henri afterward protested at the large amount of amateurish work and was critical of the more radical moderns. During the war the organization languished, although it continued to hold annual exhibitions. When it renewed activities in the postwar period, it was dominated by the more conservative elements, and the few former moderns who continued to exhibit had begun to shift their style toward more realistic interpretations of the American scene.

The Armory Show had put the custodians of orthodoxy on the defensive, but the unforeseen attention focused on European innovation, at the expense of native art, was the signal for the beginning of a retreat from internationalism. The contagious idealism kindled during the early Stieglitz period was mislaid in the war. The high expectations of one generation were exchanged for the caution and skepticism of another. Randolph Bourne wrote bitterly but prophetically in his war diary in 1917: "The war . . . or American promise. One must choose. . . . For the effect of the war will be to impoverish the American promise."

In the twenties a new mood of disenchantment set in, and modernism no longer served as a summons to action. Nor was the American artist concerned any longer to test himself by European standards, by the esthetic criteria of a culture which the war had convinced him was in its decline. Interest in the American scene as a reassuring source of common experience revived, but often with an addiction to its grotesque aspects. Experimental art lost its purpose and collective meaning, and for most artists modernism became a matter of imitative clichés, easily mastered and easily discarded. The Armory Show was robbed of its potency; a few of the sterner spirits survived the postwar crisis in painting, however, and, building on the modern legacy, fashioned their own distinctive styles in the decade that followed.

5

Innocents at Home and Abroad

"Marin is no longer translating the concrete into the abstract, he has learned to think in the latter. One accepts what is seen without any need of conjecture. One can enjoy freely the spiritual appeal of the expression."
—Charles Caffin, *Camera Work,* 1916

"John Marin and I drew our inspiration from the same source, French modernism. He brought his up in buckets and spilt much along the way. I dipped mine out with a teaspoon, but I never spilled a drop."

—Charles Demuth

The eager American acceptance of the experimental which had kindled so many hopes during the first years of 291, bore fruit in the decade after the controversial Armory Show despite the many hostile rumblings that exhibition had set off. Out of their contact with advanced Parisian painting, first *in situ* and then at home under Stieglitz's auspices, a growing number of American artists had already begun to show radical new styles before 1913. Some of the artists who made the most significant contribution to the first flowering of an advanced art were Max Weber, Marsden Hartley, Arthur Dove, John Marin and Charles Demuth.

Their painting spans a long and often contradictory period, from the lusty birth of innovation through the virtual extinction of modernism as a collective effort in the twenties and thirties, to the emergence of a new generation of abstract artists of conviction in the early forties. As had happened often in the past, the provincial innocence of our first wave of moderns was a source of both strength and weakness. It shielded the artist from the theoretical preoccupations of advanced European movements, from group manifestoes and polemics, in some cases preserving an essential individualism which proved most refreshing. On the other hand a lack of depth in their commitment to modern forms worked against even our best artists, and ultimately betrayed them into a shallow eclecticism. In the prevailing conservative artistic atmosphere of the post-bellum period, the modern painter and sculptor were, on the whole, unable to resist the pressures of philistinism and an imitative, pedestrian realism.

No individual American artist can be singled out as the pioneer of advanced styles. The early years of the modern movement are somewhat obscured by public interest in the paintings of the realists, in John Sloan, Henri and other members of the Eight. The first to react to the more sophisticated European styles may have been Alfred Maurer, who was living in Paris in 1900 and was by 1904 a welcome visitor in the rue de Fleurus apartment of Gertrude and Leo Stein. In 1907 and 1908 Maurer's rather fashionable salon painting manner, which took its cue from Sargent and from Maurer's American teacher, William Merritt Chase, began to change under the influence of Matisse's Fauve painting. Maurer was probably introduced to Matisse's new style through the Steins who had begun to collect the French artist's work after the Autumn Salon of 1905 where the Fauves first exhibited together. Max Weber and Patrick Henry Bruce also established their claim as pioneers when they joined Matisse's first painting class in 1908. And so, too, did Arthur Dove, who arrived in Paris in 1907, and Arthur B. Carles, both of whom, however, became aware of new currents in painting through Maurer.

By 1910 John Marin had been abroad five years and was in the Austrian Tyrol, at Kufstein, doing water colors of mountain scenery in an extremely free and improvisatory manner. Back in America in 1910, after two years abroad, Arthur Dove painted what was probably the country's first entirely non-representational painting, *Abstraction Number 2* (Collection of the Downtown Gallery, New York). It coincided in time with the first of Wassily Kandinsky's abstract paintings, although Dove's precocious discovery of abstraction now seems to have been fragmentary and inconclusive, since it did not develop into a consistent abstract manner in the immediately following years. In 1909 when Alfred Stieglitz gave Marsden Hartley his first one-man show, the New York art dealer could write in *Camera Work* of the *avant-garde* look of Hartley's Van Goghish landscape: ". . . his interpretation of sky, mountains and woods in brilliant coloring is of a decorative rather than realistic effect."

The exposure to Fauve painting in Paris, then, seems to have been the first inspiration of America's advanced painting; but Stieglitz's exhibition of Cézanne's water colors and Picasso's Cubist drawings and paintings in 1911 became an even more important influence. The Armory Show, the appearance of Picabia in New York at that time, and the presence of Marcel Duchamp in America after 1915, were also decisive factors in establishing European artistic viewpoints in this country.

It was perhaps the painter Max Weber who in the beginning best understood, and conveyed, the new European sense of art, through his paintings and declarations. Indeed, he more than any of his countrymen showed, through the first two decades of his art, that professionalism in medium and instinctive grasp of formal principle which have traditionally been associated with art emanating from Paris. If, in retrospect, his career now seems marked by eclecticism and a constant shifting of esthetic ground, he has also in the past demonstrated a seriousness about painting that made more consistent talents seem narrowly provincial in their limitations.

Weber was born in Russia in 1881 and emigrated to America with his family at the age of ten. His serious artistic education began at the Pratt Institute in Brooklyn when he took Arthur Wesley Dow's celebrated composition course. Dow was one of the pioneers of the new interest in oriental art, and he had been at Pont-Aven in Brittany with Gauguin and Emile Bernard. His interest in the decorative styles of Japanese art and in a non-naturalistic use of color, as exemplified by Gauguin and the Nabis, made

him an enlightened and vital teacher. He was also one of
the few members of the teaching profession who later
came vigorously to the defense of the Armory Show, and
thus faced extreme public censure.

By 1905 Weber had saved enough money from teaching
art to go to Paris. His arrival coincided with the public
debut of Matisse and the other Fauve painters who had
broken through the fetters of naturalism and a doctrinaire
Neo-Impressionism to paint with a new freedom and intensity of color. 1905 was also the occasion of a large
Cézanne exhibition at the same celebrated Autumn Salon
where Matisse and his friends made history. Cézanne's
paintings were shown again even more extensively in the
following two years, and by 1908 he had become the acknowledged inspiration of the early Cubist paintings of Picasso and Braque. That year Weber came directly into contact with advanced French painting when he enrolled in
Matisse's private *Académie;* he had already become an admirer and intimate of Henri Rousseau. On the eve of Weber's departure from Paris for America at the end of the
year. Rousseau held a soirée for him. Later the French
painter is reported advising Weber not to "forget nature."
It was Weber who introduced Stieglitz to Rousseau's painting and was responsible for the French primitive's first
American exhibition early in 1911 at 291. As Stieglitz wrote,
". . . Weber . . . first sang the hymn to Rousseau in America. Weber's daily songs were: *'Cézanne, cet homme'* followed by *'Rousseau, cet ange.'* "

The combined influences of Cézanne, Matisse, Rousseau
and Cubism were to shape Weber's early style; such influences were little in evidence, however, when he held his
first American one-man show in the cellar of a New York
framing shop early in 1909. It was Stieglitz who acted
as the decisive catalyst in Weber's more radical stylistic
ventures. The two men met in the fall of 1909 and Weber
went to live for a brief period at 291, assisting Stieglitz
in hanging his shows. In 1910 he was included along with
Dove, Marin, Hartley and Maurer in 291's first group show
of native moderns, "Younger American Painters." The ex-

hibition invited the earliest press attacks on the emerging American modernists, and was described as a hoax and an "insult to the public." This violent reaction marks the dishonorable beginning of a series of bellicose deprecations which greeted Weber's successive exhibitions. At this time the artist's interests were widening in line with the new esthetic viewpoints he had absorbed abroad. Perhaps it was Picasso's Negro period that now drove him to investigate Mayan and Aztec sculpture, the totems of Pacific Indians and other examples of primitive art in New York's Museum of Natural History.

He also began to contribute articles to *Camera Work* on the relevance of primitive cultures to modern sensibility. And with considerable eloquence he set forth his views on the dynamic, new spatial concepts that were behind the Cubist movement. In an article rather awkwardly entitled "The Fourth Dimension from a Plastic Point of View," he wrote: "In plastic art there is a fourth dimension which may be described as the last consciousness of a great and overwhelming sense of space-magnitude in all directions at the same time."

By 1910 Weber had begun to show his own individual interpretation of the drastic simplifications in form and color and the strong, rhythmic outlines of Matisse's art. Matisse's influence persisted until as late as 1913 in such paintings as *Decoration with Cloud*. Between 1910 and 1912 Weber also experimented with Cubist structure and composed more aggressively. *The Geraniums* of 1911 shows a fine understanding of early Cubism; the two compact female forms resemble Picasso's figuration of 1908 and 1909. Weber, however, achieved a distinctive personal synthesis of the abrupt, angular Cubist style with Matisse's brilliant, sensuous palette. In the masks and resigned attitudes of his figures there are elements of caricature and a touch of poetic melancholy which bear the stamp of an individual artistic temperament. Weber was at pains to link the painting with the Cubist mystique of geometric fragmentation and enumeration, describing it thus: "The conception and the treatment spring from a search of form in the crystal." But his mannered elongations of form are probably also related to the profound impression made upon him by the art of El Greco during a trip to Spain. The rather tender and wistful characterization of the figures, for all their formalism, perhaps grew out of Weber's awareness of himself as a Jew, a consciousness of origins that was to play a large part in his choice of themes in his later years.

The reactions of critics to Weber's new paintings, shown at 291 in a one-man show in 1911, were of an almost hysterical violence. One writer found that his forms had "no justification in nature" and compared them to "the emanations of someone not in his right mind." Another was aghast at the artist's "brutal, vulgar and unnecessary display of art license." And still another incensed puritan ungenerously wrote: "Such grotesquerie could only be acquired by long and perverse practice." Weber's wistful, tentative Cubism provided the philistine press with their first solid target prior to the Armory Show.

Among the modern paintings at the Armory Show, Duchamp's *Nude Descending the Staircase,* Picabia's *Procession at Seville* and Stella's Futurist, *Battle of Lights, Coney Island* (Plate 6), came to exert the most seminal influence on American painters. The intense activism of surface in these works, as compared to the more contemplative emphasis of orthodox French Cubism, touched a sympathetic artistic nerve in this country. They seemed to crystallize the heightened sensations with which American artists were now trying to express the explosive character of urban experience. The multiplicity and energy of metropolitan life were given form by Weber in a new Cubist-Futurist vocabulary which employed violent, kaleidoscopic effects, suggesting movement and a mood of agitated apprehension. In many of the paintings executed between 1915 and 1917 Weber brilliantly communicated a new sense of release and energetic excitement, even when his formal synthesis contained so many elements that the picture surface seemed to buckle under the load. *Chinese Restaurant* (Plate 7) of 1919 is surely one of the more ambitious and interesting American paintings in a period notable for boldly experimental work. While it may be judged an uncertain esthetic success, owing to its glaring stylistic inconsistencies, it is nevertheless a remarkable and convincing demonstration of a vital native application of Parisian esthetics. It conveys an authentic experience.

On the one hand the painting seems to announce itself as a venture in decorative Cubism, and its rich, ornamental surface and varied patterning can be related to the collage. These effects, however, curiously co-exist with pockets of fluid, transparent space where we catch glimpses, in shallow depth, of the multiple images and fragmentary geometric structures of Analytical Cubism. There is also a plan of episodic, visual sequence that suggests the paroxysm of Futurism, and its effort to capture kinetic sensations. Yet the picture has an undeniable impact, perhaps because it quite literally re-creates Weber's own agitated, vertiginous impressions of the bizarre décor of his subject. "On entering a Chinese restaurant from the darkness of the night outside," he wrote, "a maze and blaze of light seemed to split into fragments the interior and its contents, the human and the inanimate. For the time being the static became transient and fugitive—oblique planes and contours took on vertical and horizontal positions, and the horizontal became oblique, the light so piercing and luminous, the color so liquid and the light and movement so enchanting! To express this, kaleidoscopic means had to be chosen."

Through 1917 Weber continued to experiment in a Cubist-Futurist idiom. After that date, in response to the same revival of interest in naturalism then being experienced abroad, he began to incorporate more and more realistic descriptive detail into his painting, with more damaging disunity to his style. The return to the traditional assurances of naturalistic allusion, which in the case of Matisse and Picasso provided a temporary respite from a heroic period of adventurous experiment, seemed to rob Weber's art of its whole momentum and coherence. Caught in the crosscurrents of movements and counter-movements, and their muffled echoes in America, Weber in the early twenties emulated Picasso's inflated neo-classical style. Then he painted landscapes in a manner that combined the palette of Cézanne with a coarser pigment surface and an

Expressionist vehemence in handling. He became a lapidary of jeweled color and thick, shining paint paste, but something of his original fine energy seemed to have been lost, despite the new emphasis on voluptuous surface. Weber's mood became retrospective, his performance repetitive, if more obviously dramatic.

In the forties Weber painted more schematically in fluid oil wash, taking his figure style perhaps from Picasso's *Guernica,* and lacing his overworked surfaces with a network of line. His subjects generally were Talmudic scholars engaged in argument, or moving in fantastic gyrations whose plastic motivation or symbolic meaning were not altogether clear. A restless graphic activity was unable finally to compensate for a small inventive capacity and a curiously thin atmosphere. What friendly critics have described as Weber's capacity in such paintings to rise to religious ecstasy can be interpreted less generously as an impoverishment of content and a desperate search for viable pictorial means. Some facile critical appreciations of this inadvertently grotesque late style, and the effort to equate it with Weber's earlier work, do a disservice to the high creative level of his first decade of painting and reduce the stature of the artist as a whole.

Weber's recent work is unrelated in character or general significance to his painting of the period of *Geraniums, The Chinese Restaurant,* or even to his Expressionism of the early twenties. The rapid deterioration of advanced styles, leaving a vacuum which neither naturalism nor eclecticism can convincingly fill, has not been an unusual phenomenon in the history of modern art. It is the high price exacted from the individual creative spirit by a continuing revolutionary period in the visual arts.

The paintings of Marsden Hartley similarly show the generative powers of the first modern impulses received from Europe and, with modifications, the same pattern of isolation from the European mainstream, compromise and a sharp decline in the artist's critical capacity. Hartley had begun in 1908 to paint his own free version of Segantini's academic Impressionism, with its "stitchings of color." Then in 1909 he exhibited work at 291 which had become more concentrated formally, unified around a style that suggested both the expressive, rhythmic pigmentation of Van Gogh and the more somber tonalities of Ryder. Hartley was abroad in 1912, and there he experimented with Cubism; he then loosened his style, in contact with the high-keyed colors and the more inspirational abstract art of Kandinsky and the members of the Blue Rider. That year, at the invitation of Franz Marc, he showed with the Blue Rider, in the first German Autumn Salon in Berlin, organized by Herwarth Walden, editor of *Der Sturm* and one of the important early champions of modern art.

By 1915 Hartley had arrived at a personal synthesis of the emblematic insignia and ornament of decorative Cubism, and the fluid movement and intense spectrum colors of Kandinsky's first abstract style. His new work was bold and aggressive, incorporating references to German militarism, in such repeated symbols as the Maltese cross, within a scheme of strident, spectral color, often set off by ragged areas of flat black. The next year he moved toward a new austerity and experimented with flat, slab-like arrangements of rectilinear shapes, somewhat Constructivist in spirit. His palette was softened toward pastel and neutral hues, and he employed blander forms, held in subtle tension despite their drastic, geometric simplicity. Very few of his paintings of this brief period now exist; those that are still accessible show a distinction in color, and a most interesting balance of elegance with a stolid, forceful simplicity. They also indicate a powerful, assured grasp of abstract idioms that for a variety of cultural reasons soon atrophied in the unstable atmosphere of American art.

Like Weber, Hartley seemed for a brief period able to find his integrity and individuality as an artist within the radical structural language of European abstraction. He expressed his emotions forcefully and with a distinction that eluded him in later years when he sought a more obviously personal artistic identity, and worked within a more mannered style. Following the general tendency of the twenties to return to the object and to nature, Hartley rediscovered Cézanne around 1926, a Cézanne, however, whose vibrancy and tenuousness he hardened into em-

phatic decoration and an enameled, facile coherence of
form. Beginning in 1931 with his "Dogtown" landscapes
painted in the vicinity of Gloucester, he worked in a simplified, rugged Expressionism, curiously cold, passive and
inert despite its drastic outlines and vivid color contrasts.
Only between 1908 and 1917, that is, before he had resolved his period of experiment and before he had begun
to state all too succinctly his own sharply circumscribed
artistic personality, did Hartley demonstrate an impressive
vitality and invention. After that period he made his real
reputation in the predictable style that has won him his
widest public following.

Arthur Dove's was a more consistent performance, if
more limited in range, than either Hartley's or Weber's.
Once he arrived at the new language of abstraction, he
pursued it to its radical conclusions and never recanted.
Dove had been in Europe between 1907 and 1909. Through
Alfred Maurer and Arthur Carles he was in contact with
the work of the contemporary French vanguard. By 1915
he had firmly established himself in a painting genre of
flowing, amorphous shape, muted color and repeated
rhythmic accent. As early as 1910 he tentatively approached
abstract modes in a loose geometric style, and then, the
following year, moved into a freer manner, but one also
that renewed contact with nature, in such pastels as *Nature
Symbolized, No. 2.* His forms were related after 1915 to
the soft color masses of the Synchromists, to Kandinsky,
and more ancestrally, to Gauguin's arabesques and the
fanciful organic shapes of *Art Nouveau.* During his earliest
phase Dove painted in a restrained, monochromatic palette accented by sober earth colors. Later he used more
resonant tonalities, but always retained neutrals, tans and
velvety blacks as a foil for his more intense hues. Like
the early Kandinsky of 1910-1914, Dove used colors and
forms to suggest an attenuation of naturalistic shapes and
a diffusion of local colors taken from some actual scene.
He painted the disembodied elements of a dream-landscape
that had begun to blur, to distend and to take on mysteri-
ously heightened powers as an abstract composition. Dove
transposed but did not entirely eliminate his landscape im-

pressions, and his living, organic forms constantly evoked
nature, analogically if not more directly. Of his paintings,
he wrote: "I should like to take wind and water and sand
as a motif and work with them, but it has to be simplified in
most cases to color and force lines and substances just as
music has done with sound."

Dove's mood of poetic reverence in the presence of
nature, that sense his paintings convey of saturation in
landscape color and of a strong underlying relation to real
experience, was mingled with other psychological manifestations. His expanding circular shapes, graduated in concentric bands of diminishing color-intensity, suggested both
a symbolic representation of the effects of light and a mood
of mysticism, as if the artist were intent to lose himself
in the dark flow and pulse of organic nature. In his statement for the Forum Exhibition Catalogue he had declared
his artistic aim was to find visual symbols which espoused
both the inner stirrings of the self and external nature: "to
give in form and color the reaction that plastic objects and
sensations of light from within and without have reflected
from my inner consciousness. . . . My wish," he continued,
"is to work so unassailably that one could let one's worst
instincts go unanalyzed. . . ." One is reminded of the statements of another artist to whose work Dove's bears certain
spiritual affinities, Odilon Redon. The Frenchman had
written of his dreaming, symbolist art: "I intend an irradi-
ation which seizes the spirit and escapes all analysis." The
play of non-aggressive, rhythmic shape and the mood of
mystic imminence in Dove's paintings struck a balance
between the fantastic-symbolist modes of turn-of-the-century art and the more vital, flowing color bands of his contemporaries, the Synchromists.

An effort has been made in recent years to relate Dove
to mid-century directions in abstract art, but the comparison is strained by the diverse aims and the unrelated artistic
backgrounds of painters of the first and the contemporary
periods of abstraction. Any resemblance, for example, between the paintings of Dove and Clyfford Still, or the Mark
Rothko of an early phase, must remain superficial despite
surface similarities in appearance. Dove worked within one

of the viable blueprints of early modernism, a form of synthetic, rhythmic abstraction inherited from Kandinsky, and perhaps Delaunay, but minus their brilliant spectrum colors. His repertory of devices was limited, his forms often seemed decoratively stylized rather than plastic or organic, and they projected a consistent symbolic intention, an esthetic he shared with the more literal-minded Georgia O'Keeffe. Dove's ragged edges and engulfing black shapes, which rise and fall like some impersonal tide, share with the effects of Still and Rothko a parenthood in Kandinsky, Arp and "biomorphic" abstraction. Dove's artistic universe, however, is closed and static; his forms are more ready-made and often reject sensation entirely in favor of a stereotyped formalism. While his work is not without distinction and individual accent, it does seem calculated, using a handed-down method to proceed toward a preconceived and clearly envisioned goal. In his best work, one feels the operation of a strange, luminous subjective consciousness, but it is nonetheless firmly planted in and fixed on external reality.

The contemporary American abstract artists derive from the same general sources but their painting refers to its artistic origins far less formally and explicitly. They address themselves to fresh sensation which arises from the very process of creating itself, from the pure, physical act of manipulating paint matter. Their emphasis is on method and on the fertility and inventiveness of the artistic act, rather than on some experience external to the work of art. Dove's felicity as well as his limitations lay precisely in his easy mastery of a "received" and already articulated language of abstraction. The contemporary painter, for reasons that will become clearer in subsequent chapters, has renounced such stereotypes and has tried to make a fresh start, guided by little more than his own immediate sensations and impulses. His art is powered by a new dynamism and nourished by a more meaningful atmosphere of artistic freedom.

Another aspect of Dove's art that distinguishes it from the present generation is the collage. This he converted into a personal, intimately expressive form. Employing fragments of everyday reality, he evolved a tender poetry of the commonplace, distinguished by its simplicity, good humor and lyrical grace.

Of all the artists from America's first period of modernism, John Marin seems nearest to us and to present-day sensibilities, although he has not been a direct influence on contemporary art. This may be explained in part by his fierce attachment to values of freedom, to a traditionally American romantic individualism, and in part by his remarkable tactile sense. The lyrical effusions so often associated with his art, or his scintillating mastery of the watercolor medium, interest present-day artists less than Marin's expressive surfaces. Late in his life when Marin had begun to work more consistently in oils, he told a biographer that he wished "to give paint a chance to show itself entirely as paint." This insistence on the stubborn, irreducible, material reality of paint has become the very heartbeat of contemporary artistic creation in America. It is one of Marin's most considerable contributions to the art of his time, and is also a latter-day extension of the new mood of candor about pictorial means that had begun with Manet and the Impressionists. If Marin engages the interest of vanguard artists today or commands their respect, it is because he managed in his art to further significantly the destruction of traditional illusionist means—to carry forward the vital rehabilitation of those "painting techniques, whose principal sin," the poet Mallarmé had parenthetically observed in 1874, "is to mask the origin of this art which is made of oils and colors."

A measure of Marin's remarkable malleability is that he can be related to both the first and second phases of American modernism. A statement made by the artist in 1947, when Marin renewed his earlier mood of radical esthetic experiment, now seems prophetic of the aims of the Abstract Expressionists; he then wrote: "Using paint *as* paint is different from using paint to paint a picture. I'm calling my pictures this year 'Movements in Paint' and not movements of boat, sea, or sky, because in these new paintings, although I use objects, I am representing paint first of all, and not the motif primarily."

The other living link between Marin and the contemporary generation is his intense love of personal liberty. In his passionate pursuit of artistic freedom Marin quite often has consciously played the role of the eccentric individualist, adapting himself to the popular image of the shrewd, laconic Yankee who scorns the highfalutin and pretentious, mistrusts intellectualism, and affects a picturesque and slightly fantastic style. A friend, Loren Mozely, has described him as "an American original." Mozely has stated that Marin's "letters as well as his speech are full of tasty Yankee expressions such as 'Cracker-jack,' 'High Cockalorum,' 'Hum-Dinger.'" The paradox of Marin, as of so many American artists, lies in the combination of an aggressive native pride carried to the point of an almost gleeful provincialism, and an abiding respect for the cosmopolitan spirit. His art reflects and unites these warring impulses. Writing to Alfred Stieglitz in 1927, in a loose, Whitmanesque prose, Marin all too readily admitted the contradictions within himself, but with that characteristically disarming candor and energy which make his self-fascination seem expansive and creative rather than restricting:

> "Curiously twisted creature.
> Prejudiced as Hell.
> Unprejudiced as Hell.
> Narrow-minded as they make 'em.
> Broad-minded next minute.
> Hating everything foreign, to a degree, with
>   the opposite coming in, time and time.
> A shouting spread-eagled American.
> A drooping wet-winged sort of nameless fowl
>   the next.
> But, take it easy, whoa there, pull up. . . ."

Marin came to modern art relatively late and after considerable hesitation. He had apprenticed himself to an architect (a fact which has often been used inconclusively to explain his feeling for decisive pictorial structure), and then actually practiced as an architect before settling on painting. At the age of twenty-eight he began to give art his whole attention, entering the Pennsylvania Academy where he worked under William Merritt Chase and Thomas Anschutz. There he met Arthur Carles who later shared his interest in advanced European art and became a close companion in Paris. From 1905 to 1911 Marin lived abroad and made a considerable reputation from his etchings of European monuments executed in a delicate, atmospheric style which suggests Whistler's tonal refinements and estheticism. But even in his early European *Wanderjahr,* when he seemed to be compiling a careful notebook on the European past with much emphasis on unspectacular, descriptive detail, Marin's more wayward impulses erupted. An etching of the Cathedral at Rouen shows his restless, nervous energy shaking itself loose in a characteristically soaring transcription.

By 1908 he had begun to use fresh color and exercise a new freedom in the water-color medium, in his own more intense and loose adaptation of Impressionist technique. His *London Omnibus* of that year treated a commonplace scene with a freedom and vigor which forecast a new direction in Marin's art. In 1910 at Kufstein in the Austrian Tyrol Marin executed a series of scenic water colors of an even more inventive and improvisatory nature, using merely suggestive color diffusions and an incisive, fragmentary technique to indicate position and form. This transitional style, diffuse and accented at once, oriental in its economy, is reminiscent of the Neo-Impressionist manner employed in water colors by Matisse and Marquet in 1904, as they stood at the threshold of a more explosive Fauve manner. There is no direct evidence that Marin was aware of the Fauves, but through his friends Alfred Maurer and Arthur Carles, he undoubtedly absorbed something of the growing sentiment of freedom, if not the actual technical viewpoints of the contemporary Paris art world.

In 1909 Marin held his first one-man show at the Stieglitz gallery. This exhibition enjoyed a *succès d'estime.* Writing in *Camera Work,* Paul Haviland declared that Marin's water colors were "pronounced by authorities" to be "the best examples of the medium which have ever been shown in New York." And the critic Charles Caffin, scenting the abstract bias of his work, wrote: "Consciousness of facts disappears in a spiritualized version of form and color."

Only in 1911 and 1912, however, after he had passed his fortieth birthday, did Marin's modernism decisively announce itself in a dynamic new graphic style, with the first of his etchings of the Woolworth Building and the Brooklyn Bridge. Like Weber, Hartley and Dove, he was undoubtedly deeply influenced at a critical moment in his development by his association with Alfred Stieglitz. At 291 he had had the opportunity in 1911 to see and examine at his leisure exhibitions of Cézanne's late water colors and the early Cubist drawings and water colors of Picasso. The importance of exposure to this work was later pointed out by Charles Caffin in the *New York American*. Describing the transition in Marin's style from his anecdotal, European etchings, he wrote: "Then the exhibition at 291 of Cézanne and Picasso water colors and the talks in the gallery that they stimulated opened up to him the suggestion of abstraction as a motive. He spent a summer in the Tyrol, seeking to discover the principles of abstract expression in the study of mountain scenery. Then he returned to New York and for a while tested his experience and enlarged it by studying the colossal aspects of the city's skyscrapers." Marin's new manner drew on the spontaneous color effects and the heightened sensations of the Fauves; on the structure of Cubism, and perhaps most deeply of all, on Cézanne's water colors. These influences were ignited by the artist's intense and individual reaction to the dynamism of New York, a New York in the midst of a building boom. Such landmarks as the Manhattan Bridge, the Woolworth Building, the New York Central Railroad Terminal had either just been completed or were in construction. In these rising structures Marin found a concrete manifestation of the spirit of explosive growth, vitality and romantic hope of America, and his impressions had a fresh impact after his prolonged absence on the continent. An ability to compose rhythmically, by accents, to use fine, tense line, and to register vision with utmost rapidity and brevity were brilliantly demonstrated in these early etchings. It was part of Marin's special and more obvious gift that he could toss off the evocative, lyrical fragment with little apparent effort or meditation.

The huge industrial travail and growth of America particularly seemed to strike a responsive chord. To Stieglitz he wrote in 1913: "You cannot create a work of art unless the things you behold respond to something within you. Therefore if these buildings move me, they too must have life. Thus the whole city is alive; buildings, people, all are alive; and the more they move me the more I feel them to be alive." Marin found an optimistic song in the "tall office building," just as Louis Sullivan had, and he answered with a passionate "yes" the challenge of machine civilization at a time when it still had the power to exalt young artists.

The sense of new energies in our life and culture undoubtedly had much to do with liberating Marin's art. Yet perhaps the plastic tensions in his work were based even more profoundly on his assimilation of the dynamic principles of European pictorial forms. As early as 1916 Charles Caffin had called attention to the structural integrity and the solid grasp of abstraction in Marin's art, quite apart from the convulsive, Expressionist character and native stridency later critics tended to emphasize. Caffin wrote: "The various planes and surfaces of the transparent edifice are locked together with the logic of the builder who makes provisions for the stresses and strains of his assembled materials. I might illustrate the effect of this organic orderliness by the analogy of a person studying a foreign language, when he no longer consciously translates the words and idioms from one tongue to the other, but thinks freely in the new one. Marin is no longer translating the concrete into abstract, he has learned to think in the latter. And his freedom reacts upon onself. . . . One accepts what is seen without any need of conjecture. One can enjoy freely the spiritual appeal of the expression." Among the first American moderns, Marin successfully and consistently "learned to think" in a new language of abstract signs and symbols, and to give his structures a concrete pictorial power.

In 1914 Marin began to summer on the Maine coast,

which was to become one of his favored painting locales. His first water colors based on nature showed more reticence than those he had done from urban motifs. Their delicacy of tone and atmospheric effects, despite the use of broken color, related these works more to his experiments in the Tyrol than to the explosive New York views done in his new graphic style. Around 1919 landscape and city views became unified around an abstract, structural core as Marin began to simplify radically, employing what he described as "frames within frames," a free system of rectilinear compartments whose emphatic outlines prevented his "movements" from sliding off the edges of the picture. "When I got what I wanted," he later wrote, "I nailed the stuff down in those frames." From the twenties to his death in 1953 Marin continually drew on nature for his motifs. He was fascinated by the rugged contours of the Maine landscape and the sea, but he transposed his impressions into abstract pictorial design. By way of explanation he wrote: "Seems to me that the true artist must perforce go from time to time to the elemental big forms—Sky, Sea, Mountain, Plain—and those things pertaining thereto, to sort of re-true himself up, to recharge the battery. For these big forms have everything. But to express these, you have to love these, to be part of these in sympathy."

During the early thirties Marin began for the first time to work consistently in oils, and to make the resistances of the pigment as physical medium do some of the structural work that his more explicit, graphic organization had previously done. His more fluid approach showed a remarkable freedom for a period when abstract and nonfigurative idioms were still dominated by the geometric prejudice of Cubism. By the late thirties and forties, Marin no longer pinpointed expressive effects with graphic descriptive fragments, but depended almost exclusively on a few salient movements, large planes of color, and the expressive potential of the paint itself. His effects were coarser, in obedience to a broader principle, and his strength lay in his intense, vital surfaces, which more than compensated for the elimination of descriptive interest. The references to nature, to a ship's sail, a gull, a horizon line, seemed, indeed, to have been interpolated as an afterthought, or to function entirely as indicatory signs, establishing direction, movement or some necessary plastic accent. In *Off Cape Split, Maine,* executed in 1938, the effort "to show paint as paint" and the intensification of the painted surface command our attention, rather than the suggestion of a ship dancing on the sea. Marin did not wish to free himself from nature completely, and he remained, even in this last phase, as visual as he was architectural, conveying a heightened, transposed "impression," but an impression nevertheless. Yet, his combination of condensed sensation and abbreviated structure puts him in closer relationship to the spirit of Cézanne than to the other early American moderns who emulated Cézanne's elevated formal language. There is something of Cézanne's later delicacy of color in Marin's water colors and in his variety of soft pinks, powder blues and violets, which have the chromatic refinement of eighteenth-century porcelain.

While Marin's oils today excite the greatest interest among contemporary artists and show an admirable freedom, it was in the water color that he remained the most decisive. When he used oil pigment, he handled it with a swiftness and lightness, and with those summary, spontaneous indications of movement, that seem more appropriate to the water-color medium. He showed no very profound desire to explore the material possibilities of the weightier medium, or to seek a more grave and substantial articulation of form, despite his vital tactile sense. Marin's instinctive lyricism compelled him to feel the least burdened by the paint vehicle, to wrest the mind and senses free from its material properties. Taking his cue from Cézanne, however, he learned to use water color to create plastic structures, giving the medium a refreshing new vitality and a peculiar American integrity. At the end of his life, like Cézanne, he surrendered himself to broadly lyrical impulses based merely on rhythmic color phrase and accent, thereby returning to the impetuous romantic mood of the decade between 1910 and 1920.

Another artist superb in his mastery of the water-color medium was Charles Demuth. Like Marin, he was aware of Cézanne and followed his method of using delicate touches and dilute washes to create a structure of colored planes. For Demuth the lighter medium also allowed of certain reticences much less admissible in oils, and he actually seemed to be stimulated creatively by the limitations of the medium. Its possibilities for fine effects and clarity seemed to gibe with his own temperament, with a certain fastidiousness and an intense, if narrow, sensibility. Demuth once remarked with customary insight and modesty: "John Marin and I drew our inspiration from the same source, French modernism. He brought his up in buckets and spilt much along the way. I dipped mine out with a teaspoon, but I never spilled a drop."

Thirteen years Marin's junior, Demuth was more urbane and reserved in manner, with something of the expatriate dandy about him; his art was as much a matter of intellect, decorum and fine style as Marin's was of instinct, fancy and impulse. Demuth was born in 1883 in Lancaster, Pennsylvania, and his painting embodies something of the cleanness of line and the simple, formal elegance of Pennsylvania Dutch folk art. Many of his works were inspired directly by the orderly colonial architecture which filled the landscape of his childhood and youth. This early environment seems finally to have dominated a contemporary sophistication acquired in the capitals of the world and in the Stieglitz circle. Some self-imposed puritanical restraint, in conjuction with delicate health, prevented him from realizing the fullest sensuous possibilities of his art. His art is fragile and cold rather than robust, but it shows a perfection of taste, an aristocratic grace and, at its best, unexpected strength. Demuth's achievement is the more remarkable since, unlike Marin, Weber, Dove, Hartley, Stella and others, he did not absorb an expatriate experience and then use it to illuminate the dynamic American present. Rather, he sheltered behind the European sense of art and used Parisian esthetics as a guard against native experience, which he approached in a spirit of ironic detachment. Demuth's life and art provide a Jamesian parable; where Marin and others tried to match their own heightened responses to the American scene with bold esthetic experiment, Demuth shrank back from American materialism and, indeed, from any kind of extravagance, looseness or excess. A fellow student of his, Rita Wellman, has described this spirit of critical detachment, and the corresponding emphasis on artistic values for their own sake: "When we were young, we were very old. We were all bored with life: knew everything there was to know, and only condescended to give our time and talents to painting because it seemed to our jaded spirits the one respectable calling left."

In 1905 at the age of twenty-two Demuth enrolled at the Pennsylvania Academy and, following in the footsteps of Marin, Carles and Maurer, worked under Thomas Anschutz. He spent a year in Paris in 1907 and then in 1912 went to Europe again, for a two-year period. He may have been aware of the Fauves and the Cubists while abroad, but he didn't show any direct evidence of the new experimental moods until his return to America. In 1915 he was doing delicate but rather freely handled water-color landscapes that suggested Marin's influence, and fragile flower pieces whose tinted colors may have been a recapitulation of Rodin's water colors. Rodin had been shown at Stieglitz's gallery in 1908 and again in 1910. Even in these very early paintings Demuth revealed a delicacy of style and sentiment that were to remain characteristic of his art.

That same year he began a series of water-color illustrations for Emile Zola's *Nana,* one of the early and most shocking declarations of French naturalism. During the next four years, for his own amusement and with no publishing venture in prospect, Demuth illustrated Henry James's stories, *Turn of the Screw* and *The Beast in the Jungle,* Poe's *The Masque of the Red Death,* and other writings. These illustrations not only revealed a lively romantic taste and literary imagination, but the greatest deftness in the water-color medium. Although the illustrations were informal and free in style, the play of delicate stains and blushes of tone against sinuous curvilinear contour suggested a certain mild perfume of the romantic decadence. Demuth admired the graphic styles of both Aubrey Beardsley and Toulouse-Lautrec, their aristocratic attenuations and taste for a picturesque "wickedness." He was closer perhaps to Lautrec in his more vital color and supple line. Most of all, these water colors suggest Pascin, both in manner, and in the mingling of sensitive mood and sophistication.

Had Demuth done only these illustrations, his claim to our interest would be only that of a rather limited illustrator, if a brilliant one. From 1917 to 1919, however, he executed a far more ambitious series of water colors of vaudeville and nightclub performers; in these he passed beyond illustration. The preciosity of his early style, with its thinness and artificial quality, gave way to more decisive composition, forceful color and a new expressive power, as he pitted himself against action in the real world rather than the closed world of the literary imagination. Like Toulouse-Lautrec, Demuth was physically incapacitated to a degree, first by lameness and then after 1920 more seriously by diabetes. The grace and agility of the acrobat and theatrical performers may have had a particular appeal to this artist who was by temperament and constitution barred from a strenuous physical life. He showed action caught in the spotlight's glare, heightened by the illusion of the theater, as Lautrec had done, and his chosen themes became in a sense a metaphor for the artistic life.

Some time after the Armory Show, and in contact with Alfred Stieglitz, Demuth had begun to engage in more drastic experiment. His *Art Nouveau* serpentines and free color-stains were formalized, and he moved toward a more abstract rhythmic structure of line and color mass, suggesting the new influence of Dove, O'Keeffe and the Synchromists. He did not go far toward abstraction but did show a lively awareness of its contemporary manifestations, using a circular center of light and intense color in graduated, concentric bands at diminishing intensity to frame his action. In *Acrobats* (1919) a spotlight forms a loose figure eight of yellow and orange, dying away into mauve, against which the tense dark-colored silhouettes of his riders' arched bodies bend and strain. James Threll Soby has suggested, most appropriately, that Demuth's soft, elegant circular frames owe something to Fragonard and the rococo garland. Undoubtedly, they are also allied to the flowing, vegetal forms and the "symbolic" representation of light of his American contemporaries, Dove and O'Keeffe. Demuth's art was unique in that it created a tension between a form of "soft" abstraction, with its possible spiritual implications of passivity and mystery, and lively action.

A complementary style of "hard" abstraction, deriving from Cubism, emerged during a trip to Bermuda in 1916. In architectural studies, and seascapes such as *Bermuda No. 2 (The Schooner)*, Demuth began to use directional lines and analytical planes in a new Cubist-Futurist vocabulary of form. He parted company with his European derivations, however, in the effort to create within the new architectonic discipline, diaphanous effects of light. He interpreted his motifs as flattened prismatic shapes, extending their edges flatly, attenuating and recomposing them in a criss-cross weft of intersecting diagonals and shafts of light, like a night sky raked by searchlights. This was the method of Lyonel Feininger, the American-born modernist who spent his formative youth and maturity in Germany, and was associated there with the Blue Rider and the Bauhaus. Feininger's art, however, communicates an atmosphere of mystical contemplation, is apparitional in form and inward in mood suggesting a relationship to north European modes of feeling.

For all its charm, finesse and structural integrity, Demuth's art of this period has no very profound spiritual resonance, nor was it meant to have. It is conceived in a more bland, objective and even functional American spirit, retaining a canny hold on concrete visual facts. The selection of visual data, in Bermuda comprised of ships, wooden cottages and later of the trim lines of Pennsylvania domestic architecture and the simple logic of industrial forms, is significant in itself. For Demuth was attracted, it would seem, to those aspects and surfaces of life whose structural simplicity and sober plainness he could match in an art that, while it lent itself to subtlety and refinement, allowed a minimum of sensuous elaboration.

In 1919 in his Provincetown motifs, Demuth began to use tempera and about 1920 worked in oil, reserving it particularly for his industrial landscapes where more massive and weighty effects seemed in order. But whatever the medium, he still employed it sparingly and dryly, with the least possible indulgence of his own pleasurable sensation in its manipulation. Demuth's own variant on the "new objectivity" was achieved by suppressing any wayward painterly sensuality, and there was a certain crisp American literalism at the core of his most abstract transpositions of motifs from nature or from the contemporary industrial landscape.

Even in such a fine native application of Cubism as *My Egypt* (1925), one feels that Demuth was not so much concerned to spiritualize matter, in the sense either of the motif—a grain elevator—or the pigment itself, as he was to dematerialize it, to reduce everything to its minimal expressive equivalent in art. The same intense and often hollow interest in the cold, disembodied visual fact became even more central to the art of the group later called the "Immaculates": Charles Sheeler, Preston Dickinson and Niles Spencer. They scrupulously regroomed the American industrial environment in styles that struck an uneasy balance between an ascetic, decorative Cubism, and photography. This dry and literalistic tradition continues in our own time in the puzzling manner that has been called "magic" or sharp-focus realism—puzzling because the style combines intense realism with either slick-magazine illustrative conventions or a pastiche of old master draftsmanship. The fantasy, or literary and symbolic overtones of such paintings, however, do not disguise their kinship with a deep American tradition of adulating the disembodied visual fact. Such painting evolves out of a basic puritanism and mistrust of hedonism which has been the core of much American artistic sensibility. The denial of the sensuous character of the material means of painting has probably been one of the most identifiable marks of American provincialism, and its most damaging weakness, from the journeymen painters of the eighteenth century to Winslow Homer, from Charles Demuth and Charles Sheeler to Ben Shahn and Andrew Wyeth. It may also be one of the hidden reasons for the American predilection for water color. Demuth, however, brilliantly skirted the pitfalls of asceticism and matter-of-fact literalism, relying upon the natural delicacy of his perceptions, and a certain irony and wit to sustain and nourish his art. The qualities of wit, impertinence and ironical intelligence in his work may have been set free by contact with the painting and person of Marcel Duchamp.

He became friendly with Duchamp shortly after the French artist's arrival in New York in 1915. Perhaps it was his influence that led Demuth to append such mildly satirical titles to his free adaptations of industrial forms as *Incense of a New Church* and *The Home of the Brave*. Demuth also used numbers and letters in an inappropriate pictorial setting in his paintings to create a sudden evocation of everyday reality, often with ironic intent. He did not carry Duchamp's interest in mechanical forms to the point of pure abstraction nor did he go so far as to engage in the buffoonery and nonsense-play of the official Dada movement. His protest against the degradation of values under industrialization was arch and oblique—some factory chimneys lurking in the background of a landscape, a mocking commentary in a title, but little beyond that.

Nor did Demuth use his art to discredit the "noble means" of traditional art. To do so would have been, by implication, to attack himself, since American visual traditions had scarcely been established, and the individual artist could not afford to mock something he was in the process of building himself. In a nation where the machine was identified with the American promise, and still seemed part of a complex story of a people's deliverance from the wilderness; in a nation where the assurances of a cultivated existence had not been altogether won, American artists unconsciously checked the too violent expression of their own or their society's disorders. They could not yet risk those adventurous excursions into the unmarked mental regions where Dada's disquieting puns and iconoclasm came to birth. More youthful in spirit, more sanguine and idealistic, the American artists were not yet prepared to admit the possible boredom of modern life. And they had had no Baudelaire nor a Symbolist movement to teach them the spiritual uses of ennui. It took two world wars and a discernible increase in the violence and tensions of contemporary life to release the American artists' more rebellious impulses in some systematic, creative fashion.

Demuth's approach to Duchamp's innovation was also limited and restrained by his own mandarin sense of style, and by a pervasive good humor. He is closest to Dada perhaps in his handsome homage to the poet William Carlos Williams, *I Saw the Figure 5 in Gold,* belonging to the Metropolitan Museum of Art. The title is taken from the first line of a poem by his friend. The painting, remarkable in many ways, shows an artificiality and a free use of association and symbol that indicate a tie both to decorative Cubism and to Duchamp. It mingles the visual, the auditory and extra-pictorial associations for dramatic purposes, giving the composition an unexpected urgency, and even blatancy. The golden number five is repeated and recessed against a violent red, rectilinear shape which throws it back again, like an echo reverberating from a wall. Out of the bright visual center of clashing, intense color stream shafts of cool blue-grays, muffling the total brilliance and giving it an added sonority. There are schematic indications of a city street scene, bent to fit the curves of the number five. The effect is kaleidoscopic, a little like watching a revolving pinwheel, alternately brilliant and somber, or it can be related to the cinematic illusion created by a rapidly magnified, rotating title, or an aggressive credit line, that seems to come rushing rapidly out at the audience from the movie screen. Yet Demuth's illusion is relatively uncomplex; he doesn't appeal to chance and accident or allow his forms to proliferate in strange, metamorphic births as the Dadaists did. He starts with a small visual idea, maintains it on a highly conscious level, and stills any disruptive psychological overtones.

Demuth's fine sense of color, at once delicate in tone and structural, was again evident in the more realistic water colors of flowers and still life which preoccupied him in the last decade of his life. These themes provided a welcome lyrical relief from his industrial themes, and from the more exacting labors of oil painting. But the fanciful quality and freedom of his earlier water colors gave way to a colder efficiency and precision and often to a more commonplace literalism, as if in recognition that the mood of esthetic experiment had passed out of the American artistic atmosphere. For the pioneers of modernism, their own art had become a matter of individual direction. Demuth seemed in the paintings of his last years to address himself to an ideal of impeccable workmanship, showing a new dryness of execution; and he returned to more emphatic descriptive color. In some of his still lifes, however, he again evoked Cézanne with color which is at once tensely structural and delicate in its nuance.

His adherence to the formal principles of modernism, even threatened as they were by the cross-currents of a confused and contradictory post-bellum atmosphere, and then by his own academicism, nevertheless distinguishes Demuth from many of the other innovators who emerged after the Armory Show. He was an artist of restricted and confined sensibility who found it necessary to concentrate all his resources at one point, as it were. But for continuous creative impulse, and for his distinction as a stylist, Demuth must stand in the first rank of the pioneers of twentieth-century American art. Some time after Demuth's death, Marcel Duchamp generously acknowledged his artistic contribution with these words: "His work is a living illustration of the disappearance of a 'Monroe Doctrine' applied to art; for today, art is no more the crop of privileged soils, and Demuth is among the first to have planted the good seed in America."

6

American Scenes and Symbols

"Among democratic nations, men easily attain a certain equality of condition, but they can never attain as much as they desire. It perpetually retires before them . . . and in retiring draws them on. . . . To these causes may be attributed that strange melancholy which often haunts the inhabitants of democratic countries in the midst of their abundance, and that disgust at life which sometimes seizes upon them in the midst of calm and easy circumstances."
—Alexis de Tocqueville, *Democracy in America,* Part II

"Paris school, abstraction, escapism? Nope, just color-space compositions, celebrating the resolution in art of stresses set up by some aspect of the American scene."
—Stuart Davis, on his own painting

Even as America's mood of experiment in art reached a decisive peak shortly after the Armory Show, a limited reaction was in the making. After World War I, a conservative atmosphere reasserted itself more strongly until finally the center of gravity in art shifted once again, away from Europe and artistic innovation to the native scene and a revival of naturalism. The new realists shared none of the challenging rebelliousness or reforming zeal of the Eight; their art was instead cheerless, harsh, haunted by romantic nostalgia and addicted to the grotesque. It began by seeking refuge in the familiar and the commonplace, as a rebuke to the esthetic conundrums of the modernists. But the scene it disclosed was not humanly reassuring, and the reality it set forth was a world of shadows, haunted by strange forces and an atmosphere of emptiness. Like the modernists who had begun to react negatively to the machine and to the new landscape of power, the romantic realists, by quite different pictorial metaphors, told the story of the disenchantment and spiritual vacancy behind the American success story.

The new romantic realists fashioned their paintings gracelessly and unesthetically, working out of a clumsy artisan tradition and from sudden moments of vision. They lacked any profound sense of style. Pictorially, they were as limited, average and undistinguished as the humiliated landscape, broken-down architecture and drab scenes they made the stock-in-trade of their subject matter. It was an under-privileged art that seemed disinclined to draw attention to itself; yet the least attractive aspects of American life were presented without apology. The romantic realists were less interested in painting as such than in "picturing" or describing, and they rejected out of hand any commitment to formal principle or esthetic ideal. Mounting pressures of American provincialism in the post-war era once again forced devastating alternatives upon the artist, exposing a cruel division in native sensibility. He was forced to fight an increasingly lonely battle for modernism against the American grain, giving all his devotion to the integrity of his principles and consoling himself with pride in his independence, and self-knowledge. Thus, John Marin, Arthur Dove and Charles Demuth in their different ways had come to use experimentalism as a metaphor for their separate and distinguished brands of individualism. The alternative was to give up the effort of trying to stay afloat in the mainstream, and to surrender to the raw American experience. Modified by their own idiosyncratic visions, this latter course became for the emerging realists a general objective. Realism, nostalgic and romantic in the twenties, and progressively more violent in mood and more Expressionistic in form during the thirties, once again asserted itself as the dominant American tendency.

Most striking of the first realists were Charles Burchfield and Edward Hopper. Their art coincided in time and temper with the first stories and novels of Sherwood Anderson and Sinclair Lewis. *Winesburg, Ohio,* Anderson's

gallery of grotesque small-town lives, and *Main Street,*
Lewis's satire on boosterism and middle-class conformity,
appeared in 1919 and 1920. Burchfield and Hopper seemed
to work out of the same sources in American life. Lewis's
description of the typical American main street, "where
dullness is made God," establishes the tone for Hopper's
paintings of the national spiritual vacuum and his visual
descriptions of sullen, mechanical lives set in stagnant
scenes. Burchfield was an acknowledged admirer of Anderson's writing. Perhaps he was drawn to the novelist's
sentimental lyricism, his fascination with the commonplace, and his brooding introspection in the face of the
moral rot of small-town existence. Anderson's description
of himself as a writer "whose sympathy went out to the
little frame houses on often mean enough streets in American towns, to defeated people, often with thwarted lives"
is also applicable to Burchfield's artistic personality and
accomplishment.

James Thrall Soby has very brilliantly characterized
Burchfield when he describes him as "a painter of memories in an era of anticipation." In the small-town back-
waters of American life and in their decaying architecture,
Burchfield found a symbolic projection of a private ennui
that could deepen into fantasy and significant emotional
experience. He had grown up in Salem, Ohio, and then
gone briefly to the Cleveland School of Art, only to return
to Salem in 1916. Between that date and his induction
into the army in 1918, he independently arrived at a fanciful symbolic mode of expression in water color that suggests the paintings of Edvard Munch, and the melancholy,
introspective mood of much European art of the turn-of-
the-century era. Back in Salem, Burchfield wrote, he experienced a personal crisis: "A curious depression assailed
me, and I worked constantly to keep it down." Out of this
mood flowed a series of fantasies in water color which
turned the familiar landscape of his youth into a symbolic
representation of childhood fears and ghostly apparitions.
"As I progressed," the artist declared in his journal, "I
went further back into childhood memories and it became
such an obsession that a decadence set in. I tried to re-

create such moods as fear of the dark, the feelings of flowers before a storm, and even to visualize the songs of insects and other sounds."

Employing the curving forms and ornamental line of *Art Nouveau*, Burchfield created a hallucinating atmosphere in which everything in nature was freely distorted and became vaguely menacing: windows and doorways of houses doubled as eyes or mouths; flowers were faces; all nature joined a ghostly retinue of fearful presences. This vein of depressed fantasy and dream had been explored with signal success by many north European artists around 1900; it was Burchfield's achievement to give validity to the same mood within the more restricted pictorial scheme of the water color in the American landscape some thirty years later. His awareness of and attraction to the brooding spirit of the North was made clear in his journal, where he later wrote of the imaginary locale that had always haunted him, of "some fabulous Northland unlike any place on earth—a land of deep water-filled gashes in the earth; old lichen-covered cliffs and mesas, with black spruce forests reflected in the pools, against which white swans gleam miraculously. This romantic land of the imagination, the mysterious North that has haunted me since I was a boy—it does not really exist, but how did it come into being?"

It is the author's opinion, however, that Burchfield's literary imagination more often than not outstripped his power to create convincing illusion, and the pictorial results were not always commensurate with his fine inspiration. In such water colors of 1916-1918 as *Church Bells Ringing, Rainy Winter Night* or *The Night Wind* the artist's grotesque fancies and expressive means achieve the unity of a style. Many of his other works even in the same period are singularly lacking in atmosphere and bear no stamp of individual vision. They show a curious and often meaningless penmanship embroidery, as if the artist were at a loss and fell back disconsolately on a random, half-hearted inventiveness of linear detail.

After 1921 when he moved permanently to Buffalo, Burchfield began to document the American scene in a more objective manner. He painted the great vacant façades of the homes of the Awkward Age, and in his treatment of these architectural relics, found a new outlet for his mood of nostalgia. Sometimes fantasy was given humorous relief by satirical caricature, particularly as he introduced figures into his compositions. At other times he used the extravagant, peaked architectural forms of Buffalo to create a more somber atmosphere. *House of Mystery,* a water color of 1924, is most probably the direct ancestor of the haunted houses of the *New Yorker* cartoonist, Charles Addams. Burchfield described it as a "house where anything might have happened, or be happening." At the end of the twenties and through the thirties his feeling for the weird became further diluted, almost as if even the grotesque were powerless to deal with the "measureless grossness and slag," in Whitman's phrase, of the American visual reality. Ramshackle house fronts, dilapidated factories and dismal back streets were set down now with little esthetic or imaginative elaboration; the artist seemed to succumb to the dull torpor, the enervating tempo, the gritty ugliness of those aspects of American life he had chosen to treat. He dealt too timidly with the harsher visual truths of American life, repeating and ritualizing them with a discouraged objectivity, and American materialism took its revenge finally by smothering his imagination.

Burchfield had set himself the task of exploring in humble visual metaphors the failures behind the American success story, the corruption of the landscape that followed in the wake of industrial progress and which most Americans had managed conveniently to ignore. The dreary tonelessness of his own art, however, too closely matched his subject matter. He began as a romantic fantast, aggressive even in his apprehension, but ended as a mild elegist of defeat. In the latter phase of his work he seemed unable to make the radical distinction between raw experience and art. To Thomas Benton, John Steuart Curry and other "regionalist" painters of the thirties, Burchfield's art may have supplied the first hint of a violent rebuke to modernism in its makeshift, illustrative style and American scene subject matter. But these artists primed Burchfield's despondency with false optimism and interpreted his subject matter as an endorsement of a new jingoism. In some of his mid-western farm scenes, such as *November Evening*, Burchfield had painted a rural America from which pioneer zest had long since vanished, leaving a vacuum of endless chores, loneliness and fears. Benton and Curry dramatized Burchfield's gnarled distortions in form, his ornamental arabesques, but brightened his palette and mood, and tried instead to re-create the heroic myth of the American west. Their mawkish, melodramatic regionalism was not as convincing as Burchfield's less self-conscious treatment of the local scene, and his unembarrassed admission of ugliness.

What Charles Burchfield was to domestic wooden architecture, and to the rural or small-town scene, Edward Hopper has been to the crassly "modernistic" America of the large cities. In the inhuman surfaces of urban life, anonymous brick house fronts, neon signs, ubiquitous diners, gas pumps, cinema interiors, and even in pavement itself, he has found metaphors for spiritual vacancy and imprisonment. Like Burchfield, he is an artist of American ennui and loneliness; unlike him, Hopper never expresses an explicit fantasy or subordinates description to free invention.

Hopper's paintings represent the revival of the anecdote, but the story they tell is always the same one. His favorite subjects are the least prepossessing, least promising visual commonplaces of American life. Their very familiarity has robbed them of their relevance to feeling. Somehow Hopper has managed miraculously to extract fresh sensation from his stagnant scenes. A motif may be nothing more than a deserted street at night, with a brightly lit lunchroom at one side, through the windows of which figures are seen sitting torpidly, not unlike surrealist dummies. In another painting the subject is a bizarre Victorian house caught in a striking angle lighting which gives it mysterious new properties. A subject that he has repeated is the interior of the modern movie "palace," painted in a manner that vividly summons up the artificial dream world of the cinema. The helpless surrender and preoccupation of the audience is heightened by contrasts in color, value and degree of definition between the amorphous black mass the spectators make, and the brilliant square of white screen. Vacuity is compounded with inanition by setting the scene off with an inattentive usherette who stands to one side, lost in her own thoughts. Despite the figure style of spare and, indeed, famished realism, there is a poetry hinted at in the color and lighting, a certain taste for luxurious sensation that won't be suppressed. With his strange, artificial quality of light, Hopper manages to create romantic atmosphere as no American realist since John Sloan has done. Hopper was in all probability directly influenced by Sloan and other members of the Eight whom he knew and for a time imitated in the earlier years of the century.

His atmosphere, however, is stifling and curiously unreal, with a strange anxiety hovering at its edges, as if the sheer inertia and immobility of his figures and scenes might foreshadow some extraordinary event. The result of his combination of bald literalism and dramatic heightening by a mysterious alchemy of light, is to give a mood of impenetrable monotony the quality of a dream. The last, pale, dying radiance of light which gives his cityscapes a dull glow suggests that romantic feeling has brushed the scene somewhere, once. A weakened echo of lavishness and mystery is enough to provide relief from the otherwise drab, routine realism and the unspectacular, everyday events depicted.

Hopper came to maturity as a painter in a period the prevailing mood of which was either insurgently realistic or experimental. In the end he set himself against both tendencies, and was a long time developing his own distinctive style. He had studied at the Chase School of Art for five years under Robert Henri and Kenneth Hayes Miller and then had gone to Paris in 1906. On his return to America Hopper participated in the first exhibition of the Independents in 1910. He witnessed, but did not take part in, the early public demonstrations of a more radical modernism at Stieglitz's gallery, the Forum Gallery and in the Armory Show. Discouraged by his own personal struggle to live by art and alienated by the more radical artistic tendencies, he abandoned painting for etching and commercial illustration from 1915 to 1923. On the basis of his first strong

artistic contacts, Hopper's deepest sympathies lay with
John Sloan's romantic mood, although he was to depend
on enervation rather than energy to convey it. In 1914
he painted *Corner Saloon,* employing a sensitive feeling and
brush to set down the red brick façades which were to become one of the ubiquitous stage properties of his art. The
commonplace subject, the suffusion of warm light and en-
riched surface effects place this New York street scene
very close to Sloan's work. Hopper later acknowledged
his debt to the older artist when he praised Sloan's ability
to render "remarkably the quality of a brooding silent interior in this vast city of ours." And he continued: "Sloan's
design is the simple and unobtrusive tool of his visual reaction. It attempts tenaciously and ever the surprise and un-
balance of nature, as did that of Degas."

The reference to Degas is unexpected but illuminating
in relation to Hopper's art; it is probably more signficant
in psychological terms than it is compositionally. For
Degas was one of the first modern Europeans to show human boredom and mental funk candidly, to paint people
as they were *unrelated* rather than related to each other.
Degas was adept at setting up compositional tensions across
empty areas of space, areas which not only figured as design elements but created a distracting mood of vacancy
and anticipation as well. Degas was too fine an artist and
far too aware of pure esthetic values to underscore the possible psychological implications of giving human action
a marginal role in his pictorial schemes. In great part this
aspect of his art, and his habit of catching his human subjects unaware as they stood self-absorbed outside of the
action, reflected a growing process of abstraction in all late-
nineteenth-century art, mirrored differently in the painting
of Manet and the orthodox Impressionists. However,
Degas's procedures also represented a new sense of the dis-
integration of the traditional concept of the individual. The
human subject had lost its centrality and was seen, esthetically, merely as one possible motif among others. More
importantly, the individual had begun to lose some of his
reality, to be transformed into a symbol or a "case," as in-

terest shifted from man to his defining environment. This process had already taken place in the naturalist and realist novels of Zola and Flaubert, and in the twentieth century it belatedly affected the American naturalist writers. Degas's art was among the first to signal visually the radical change in feeling. It was no accident that Degas should attract Hopper—an artist who gave his humanity significance only in terms of an oppressive urban environment, and made their lusterless lives a function of a stage-set modern world, in which they move dully like automatons.

Hopper was shrewd enough to know that his realism was outmoded and went against the grain of the prevailing modern tendencies, but he must have felt confident that the lack of a more contemporary sophistication need not necessarily stand in his way. He found encouragement in Thomas Eakins's example, describing him as an artist who, "in the nineteenth cenutry used the methods of the seventeenth, and is one of the few painters of the last generation to be accepted by contemporary thought in this country."

The wooden, apathetic creatures that inhabit Hopper's paintings are directly related to the lumpish figures of Guy Pène du Bois, Kenneth Hayes Miller and other American realists of his period. Perhaps they show Hopper's ineptness at significant characterization, but it is to the artist's credit that he can force us to associate them and the scenes in which they participate with the thwarted lives of Sinclair Lewis's or Sherwood Anderson's characters. Although he deals for the most part with metropolitan life and its settings, Hopper's central theme is also the ugliness and frustrations of provincial life, an existence lacking romantic fulfillment and satisfying spiritual values.

Without the precedent of Hopper, it would be difficult to conceive such varied and distinct poetic documentations of the American scene of the late thirties and early forties as those of Ben Shahn, Walter Steumpfig and Loren Mac-Iver. In styles of social realism, traditional romanticism and a magically heightened abstraction of evocative symbol and sign, these artists registered their visions on an exposed poetic nerve, and transmuted a harsh external reality: the drab surfaces, vacant back lots and visual horrors of the modern urban environment. The exploration of picturesque elements in the local scene by both Hopper and Burchfield led even more logically, and obviously, to the regionalist styles of the thirties; in mood, these two artists also anticipated the fantasy, if not the violence, of the Expressionists who later in the same decade turned a feverishly disenchanted eye on the American scene.

In his effort to combine social realism with an elliptical visual shorthand and to make this synthesis meaningful to Americans, Ben Shahn's art provides one of the more interesting experiments of the late thirties. Shahn and his art must be set against the general mood of a period in revolt against the hedonist esthetics and formalism of Paris painting. American painting was dominated by regionalism, and by local Expressionist styles. The New Deal of Franklin D. Roosevelt with its enlightened arts program had encouraged mural decoration, and a new artistic self-consciousness was emerging. Inspired by this program of public art, obsessed with social problems, and influenced by the vigorous revival in Mexican mural painting, under Rivera and Orozco, American artists had set themselves a program of national self-discovery. Curry, Benton and Grant Wood tried to create a new regional style of melodramatic realism. The passion for creating an "American" idiom led to a narrow chauvinism, with a violent rejection of European modernism (even though an artist like Benton was directly indebted to Paris painting and had been a member of the American vanguard at the time of the Forum Exhibition). In time however, there was a further reaction against the provincialism of the regionalists. Out of this repudiation emerged the modified social-realist art of Ben Shahn. It represented a militant response to both the woolly idealism of the regionalists and their blind political optimism, as well as a renewal of interest in European painting modes.

Shahn grew up in an atmosphere of left-wing radicalism. Many of his early projects in the thirties took the form of social polemic and caricature. His art took note of such controversial issues as the execution of the anarchists, Sacco and Vanzetti, and the imprisonment of the labor leader, Tom Mooney. Shahn also worked for a time in Mexico as an assistant to Diego Rivera, whose ideological and technical influence on the younger painter is apparent in work of this period.

As Shahn developed in the late thirties and early forties, he began to move from a public art of direct social criticism to a more personal art that portrayed the individual in terms of private emotional experience. Elegiac poetic content began to replace satire, and he portrayed figures of the old and homeless marooned on a park bench; children carried away by the excitement of play; lovers in a park, imprisoned by a network of fence railing and their own dream. His figures, often reduced to a significant, expressive silhouette and pressed into the maze of urban building patterns, became eloquent images of loneliness, in an art that was hard-boiled and sensitive by turns.

Flat, poster-like, and extremely denuded, his earlier imagery suggested a deceptive callousness and a photographic objectivity; but beneath the surface a sensitive poetry played. In technique, Shahn most often used tempera, obtaining effects alternately of dry incandescence and of a metallic luster. His surfaces, his colors, his expressive language of image and symbol have progressively reflected the increasing influence of Paul Klee; yet the nervous pulse of his work and its "commercial-art" blatancy are unmistakably native. Drawing on a sophisticated, semi-abstract idiom, Shahn has portrayed the American scene with interpretive imagination. He has been a poignant and effective lyricist, and always a fine reporter. When he tends, as in most of his recent painting, to emphasize wider allegorical themes rather than to consult specific incident, his art loses its tension and suffers from affectation. Its limitations and tendency toward visual stereotype have become even clearer against the background of the vigorous movement in contemporary American abstract painting.

Shahn's magical realism has been a formative influence on many younger American painters, most notably on Andrew Wyeth. Wyeth is, however, an almost clinically direct, realist reporter by comparison. He seems, in fact, to strive frankly for the absolute verisimilitude of the photograph. But the sense of loneliness and of spiritual malaise in the American scene that both Shahn and Hopper underlined have also become his themes. He sometimes approaches Shahn's manner of expressing fantasy by setting a figure starkly against an intricately embroidered expanse of nature, a nature in a state of unnatural inanition and haunted by somber forces. Wyeth's realism is airless and oppressive, both for its derivative atmosphere and for its bizarre adaption of slick magazine illustrative technique to macabre emotional themes.

In the art of a number of American Expressionists the exposed sensibility that characterizes the preceding artists achieves a higher pitch of violence and grisly fantasy. Henry Koerner uses many of Shahn's technical devices and subjects, but he has turned the American scene into a mockery of billboards, cheap amusement parks and a bored, brutish, sensation-hungry populace. Alton Pickens, perhaps influenced by the symbolism of the German Expressionist, Max Beckmann, paints human deformities in the tormented mood of a Grünewald with an added taste for modern psychological horror. In form these two artists are extremely mannered and unadventurous, for all their technical ingenuities. Their popularity is not surprising in a country where movies and comic strips cultivate and reflect a taste for violence, and where many of our best writers, William Faulkner and Carson McCullers among others, have found freaks and human degeneration a fruitful subject matter.

The work of Walter Steumpfig is also descriptive in character and depicts the American scene, but he finds an old-world beauty in the ugliness of the urban dust heap. Influenced by Eugene Berman and his brother Leonid, and in some of his compositions by Shahn, Steumpfig paints the American landscape with the nostalgia of a European. He gives a gas works or a dilapidated American façade an air of permanence, as if they were a heap of Roman ruins, and he paints with great atmospheric subtlety. A fluent craftsman, he too often presents second-hand memories of the Neo-Romantics of the twenties in Europe, and the carefully cultivated estheticism of his art is lacking in contemporary vitality.

Along with realism and traditional romanticism the dominating tendency of the thirties and early forties was a vehement Expressionism. It is still practiced by a great many American artists, although it has given ground to the revival of abstraction. Strong subjective feeling, brilliant color, and violent handling, in fact, became for a time identifying trademarks of American painting. One of the most effective Expressionist painters of the forties was Hyman Bloom. Russian-born, trained in Boston, Bloom's early work in the late thirties was full of blazing color and distortions with clear reminiscences of both Soutine and El Greco. Bloom evolved a personal symbolism of cantors, rabbis and synagogue interiors of an extraordinary vividness, aiming for stupendous color effects and rich visual sensations. His debt to Soutine was more than compensated for by the impression he conveyed of deep and sincere emotion. The iridescence of color in the exotic settings and costumes of his church that bewitched Bloom, and his interest in religious ritual, later gave way to a mode of near-abstraction. His themes began to look like interior anatomies, an abstract flesh that glowed with brilliant color as it decomposed and putrefied. Then Bloom's violent romanticism took on a more gloomy cast and he produced a series of bloated corpses and severed limbs, livid and rather frightening. Death and putrefaction of flesh still release his most exotic colors and forms today, but in an almost purely abstract manner the aim of which is to achieve a new chromatic magnificence. An accomplished craftsman with a taste for the grand manner, Bloom is betrayed by "museum memories" and his rather synthetic, unvital artistic culture.

Jack Levine was Bloom's fellow student at the Boston Museum School, and two years his senior. Like Bloom, he owed a technical debt to Soutine and to other European Expressionists. Unlike Bloom, his art is worldly and satirical, and takes its stand as an indictment of the avarice of the rich, the miscarriage of justice, the squalor of official public life. Though he blurs, distorts and paints with lavish abandon, Levine is essentially a realist reporter. Even his most violent distortions cannot dislodge a certain literalism, as if his inventions were superimposed on an armature of photography. His inflamed social conscience and satirical themes now give his art a period flavor of the thirties, and seem remote from present-day artistic preoccupations. Levine's palette has lightened, and his effects have become elaborately illusionist; he paints now in thin washes, creating a fine filament of form and atmosphere in an elaborate effort to give his subjects a quality of mystery.

Both of these gifted technicians, Bloom and Levine, have experienced the same sentimental education, and have drawn parallel conclusions from it. They brought rich and exotic foreign backgrounds to Boston's atmosphere of priggish gentility; both insisted violently on their capacity to feel, to live intensely through the senses in their art. Both were in the social and cultural position of the outsider. And they carried their attitudes to the utmost limits with a typical American feeling for extremes: Levine's sense of social outrage turned the society he portrayed into a gallery of grotesques; Bloom's disenchanted mood produced cadavers and a morbid awareness of the corruption of the body, and of death, in the form of ectoplasmic abstractions.

In America the contemporary artist is not on the best of terms with life, even though the material comforts of existence are probably more accessible to him here than elsewhere in the world. Indeed, the pressures of materialism and the deeply rooted American psychology of the utility of all products, including the cultural product of art, often undermine the artist's position. On the one hand the artist is made acutely aware of his separation from shallow popular culture, and his creativeness is threatened by this sense of isolation. On the other hand he may also be unconsciously affected by the corrupted visual currency of mass media, of advertising art, and driven into slick and synthetic expression. The "skin" of American realism, fantastic art, and Expressionism, often has a distinctly native look, a photographic or commercial-art finish, and an air of deceptive callousness, as if the artist were not only unable to release his basic human sympathies but was even afraid of betraying any obvious affection or regard for the material possibilities of the medium itself. The later careers of Bloom and Levine seem to have been an acting out of violent repentance for their early sensuality in paint. Levine's art has become more and more synthetic and immaterial; Bloom permits himself a taste for luxurious sensation only in a rather contrived atmosphere of the charnel house.

A fantastic realism or Expressionism rather than Surrealism have been the usual forms which the more violent reactions to the American experience have taken. Official Surrealism, with its dreams, romantic disorders and bizarre inventions, has only touched America lightly. In Europe Surrealism positively represented a new liberation of sensibility in the continuing revolution of modern art and an assertion of the artist's prerogative to paint as he wished, to create and dream, even if his dreams · reflected personal anxieties or the collective nightmare of the postwar epoch. In America, which ironically prides itself on the freedom of the individual, the artist has been in many subtle ways barred from making such radical appeals to freedom. When he takes his stand too distinctly outside the optimistic folkways of American society, the artist is subjected not only to violent criticism, but also to a destructive process of inner erosion. He suffers from a lingering sense of guilt. In a utilitarian culture which has still a hard puritanical core, daydreams and chimerical visions are not easily tolerated. At least they are not usually set forth in explicitly "high" art, but reserved for the fantasy-life of the cinema or the lonelyhearts columns. By mutual consent of artist and public, Surrealism is frowned upon. It has, however, forced its way into American art through the back door, in the more violent forms of realism and in much of the "symbolist" abstract painting of the early forties.

The notable lack of success of the movement in this country also stems from the fact that the general frame of reference and many of the arcane images of European Surrealism are alien to the American spirit. It takes a highly conscious effort on the part of the American artist to recover some sense of what Nathaniel Hawthorne called a "picturesque and gloomy wrong" in his own past, that awareness of evil which has been one of the main sources of Surrealist inspiration. No painter has been able to draw on the formal culture and puritan repressions of New England for this sense as have so many of our great writers. Our artists' indifference to their past has been most interestingly described by the contemporary abstract painter, Robert Motherwell. Speaking of Max Ernst, Motherwell has written: "His art depends on a sense of the vicious past. To the American mind nothing could be more alien. . . . Such images as a black mass, a bloody nun, an invader from the east cannot arouse deep feelings in most of us . . . for better or worse most Americans have no sensation of being either elevated or smothered by the past. . . . Consciously abandoning the past is the essentially American creative act; we painters here remain indifferent to the objects surrounding us. Our emotional interest is not in the external world, but in creating a world of our own. . . . It is from this reasoning that we can account for the fact that objectless painting, that is, various modes of abstraction, appeals more to the most modern American painters than Surrealism."

The American artist literally closest to Surrealism has been Peter Blume. His earliest paintings, such as *Parade* of 1930 and *South of Scranton,* combined free association, fantastic imagery, and the precisionist surfaces of Sheeler and the "Immaculates." In recent years he has mixed a more illustrational realism with bizarre and ambitious allegory. He paints with the scrupulous care of a fifteenth-century Flemish craftsman, and he is an astonishing technician. Blume is also an effective polemicist in such a painting as *The Eternal City,* a violently satirical evocation of Rome under Italian Fascism, with Mussolini burlesqued as a jack-in-the-box. But Blume, it seems, feels compelled to paint for a popular audience, in terms of immediately comprehensible visual facts. His carefully wrought surfaces and virtuoso technique often seem merely a maneuver calculated to distract attention from a small inventive capacity. Man's struggle with hostile nature and his effort to build a new world are the grandiose themes of the artist's recent large painting,

The Rock. For all its elegance of detail, its vivid presentation and reminiscences of the old masters, the painting is remarkably bleak; it is a manufactured dream-allegory designed to please an audience accustomed to science-fiction fantasy, in the author's opinion. Blume is a technically accomplished artist of deep and sincere conviction, who, like another Surrealist, Salvador Dali, has perhaps become too conscious of the public he serves.

The pressures on the American painter to produce a facile, smoothly manufactured artistic object, and the general lack of appreciation that awaited those artists who did not submit to popular taste, have resulted in the adoption of extreme esthetic positions. Personal mysticism, based on an inward poetic vision, has been one fruitful avenue of exploration for a number of Americans. At the other pole, there was apparent in the middle and late forties a growing mood of dynamism and a radical, new atmosphere of freedom among abstract artists. In the middle ground between the intensely private romantic, and the abstract artist, a number of painters have worked as eclectics, keeping alive the contact with international idioms. Stuart Davis, notably, has been one of the few artists who remained above the factional battles of the regionalists and Expressionists in modernism's dark days, during the twenties and early thirties. He maintained a meaningful continuity between America's first phase of experiment and contemporary abstract styles.

Among those artists who have attempted to delineate an intensely personal world, concentrating all the resources of their sensibility at one point, Morris Graves and Loren Mac-Iver are perhaps the most interesting. Their small, passionate utterance and romanticism are in a distinct American artistic tradition, recalling the confined but powerful sensibility of Ryder and the poetess, Emily Dickinson. In Morris Graves, too, an entirely new American regionalism is represented. He has traveled briefly in Europe and Japan, but otherwise has spent his life in Seattle. Like the art of his neighbor, Mark Tobey, Graves's paintings have been associated with the Pacific Northwest. Both Graves and Tobey have been strongly drawn to Oriental philosophy and art. Tobey has made a study of Japanese calligraphy and is known for his "white writing," a delicate, automatic, non-representational script, which is probably as indebted to Paul Klee as it is to the art of the East. Graves's art is, by contrast, imagistic and particularized, though it has been somewhat influenced by the witching atmosphere and many of the devices of Tobey's style.

A deeply religious man and a serious student of Vedanta, Graves has made a tender, lyrical poetry from such images as a pine tree tremulously holding a full moon in its branches, or tiny birds and snakes, images which seem to be secreted rather than painted on the canvas or paper. His art is rapt, visionary, hypnotic. Its mystical mood is best caught in the nature poetry which D. H. Lawrence wrote in the New World. In recent years Graves's mysticism sometimes raised a communication problem for all but the rare, indoctrinated religious spirit like himself. For his technique so closely imitated that of the East, even to the use of scrolls and the cultivation of an archaic patina, that his art has often seemed a replica of ancient Chinese or Korean painting. In some of his more recent paintings, however, Graves has returned to a more traditional western expression, employing dryly opulent color that recalls Redon. Such recent ventures as *Fox with Phoenix Wing* or his more abstract works have less of an air of preciosity.

Loren MacIver has become one of America's better known women painters. An imagist poet in paint, she finds unusual pictorial associations in commonplace objects and impressions: in the pattern and rainbow reflections of a gutter oil slick, in a bunch of flowers blooming on a garbage heap, or in the sad phantom-face of one of America's famous clowns. Her paintings attempt to recapture the ecstasy of enchanted moments, a remembered pleasure on the edge of some sad, cold reality. Their soft, smoky pastel shades and gleaming, lapidary lights are given substance by the artist's instinct for abstract design. MacIver's sensibility is intensely feminine, like Virginia Woolf's or Katherine Mansfield's. The city air for her is full of bright images and vivid discoveries that would elude all but the most elfin temperament. During a trip to Italy in 1952 she was dazzled by the visual splendors of Venice, and painted the city as an airy dream-impression, with a delicate necklace of façades dancing in a heat shimmer, punctuating a broad expanse of cool blue lagoon and sky. Her art owes much to Paul Klee's innocent wonder before experience; it similarly creates a world in microcosm, an enchanted garden where the commonplace becomes transformed into the marvelous at the wave of a wand. But she often forces her visions and mysteries, depending on pictorial effects that are synthetic. Much more so than Graves, MacIver thinks in terms of the image rather than paint, with the result that her imaginary garden often produces only artificial flowers.

The common link between all the preceding artists, despite the variety of styles and moods, has been a preoccupation with subject matter, with images either sacred or profane, literal or fantastic. Drawing on the American scene, the artists of the twenties and thirties for the most part attempted to give visual substance to their feelings within the framework of external reality. Even Morris Graves's visionary art would fit into this general scheme at least insofar as he, too, used legible images. While his art is not directly connected with the American scene, its very remoteness from common everyday reality, its intense individuality, and its mood of nostalgia may be taken as a rebuke to his admittedly hostile surroundings. As an artist of narrow romantic sensibility who cultivates exceptional states of mind, he has also taken the route of evasion when confronted with the most radical modern painting, just as those artists have done who more obviously found refuge in external reality.

A cardinal rule of art history is that at any given period certain styles and prescribed pictorial means are more fruitful and productive than others, and that these engage the efforts of the most serious contemporary artists. In our own time the repudiation of illusionism, the rejection of the anecdote, a concern with pure pictorial values, all those tendencies associated with the collective visual revolution known as modernism, have acquired the status of a program for the most convincing artists. Those artists who have turned their back on the form-language of modernism and revived traditional procedures and esthetic values of the past have been threatened by academicism and second-hand effects.

They settled for less than what the most adventurous and courageous artists of their time sought. And they have often succeeded only in cutting themselves off from the main sources of vitality in contemporary artistic culture. It is, therefore, ironic that the artist who perhaps has drawn the most vitality from the American scene, and whose art over the past three decades has been almost unique for continuous creative impulse, should be the confirmed abstractionist Stuart Davis.

Like Hopper, Davis dates from the period of the first realists, the Eight, many of whom he came to know as a boy in Philadelphia. His father was Edward Davis, art director of the *Philadelphia Press,* and it was under him that Shinn, Luks, Henri and Sloan first worked as artist-journalists. In 1910 at the age of sixteen, Davis began to study painting in New York with Robert Henri, the guiding spirit and spokesman for the new realists. Davis has acknowledged Henri's stimulating influence as a teacher and expressed his appreciation of a liberal viewpoint so opposed to the stultifying academic outlook found in most art schools of the period. But he later qualified his enthusiasm when he told an interviewer that "the emphasis on 'anti-artistic' subject matter, which was implicit in the whole Henri idea, tended to give subject matter, as such, a more important place than it deserves in art. . . . Reliance on the vitality of subject matter to carry the interest prevented an objective appraisal of the dynamics of the actual color-space relations on the canvas" and he added: "I became vaguely aware of this on seeing the work at the Armory Show, but it took years to clarify the point."

After working with Henri for three years, Davis was painting in a manner of simplified realism. Soon after leaving school he joined Sloan, Coleman and other artists of the new realist camp as an illustrator for the old *Masses,* then under the editorial direction of Max Eastman. In 1916 he withdrew from the magazine, with these artists and two others, over policy differences. Art Young, the art director of the *Masses* and victor in the ideological scuffle, issued a statement at the time of the rupture coining the phrase that led to the most famous of the various epithets used to describe the realists: "The Ash Can School." In the *New York Sun* on April 8 he was quoted as follows: "The five dissenting artists want to run pictures of ash cans and girls hitching up their skirts in Horatio Street—regardless of ideas—and without title."

The break with the *Masses* apparently confirmed in Davis growing doubts about realism and descriptive subject matter already stirred by the Armory Show. In later years he described the impact of America's first wholesale introduction to modernism: "The Armory Show was the greatest shock to me—the greatest single influence I have experienced in my work. All my immediately subsequent efforts went toward incorporating Armory Show ideas into my work." By 1919 Davis was painting landscape in a freer, expressive manner derived from Van Gogh, and had, in his own words, "learned to think of color more or less objectively so that I could paint a green tree red without batting an eye." In the preceding years Davis had conducted explorations of New Jersey night-life in the company of another young painter who also felt an allegiance to the new naturalist school, and wished to go to actual life for artistic material. Now Davis found in the Post-Impressionists Gauguin and Van Gogh, and in Matisse, "the same excitement" which he had gotten "from the numerical precision of the Negro piano players in the Newark saloons." Thus had Davis begun to make his own relation to the American scene, and to its spirit of dynamism, at the level of popular culture. Since then he has always tried to convey in his art something of the vitality he felt so keenly in jazz music.

In 1920 Davis moved toward a more uncompromising non-representational art, using "a conceptual instead of an optical perspective." The following year he was executing such works as *Lucky Strike,* his own vital, painted version of the Cubists' *papier collés.* In 1927, he began the first of a series of abstract variations in the spirit of decorative Cubism based on the motif of an egg beater, an electric fan and a rubber glove. In these paintings Davis drastically simplified his forms, eliminating all but the most schematic descriptive content, and reducing it to a system of flat planes and geometric shapes. "I felt," he was later to say, "that a subject had its emotional reality fundamentally through our awareness of such planes and their spatial relationships." The next year he went to Paris, where he found his radical experimental mood confirmed; he returned to his native land in 1929 and was immediately depressed by the "gigantism" and inhumanity of New York City. He was convinced, nevertheless, that as an American artist he "had need for the impersonal dynamics of New York City." His continuing variations on the egg-beater theme showed an even more simplified graphic style, with larger planes of solid, bright color relieved by a supple tracery of line.

During the thirties and forties, Davis's style became more abstract, but denser in its linear detail, full of cadenced movement and restless surface activity. Even in his more abstract inventions, however, he depended on locale, introducing a cursive, running script of lettering fragments taken from signboards, and glimpses of some characteristic American shop fronts, houses or streets.

Although he is indebted to decorative Cubism and perhaps most of all to Léger (whom he once described as "the most American painter painting today"), Davis has given a distinctly native inflection, a special lightness and an altogether personal, whimsical humor to his European sources. If his painting may sometimes seem too much in the spirit of the poster and a form of merely graceful decoration, he has shown an impressive, structural color sense from the first. "I think of color," he has written, "as an interval of space—not as red or blue. People used to think of color and form as two things. I think of them as the same thing, so far as the language of painting is concerned. Color in a painting represents different positions in space."

Davis added a cleanness of line and sparkling, extrovert color to Parisian idioms. A man who has expressed a partiality for jazz and other popular art forms, he has sought also to inject brisk new rhythms and an irreverent gaiety into abstract painting. For the stage properties of Cubism, the pipes, mandolins, and harlequins, Davis has substituted the surfaces of American life: ensembles of gas pumps, colonial houses, local street scenes, disembodied lettering and signs. Some of his more abstract, irregular silhouettes

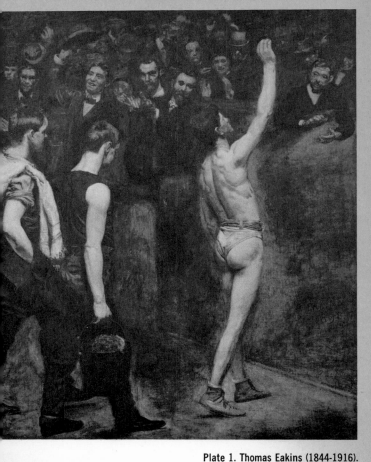

Plate 1. Thomas Eakins (1844-1916).
SALUTAT.
1898. Oil, 50 x 40".
Addison Gallery of American Art, Andover, Mass.

Plate 2. John Sloan (1871-1951).
THE HAYMARKET.
1907. Oil, 26 x 31⅞".
The Brooklyn Museum

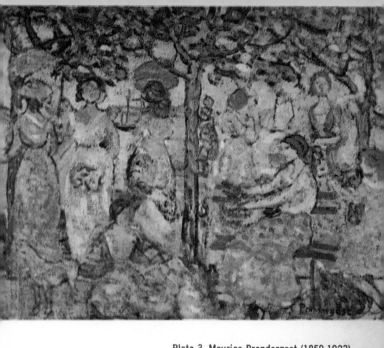

Plate 3. Maurice Prendergast (1859-1923).
ACADIA.
1922. Oil, 31¾ x 37½".
The Museum of Modern Art, New York,
Mrs. John D. Rockefeller, Jr. Fund

Plate 4. William Glackens (1870-1938).
CHEZ MOUQUIN.
1905. Oil, 48 x 39".
The Art Institute of Chicago

Plate 5. George Bellows (1882-1925).
STAG AT SHARKEY'S:
1909. Oil, 36¼ x 48¼".
The Cleveland Museum of Art,
Hinman B. Hurlbut Collection

Plate 6. Joseph Stella (1880-1946).
BATTLE OF LIGHT, CONEY ISLAND.
1913. Oil, 75¾ x 84".
Yale University Art Gallery,
Société Anonyme Collection

Plate 7. Max Weber (1881-   ).
CHINESE RESTAURANT.
1915. Oil, 40 x 48".
The Whitney Museum of American Art, New York

**Plate 8. Stanton MacDonald-Wright (1890-   ).
CONCEPTION.**
1915. Oil, 30 x 24".
The Whitney Museum of American Art, New York

Plate 9. John Covert (1892-   ).
BRASS BAND.
1919. Oil and strings on board, 26 x 24".
Yale University Art Gallery, Société Anonyme Collection

Plate 10. Marsden Hartley (1877-1943).
"E".
1915. Oil, 48 x 47¾".
The estate of the artist,
courtesy of A.P. Rosenberg & Co., Inc.

Plate 11. John Marin (1870-1955).
LOWER MANHATTAN.
(Composing derived from top of Woolworth.)
1922. Watercolor, 21⅝ x 26⅞".
The Museum of Modern Art, New York.
Acquired through the Lillie P. Bliss Bequest

Plate 12. Arthur G. Dove (1880-1946).
PLANT FORMS.
1915. Pastel, 17¼ x 30".
The Whitney Museum of American Art, New York.
Gift of Mr. and Mrs. Roy R. Neuberger

Plate 13. Man Ray (1890-   ).
THE ROPE DANCER ACCOMPANIES
HERSELF WITH HER SHADOWS.
1916. Oil, 52 x 73⅜".
The Museum of Modern Art, New York.
Gift of G. David Thompson

Plate 14. Stuart Davis (1894-   ).

URSINE PARK.

1942. Oil, 20•x 40⅛".
Collection International Business Machines Corporation, New York

Plate 15. Niles Spencer (1893-1953).

TWO BRIDGES.

1947. Oil, 28½ x 45½".
Collection Mr. and Mrs. Roy R. Neuberger, New York

Plate 16. Charles Demuth (1883-1935).
BUSINESS.
1921. Oil, 20 x 24½".
The Art Institute of Chicago,
Alfred Stieglitz Collection

Plate 17. Charles Sheeler (1883-   ).
CLASSIC LANDSCAPE.
1931. Oil, 25 x 32¼".
Collection Mrs. Edsel B. Ford,
Grosse Point Shores, Michigan

Plate 18. Edward Hopper (1882-   ). EARLY SUNDAY MORNING. 1930. Oil, 60 x 35⅛". *The Whitney Museum of American Art, New York*

Plate 19. Ben Shahn (1898-   ). HANDBALL.

1939. Tempera, 22¾ x 31¼".

The Museum of Modern Art, New York, Mrs. John D. Rockefeller, Jr. Fund

Plate 20. Gaston Lachaise (1882-1935).
STANDING WOMAN.
1932. Bronze, 91" high.
The Museum of Modern Art, New York,
Mrs. Simon Guggenheim Fund

Plate 21. William Zorach (1887-   ).
CHILD WITH CAT.
1926. Tennessee marble, 18" high.
The Museum of Modern Art, New York.
Gift of Mr. and Mrs. Samuel A. Lewisohn

Plate 22. Morris Graves (1910-   ).
BLIND BIRD.
1940. Gouache, 30⅛ x 27".
The Museum of Modern Art, New York

Plate 23. Mark Tobey (1890-   ).
TUNDRA.
1944. Tempera, 24 x 16½".
Collection Mr. and Mrs. Roy R. Neuberger, New York

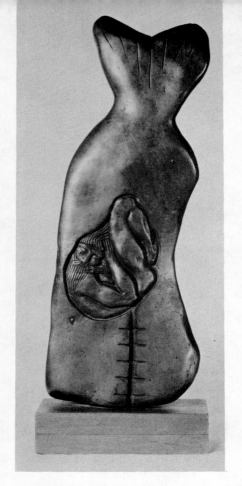

**Plate 24. John B. Flannagan (1898-1942).
JONAH AND THE WHALE.**
1937. Bronze, 29½" high.
The Minneapolis Institute of Arts

Plate 25. Theodore Roszak (1907-).
SPECTRE OF KITTY HAWK.
1947. Steel brazed with bronze and brass, 40¼" high.
The Museum of Modern Art, New York

Plate 26. Arshile Gorky (1904-1948).

WATERFALL.

Ca. 1943. Oil, 60½" x 44½".
Courtesy Sidney Janis Gallery, New York

Plate 27. Jackson Pollock (1912-1956).
NUMBER 12.
1952. Oil and aluminum paint, 101½″ x 89″.
Private Collection, New York

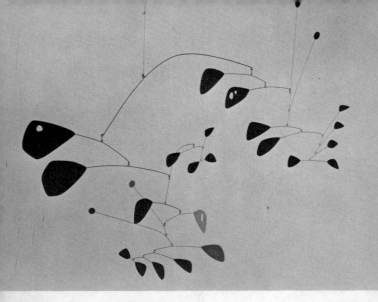

Plate 28. Alexander Calder (1898-   ).
SUMAC.
1952. Sheet metal and wire, 52" high.
Collection Frederick Seacrest, Lincoln, Nebraska

Plate 29. David Smith (1906-   ).
AUSTRALIA.
1951. Steel, 107" wide.
Owned by the artist, Bolton Landing, New York

Plate 30. Willem de Kooning (1904-   ).
COMPOSITION.
1955. Oil, 79⅛ x 69⅛".
The Solomon R. Guggenheim Museum, New York

Plate 31. Hans Hofmann (1880-   ).
EXUBERANCE.
1955. Oil, 50 x 40".
The Albright Gallery, Buffalo

Plate 32. Herbert Ferber (1906-   ).
CREATION.
1957. Brass brazed with brass, 69 x 42".
Fairmount Temple, Cleveland

Plate 33. Franz Kline (1910-   ).
THIRD AVENUE.
1954. Oil, 25 x 37¾".
Collection Mr. and Mrs. B. H. Friedman, New York

Plate 34. Robert Motherwell (1915-). THE VOYAGE.
1950. Oil and tempera, 48 x 94".
The Museum of Modern Art, New York.
Gift of Mrs. John D. Rockefeller, Jr.

Plate 35. Bradley Walker Tomlin (1899-1953). NUMBER 9: In Praise of Gertrude Stein.

1950. Oil, 49 x 102¼".

The Museum of Modern Art. Gift of Mrs. John D. Rockefeller, Jr.

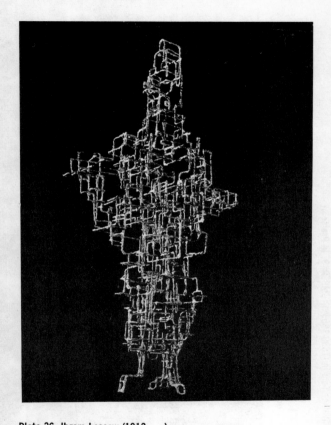

Plate 36. Ibram Lassaw (1913-   ).
MONOCEROS.
1952. Bronze, steel and chromium, 47" high.
Collection Mrs. Albert H. Newman, Chicago

te 37. Seymor Lipton (1903-   ).
THE CLOAK.
1951. Bronze and steel,
96" high.
Private Collection, New York

Plate 38. Mark Rothko (1903-   ).
EARTH AND GREEN
1954-55. Oil 91 x 74"
Collection Mr. and Mrs. Ben Heller, New York

Plate 39. Philip Guston (1913-   ).
THE CLOCK.
1957. Oil, 76 x 64".
Courtesy Sidney Janis Gallery, New York

Plate 40. William Baziotes (1912-   ).
RED LANDSCAPE.
1957. Oil, 72 x 60".
The Minneapolis Institute of Arts.

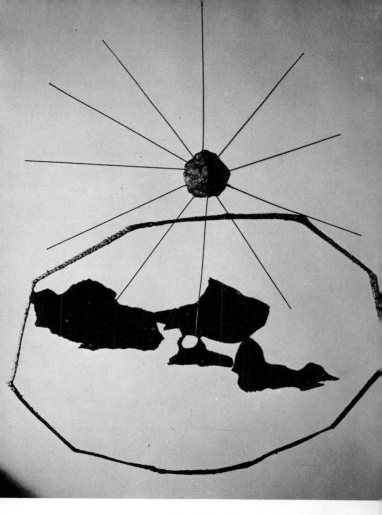

Plate 41. David Hare (1917-   ). SUNSET 2.
1953. Bronze and steel, 60" high.
Courtesy Samuel M. Kootz Gallery, New York

Plate 42. Clifford Still (1904-   ).
NUMBER 2.
1949. Oil, 91 x 69".
Collection Mr. and Mrs. Ben Heller

Plate 43. Jack Tworkov (1900-   ).
PINK MISSISSIPPI.
1954. Oil, 60 x 50".
Courtesy Stable Gallery, New York

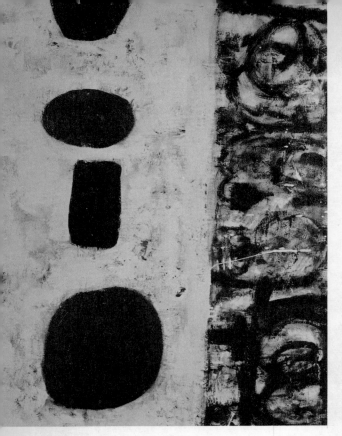

Plate 44. Adolph Gottlieb (1903-   ).

FROZEN SOUNDS 2.

1952. Oil. 36 x 48". The Albright Gallery, Buffalo

Plate 45. James Brooks (1906-   ).
GORDIAN 1957.
1957. Oil, 41½ x 89½". Courtesy Stable Gallery, New York

Plate 46. Helen Frankenthaler (1928-   ).
EDEN.
1956. Oil, 102 x 120".
Courtesy Tibor De Nagy Gallery, New York

Plate 47. Grace Hartigan (1922-   ).
BILLBOARD.
1957. Oil, 78 x 90".
The Minneapolis Institute of Arts

Plate 48. Joseph Cornell (1903-   ).
PAVILION.
1953. Painted wood, pasted paper, glass, 19 x 12".
Collection Mr. and Mrs. Herbert Ferber, New York

and his bright color seem to have anticipated Matisse's humorous and playful *Jazz* cutouts of recent years. The total artist reveals an intensity of feeling and a pictorial energy that takes his painting beyond the category of decoration. Reflected in Davis's art, too, is a twenties mood of cheerful but ironic detachment, and a deeply engrained habit of teasing American culture, all of which can be related to the poetry of E. E. Cummings. (Like Cummings, Davis has shown himself both a fine lyricist and an effective satirist.)

Davis uses scraps of lettering or abstract words and phrases to give an abrasive, contemporary quality to a painting, the shock of a suddenly evoked, everyday reality in the midst of an abstract pictorial scheme. At other times letters are identified with the individual and his emotions in an anonymous urban environment. "I often use words in my pictures," Davis has said, "because they are a part of an urban subject matter." He has described the content of one of his phrases as being "as real as any shape of a face or a tree. . . ." Thus in a modest way Davis evolved an abstract visual language which is also a sensitive recorder of real impressions—a small language perhaps, but passionate nonetheless. It is thoroughly contemporary, unmistakably American, and decisively his own.

Davis's art is one of the few links of continuity between America's first phase of advanced art and contemporary experiment. While his expression is no longer related in style or aims to present-day abstraction, in the thirties it provided a useful frame of reference and a point of support for many of the young artists who were beginning to move toward abstraction. David Smith, the sculptor, has indicated that he found stimulation in Davis's liberal viewpoint on the WPA art project, during a period dominated by regionalist styles or a somber Expressionism. Some of the more geometric abstractions by Arshile Gorky in the same era bear a resemblance to Davis's work of the egg-beater phase, as do many of the paintings of the members of the American Abstract Artists group which was formed in the late thirties.

To the generation of Hopper, Burchfield and others who drew on the local scene, Davis's art must have posed a challenge, for it provided more refreshing answers in the quest for a native art than the various styles of romantic realism offered. "In my own case," Davis has written, "I have enjoyed the dynamics of the American scene for many years, and all my pictures . . . are referential to it. They all have their originating impulse in the impact of the contemporary American environment." For the generation of emerging younger artists who would soon be moving toward even more radical modes of abstraction, Davis's work confirmed a growing resolve to search for expression outside of representational styles. Just as Alexander Calder served the young sculptors of the period, Davis became for the new painters a living proof that the pressures of provincialism could be successfully set aside. He also provided a high standard of taste, if not a direct incentive for further experiment. Throughout the period of reaction, in the twenties and during the depressed thirties, Davis painted according to esthetic principles far more strict and exacting than those of his contemporaries. The new generation of abstract artists were to find a badly needed solace and encouragement in his statement: "The act of painting is not a duplication of experience, but the extension of experience on the plane of formal invention."

7

Into the Forties: The Crisis in Painting

"Art consists in going the full length. . . . The task which the artist implicitly sets himself is to overthrow existing values, to make of the chaos about him an order which is his own, to sow strife and ferment so that by the emotional release those who are dead may be restored to life."

—Henry Miller, *Tropic of Cancer*

Since the war years the most vital development in American painting has been a fresh and underivative form of abstraction. Called "Abstract Expressionism" or "Action" painting, and identified with a rather heterogeneous group of painters known as "The New York School," this new painting genre has radically transformed our artistic atmosphere. It is generally acknowledged, and more often deplored, as the dominant American current. Perhaps the critical figure in the evolution of the new modes was the late Jackson Pollock. His name has been anathema to the public at large who have received a rather sensational journalistic portrait of him as the Peck's bad boy of technique, as an artist who splashed paint about over immense surfaces in violation of all rules and decorum. To many of the frightened, servile critics and editors of our large metropolitan newspapers and national magazines, he still represents modern anarchy, just as for many younger abstract artists he remains the heroic symbol of their new sense of liberation and hope.

Pollock has been one of the prime movers of the new abstract painting. His great contribution lay in "going the full length," in his willingness to expend himself extravagantly and profligately, often at the cost of the harmony and coherence of individual paintings, in order to take possession of the modern abstract picture.

Paradoxically, to possess modern tradition on one's own terms became for American artists at a crucial period in our painting history, during the late thirties and early forties, a way of bringing American art back into the international mainstream. Energy, sometimes reduced to an unrelenting rhythmic monotone or mere motor violence, has been one of the hallmarks of Pollock's painting. In the beginning these energies were tumultuous, self-fascinated and desperate; in the later phases of his work they have been more controlled and impersonal. The very superabundance of his pictorial energies, the expression of a power almost grotesque in relation to its situation, link Pollock to a native tradition of romantic exaggeration and hyperbole.

As a distinctly American romantic temperament, Pollock made his own individualism the theme of his art. In an early "dark" style particularly, his paintings functioned as a kind of fever chart of the ecstasies and the torments of his sense of isolation. The very fact that he felt it necessary to express his anguished sensibility in a Herculean dimension was also in the American grain. If Pollock seemed driven to register his own rancors, fancies and impulses, it was not merely as an act of self-indulgence; his was an honest record of the sensitive man's response to contemporary crisis, an effort to come to terms with a world in which traditional order and traditional values were seriously threatened. The violent emotionalism of his first style marks the rise of a new school of romantic sensibility in American art. It is new because it has synthesized indigenous modes of feeling and the vital form-language of European modernism. Pollock's tormented individualism relates him to a whole gallery of American romantics from Melville and Poe through Faulkner. His radical achievement was to make the American romantic sensibility viable in abstract art, to express it unsentimentally and without losing sight of the examples of high creativeness in modern tradition.

That Pollock was able to move into a significant advanced painting style in the late thirties, along with a number of other American artists, was due to a curious set of circumstances. Most important was the international crisis, which made the prevailing regionalist sentiment and the complacent optimism of American scene painting suddenly appear preposterously provincial. A world in dissolution deserved better of the artist than an uneasy esthetic isolationism which identified virtue in art with the rural western idyl of Thomas Benton, the backwoods folklore of John Steuart Curry, and the somewhat satirical ancestor worship of Grant Wood. The dramatic crisis in European culture drew American artists closer to the spirit of continental modernism, and migration of European intellectuals and artists to these shores renewed vital artistic contacts that had lain moribund for many years. There was a sense even by the late thirties, as John Peale Bishop has noted, that the European past had been confided to us, since we alone could "prolong it into the future." The immediate stimulation for the American vanguard came from the group of Surrealists who gathered around the dealer, Peggy Guggenheim, in the early years of the war, and from the influential teaching of the German modernist, Hans Hofmann, who had opened an art school in New York. The Federal Art Project of the WPA was another factor in the emergence of an advanced art. As a national experience in self-discovery, it both reinforced and offset the new rapprochement with modern European modes. In their eagerness to find a new way for art, Americans began again to consult continental examples; but a newly awakened sense of their own powers made them do so in a more critical and independent spirit.

Of all the artistic influences in the air, the belated discovery of Surrealism was perhaps the most important. Surrealism was one of the major lacunae in our artistic culture, and its absence left the modern American artist without a portion of the romantic patrimony. The importance of both Dada and Surrealism arose as much from their mood of romantic protest, their state of mind, as it did from their actual program or artistic devices. Although this spirit had never seized the American imagination, in Europe the Surrealists figured prominently in the continuing art revolution which sought to release the artist from the harsh compulsions of modern life, from what one critic has described as "the regimentation of men and the culture of things." (It is interesting to observe that when American abstract artists did seek in Surrealism new means to express their flight from the crude material values of contemporary life, they were driven not into an art of private dreams, as might be expected, but one of immediate sensations. They revealed themselves as sensitive materialists even as they flew in the face of contemporary materialism.)

The Surrealists, by their presence in America during the war, were to offer some very crucial hints for a new synthesis of abstract form and a romantic-feeling content. Their "automatism" and rehabilitation of instinct provided a vital alternative to the geometric design and pattern-making of the academicians of Cubism and abstract art. While the rational constructions of the Cubists had given modern art perhaps its most impressive and elevated style, by the late twenties much of the generative power of the movement had been lost or supplanted by an abstract academicism. In America a decade later, a kind of post-Cubist Byzantinism was considered our most advanced style; it was reflected in the competent, doctrinaire, non-objective painting of the American Abstract Artists group. To such currents in art, Surrealism posed the alternative of the spontaneous, of unpremeditated impulse and gave a new primacy to creative freedom. A number of Americans were quick to seize on this alternative and used it to enlarge the expressive possibilities of their art. Eventually, they subordinated surrealist intuitions completely to their own artistic needs and purposes.

The impact of the surrealist liberties on the American *avant-garde* was sharp if somewhat oblique. Pollock was undoubtedly affected by the milieu around Peggy Guggenheim, his first dealer, and his own methods were "automatic" to a degree. Later he wrote: "The source of my painting is the Unconscious. I approach painting the same way I approach drawing, that is, directly, with no preliminary studies. . . . When I am painting, I am not much aware of what is taking place; it is only after that I see what I have done."

Arshile Gorky, an elegant, mannered virtuoso in both

figurative and abstract modes during the thirties, was in the early years of the next decade deeply influenced by the unstable forms and molten space of Yves Tanguy, Joan Miró and Matta Echaurren. Later André Breton claimed Gorky for Surrealism when he suggested that Gorky treated nature "as a cryptogram." The earliest painting of Adolph Gottlieb, Mark Rothko, William Baziotes and Clyfford Still were all in varying degrees concerned with myth and with the "primitive"; and these artists worked in a form of symbolic, surrealist-tinctured abstraction. Along with Motherwell and Pollock they all relied on "accident," felicitous or disruptive, to give vitality to their creations. The American esthetic of the accidental descends in a direct line from the surrealist *trouvaille*, or lucky find.

In New York during the early forties there were two private temples of Surrealism, the Julien Levy Gallery and Peggy Guggenheim's Art of This Century. Most active and significant was Peggy Guggenheim who not only became a transmission point for the painting of international Surrealism but introduced their makers, in the flesh, to the American art scene. She made accessible to the young New York painters whose work she exhibited such artists as Breton, Masson, Ernst, Tanguy, and Matta. For the first time since Duchamp and Picabia had invaded New York in the period of the Armory Show, our artists knew what it actually felt like to live in the midst of an active international art milieu. They were able to keep abreast of the new currents, not by having recourse to the latest issue of *Cahiers d'Art* as they had in the past, but simply by listening and observing. They must have felt modern art freshly and with a new sense that they were actually living it; contact with many of the impressive reputations of Paris had done something to free them of their provincial diffidence.

More than anything else, it seems now in retrospect, the sudden efflorescence of cosmopolitanism during the war was the inspiration of the new abstract expressions. During the thirties there had been many promising hints of a new synthesis, especially in the painting of Pollock, Gorky and Hofmann, but they were not entirely decisive. The moment of crystallization had to wait until the first years of the forties, and it was only then that the search for abstract idioms assumed the unity of a sustained collective effort. Hans Hofmann had begun to splash pigment around freely on canvas as early as 1938, but his influence was not so immediately decisive as Pollock's. Gorky had in some ways anticipated Pollock, particularly when he began to paraphrase Picasso in the late thirties; but the fascination his sources held for Gorky delayed his highest creative moment until the mid-forties. For all his remarkable instincts and painterly gifts, Gorky lacked the primitive force and energy that seem necessary to bring the new in art. His remained an epicurean sensibility until the last years of his life when he suddenly seemed to catch fire from the painting atmosphere he himself had been instrumental in creating. Then his art blazed out in passionate fulfillment of his great promise.

The first and most decisive public expression of the new mood came from Pollock. Everything that had been amorphous, contingent on circumstance, and unstable in advanced painting first came into focus in his art with his first New York exhibition in 1943. The unwavering pitch at which he registered his own sensations and even revealed his uncertainties, lent a new confidence and security to the American vanguard. His spirit of monumental intransigence and dynamism helped release energies that had been pent up in American art for twenty years. Pollock's first expression was dark and narrow, haunted by obsessive themes and a self-absorbed romanticism; yet he managed miraculously to preserve a plastic painting rationale derived from the most elevated modern styles. He achieved this even as many fellow-artists, whom we now associate with him, seemed prepared to leave the high road of twentieth-century painting tradition for the byways of myth and symbolism. From the beginning there was a touch of revolution in Pollock's painting; many artists who now seem more drastic or advanced are still elaborating on some phase of that revolution. None, I think, would hesitate to name Pollock as the most critical figure in the emergence of the new genre of abstraction.

Pollock was killed in a tragic automobile accident in the

summer of 1956 at the age of forty-four. He grew up in Arizona and Southern California. Geographical impressions may very well have played a significant role in the development of his painting. He has described his delight as a youth at seeing the western landscape, immense, illimitable, unroll before him from freight trains or his old Ford. His early peregrinations filled him even in maturity with some nostalgia, as if the freedom of boyhood and the open road were best. He retained something of the restiveness of his youth and an unformulated, primitive sense of the vastness of things American. A rootless feeling which was as acute as his instinctive distaste for social restraints, real or imagined, persisted throughout his life.

As a personality he re-created D. H. Lawrence's ambiguous picture of the American free spirit in *Studies in Classic American Literature*. Lawrence was acute enough to see in American writing of the golden age a refreshing, new human consciousness, as he put it. At the same time, he suggested that the American writer, who lacked so many of the assurances of a cultivated existence and was *sui generis* a romantic, might shrink from the harsh forms of native reality and seek relief in the expression of extreme states of mind. For Lawrence the American imagination was in fugue, in eternal revolt against the parenthood of European authority and traditional values. In the need and passion to create new artistic values where none existed before, American genius fulfilled itself. "Henceforth masterless" was his half-mocking, half-admiring refrain for the new world's mystique of freedom. Impatient of European civilization and himself eager to find renewal at more primitive sources, Lawrence was able to sympathize with anti-traditional modes of feeling and expression. But he was also mindful of their limitations, and warned that the American's romantic egoism might become a prison. The estrangement of the modern writer and painter from contemporary mass culture is the more acute in America because, as Lawrence discerned, it feeds on a native habit of inwardness. Modern art in Europe has also been created under conditions of isolation ever since the Impressionists. But the alienation of the artist has been less destructive in tradition-directed culture. An urge to abstraction and the suppression of individualized feeling has always been indigenous to the American temper.

The romantic bias of Pollock's individualism and his sense of freedom as expressed in his art stand out in sharper definition when his work is compared with the abstract painting of the new European generation. No painters of the French vanguard, many of whom have felt Pollock's influence, permit themselves the liberties he takes. Barring some notable exceptions, the foreign abstract article generally still has the look of studio manufacture, and an air of knowing if shallow professionalism. Pollock's raw directness and his lack of finish strike most contemporary European critics as being in appallingly bad taste. Those painters who have followed his example in France, under the banner of *tachisme,* and have adopted his formal devices and scale, are unwilling or unable to pursue the more radical implications of his art. A traditional French hedonism, which is being given a more and more decorative elaboration today, pulls them up short on the threshold of discovery. From recent criticism in Paris of contemporary American painting, it would seem that the French for the most part see in artists like Pollock little more than a promise, and are convinced that painting only *begins* where American abstract art so suggestively but disappointingly ends. Behind Pollock's art is a conviction, equally strong, that the moment painting indulges in a derivative pictorialism, the moment it becomes a conscious artifact, it loses its creative meaning. The European finds audacity, originality and certain intriguing effects in the new American painting, but misses its inner working process.

The eruption of new creative energies may be attributed to the divided will of our art at the end of the thirties, to the often self-contradictory efforts of American painters to reassimilate modernism and also to discover themselves. A fellow painter has said perceptively that in the beginning Pollock paraphrased Picasso and then turned against his inspiration and violently eliminated all evidence of his debt. The very erasures, eliminations and emendations were converted into a viable expression, as they were during that same period in the more urbane but also more derivative work of Gorky. The American vanguard's search for authority has been a troubled one, moving between a Scylla of fashionable modernism and a Charybdis of provincial expressionism. The history of that voyage is the story of Pollock's evolution as a painter.

Pollock began his artistic education in 1929 when he came to the Art Students League in New York and studied with Thomas Benton. Benton's homely American scene realism was at the time compelling, and he was a vital personality who exerted a strong influence on his students. Although Pollock studied with him for only two years, he did not begin to shake off Benton's style until the middle thirties. It is significant that the younger artist found his independence not so much in reaction to Benton but *through* him, by re-creating, amplifying and exaggerating his first teacher's rhythmic distortions under conditions of greater intensity until his forms achieved a different order of life. In a sense, Pollock arrived at abstraction by pushing Expressionism to a point where subject matter was so improbable that there was no need to retain it. By the middle thirties Pollock found in the Mexican Orozco a more satisfying drama of violence. His paintings of this period are muddy, crude and inchoate but already stamped with genuine temperament; they still describe, if very freely, figure groups or landscape.

In 1936 Pollock began to eliminate recognizable subject matter, and replaced it with angular, non-representational shapes and thick, rhythmic coils of tarry black line, which stood out in assertive texture and relief. His color combinations of muddy blue-greens, brick reds and yellows were loud and violent; the forms, elementary in their simplicity but full of character. These paintings were still close to Orozco in spirit. Curiously enough the color schemes and rugged, plastered surfaces were similar to some Gorky still life of the same epoch, paintings which Pollock has said he never saw, however.

There is one small crayon and water-color painting from this period of a rather more representational character that deserves attention for what it reveals of Pollock's inner

struggle. It is an alternately muddy and vivid little landscape, with a black hole in the foreground holding a ladder,
and a night sky in the background lit by blood-red flames.
The artist always felt a very personal relationship to the
painting which stood as a private symbol of frustration and
hope and represented a voyage of the soul from darkness
into light. The fact that the light in the painting emanated
from a conflagration apparently signified that Pollock's
crisis would be resolved by violent catharsis.

In a sense that is exactly what happened immediately
after, first in his bold distortions based on Mexican painting and then in his rapid and aggressive assimilations of
Picasso and European modernism. In the late thirties Pollock filled notebooks with abstract anatomical themes that
were Picassoid, but with a difference. To Picasso's delimited,
contained abstract imagery of the period Pollock applied
his own expansive energies with startling and novel results.
His nervous, broken line shredded Picasso's fantastic anatomies, reducing them to a system of expressive accents or
more generalized thematic variations. Carried away perhaps by a random inventiveness in line, Pollock had begun
to create more evenly distributed effects. They broke up
the unity of Picasso's abstract figuration and were the first
step toward a later free and cursive calligraphy which dispensed with image suggestion altogether.

These drawings also revealed a tension between ugliness
and elegance, clumsiness and finesse, that has persisted
throughout Pollock's work. He often seemed to wish to
destroy his great natural gifts as a draftsman by deliberately
breaking the rhythm of his line when it had achieved only
the most rudimentary signs or configurations. If Pollock
pursued the rude and apparently incomplete statement, however, it was with a purpose of freeing himself from the
prejudice of geometric design. Even more, he sought to
repudiate *any* commitment as to style or manner; in this
early work there was, indeed, almost a fetish of non-style.
Such impersonality has disturbed many critics. It was a
necessary adjunct to a more elevated painting objective,
however: the aim to create a more inclusive, plastic point
of view which would translate even the most extravagant

emotion into convincing pictorial sensation. His sensitivity to the felt structure of drawing and later of painting in all its palpable immediacy had much in common with early Cubism, and that despite a great show of recklessness and the apparent absence of formal order.

In 1942 Pollock participated in his first New York group show, organized by John Graham at the MacMillan Gallery. Showing with him were Graham, Lee Krasner (now Mrs. Pollock) and Willem de Kooning, another unheralded member of the *avant-garde* who less than ten years later was to share the leadership of progressive American painting. Pollock showed a blue-green, expressionist-flavored abstract painting. His abstract figuration had a look of phantasmagoria and already resembled those disembodied, astral eyes which later became a key theme in his painting. In these agitated movements and grotesquely suggestive whirlpools of line Pollock found a private totem which has persistently refused to be expelled from his painting. Some time later De Kooning, too, discovered that his abstract paintings were still inhabited by an obsessive reality, the human figure of an earlier phase, or more exactly, "The Woman." Such fearful presences are not out of character with abstract expressionist painting because the genre permits wide inclusions. They also indicate that this painting has never been abstract in the more narrow, limited sense of non-objective art. It has, on the contrary, always been emotive and vital in its handling, and rich in content, a content that betrayed the exaggerated fears, the exalted moods, and the libido of its creators.* Frequently this content has sug-

---

* Edgar Allan Poe provides useful clues to the ambiguous content of Pollock's painting. An unconscious by-product of paint manipulation, this content is at once more than an expression of pure esthetic relation and less than imagery. Pollock's forms, or writing, are too emotionally charged and unstable to be contained by the first category; and they are not sufficiently articulated or explicit in reference to fit the second. They belong perhaps to Poe's realm of "fancies," which he described in *Marginalia* as follows: "There is a class of fancies, of exquisite delicacy, which are *not* thoughts, and to which, *as yet*, I have found it absolutely impossible to adapt language. I use the word 'fancies' at random, and merely because I must use some word; but the idea commonly attached to the term is not even remotely applicable to the shadows of shadows in question. They seem to me rather psychical than intellectual. They arise . . . at those mere points of time where the confines of the waking world blend with those of dreams. . . . Now, so entire is my faith in the *power of words*, that, at times, I have believed it possible to embody even the

gested a search for some hidden or lost mytho-poetic symbolism. A highly charged atmosphere survived in Pollock's freest abstract transpositions from Picasso, and these paintings often ended, as if he were powerless to prevent it, by looking like fantasias of the unconscious.

In the general rhythm of Pollock's work, imagery itself generates an abstract invention which destroys references to natural appearances. But his purer, non-representational plastic "writing" also has a backlash of suggested presences and near-imagery. Much of the power of his early work springs out of the tension of renunciation: the image is denied but something of its atmosphere and immanence remains, creating a powerful and luminous diffusion of felt content throughout the length and breadth of the canvas. It was only after Pollock had worked through and exorcised the more pointed images which referred to his own rancors and fears that he, and then many of his fellow painters, could draw with unconscious freedom on the purer or more "abstract" aspects of Abstract Expressionism.

In 1942 Robert Motherwell introduced Pollock to Peggy Guggenheim, and that year he exhibited in a group show at her gallery the painting, *Stenographic Figure*. It was a loosely knit arrangement of shapes derived from Picasso with a kind of erratic "automatic" over-writing. The colors were bizarre mauves and blue-greens, set against grays and off-whites, suggesting somewhat the high color key of Mexican *papier-mâché* decorations or the palette of Northwest Indian art. This was probably the first painting in which Pollock's vermiform shapes actually broke down into energy areas and a free calligraphy. The next year, at the age of thirty-one, Pollock was given his first one-man show at the Art of This Century gallery and with it began a prolific production that carried him through eleven exhibitions in a period of twelve years.

---

evanescence of fancies such as I have attempted to describe." One should not make the mistake, however, of considering Pollock an inspirational, paint-drunk genius, or as a creator of fantasy primarily. He had always addressed himself to medium in immediate physical and material terms. It is possible to achieve fully formed fantasy only by illusionist pictorial means which no longer prove useful to the most serious contemporary artists. Pollock steadfastly repudiated illusionist devices as a violation of modern art's tradition of concreteness and its central esthetic purposes.

From the years between 1943 and 1947 date the anatomical themes and the compact compositional schemes of such paintings as *The She-Wolf, Pasiphae* and the more abstract *Gothic*. Pollock had already begun to unify his pictures by "writing" freely over the surface with an energetic, whiplash line. He had learned to release a confused and opaque bitterness by sheer energy, by the very fury of his attack. The result was that he literally remade the abstract picture, and under new conditions of extraordinary intensity.

In *Pasiphae* and *The She-Wolf* Pollock's baroque energies took him to a new form of expression that relieved the dense, impacted surfaces of Picasso's late Cubism with the fluent, abstract imagery of Miró and such other Surrealists as Masson. To the Surrealists he owed not so much the form of his own distinctive "writing," but the notion that the painting was to be ejected as a "stream," in one seeming burst. The wiggly line and agitated movements of these two paintings recall Miró of his 1924-1926 period. Miró, however, floated his shapes on a ground, giving his pictorial incident a setting and hinting at representational illusion. His shapes kept their integrity as individualized forms despite the metamorphic transformations to which they submitted. Out of Miró's ingenious and inventive mind streamed an anarchic abundance of new life and pictorial incident, with an effect of multiplicity and particularity. Rooted in modern tradition, he could afford to play and pun, to sport with his own fears, as one critic has put it, and to make an enchantingly witty game of them. For Pollock, on the other hand, abstract painting was an altogether more solemn and even desperate matter; he felt compelled to be more savage and self-absorbed and had nothing of the artistic playboy about him. He saw the abstract picture as an elementary expression of belief, and in this conviction lay his power and originality. Pollock's paintings groped from the particular to the general, from a chaos of expressive accents to the single statement. He dissolved and fused his vague references to a chimerical subject matter into a unified, impersonal scheme. After the picture was completed, he named it for the chimera it still rather irrelevantly suggested. In the end the painting had become a continuous field of uniform accents where it was impossible to distinguish between scrolling lines of paint and phantasmagoria, the near and the far, the symbolic and the plastic.

Pollock's early style culminated in his predominantly black, vehemently pigmented canvases of 1945 such as *Night Mist* and *Totem Lesson Number II*. The latter is a large, vertical painting where he played with a grotesque abstract figuration within his own powerful system of chiaroscuro. To achieve intimations of terror within disorder and chaos seemed to be the message of this forbidding and claustrophobic work. Other paintings of the period carried Pollock's anxiety to an unrelieved extreme. After 1947, however, his gloomy and morbid intuitions were spread over a broader surface, and he surrendered most of his inner compulsions to a calm and measured lyricism. The vaguely imagistic references to his own fears and fantasies stopped crowding him and gave way to more sweeping and grandiloquent rhythms and a new clarity. His work no longer suggested presences, fearful or otherwise, or a mood of exasperation, but only a generous and impersonal flow of pictorial energy. He had won a new breadth of feeling as he learned to master larger surfaces.

Pollock's ambition carried him far beyond the traditional unity of easel painting in search of a more monumental space and a total pictorial experience. In 1948 and the early months of 1949 he painted most often on narrow horizontal canvases with irregular patches of cobalt, cadmium red and white against a dull reddish-brown ground. Even such an assertion of a Mondrian scheme of simple primary colors reflected a new objectivity. These long, narrow "scroll" paintings still retain something of the particularization, texture and sensuality of his earlier work despite their freedom, and have a balance and poise unique in Pollock's productions. *White Cockatoo* and *Summertime* are typical of this high moment; their lyricism and purity of movements remind one of the abstract yet deeply expressive gestures of the modern dance.

From 1947, the year he began to paint with aluminum and commercial paints, and to "drip" as well as brush his pigment on canvas, Pollock strained against the limits of the oil medium. He began to contrive a more radical space and invented altogether more remarkable painting effects, working on an ever more monumental scale in a grandiose personal pointillism. As Hans Namuth's dramatic series of still photographs and the film of Pollock at work demonstrated, he painted by standing over a canvas and letting paint drip on it from above until he had achieved the rhythmic movements, varied densities and textures desired. The results were probably the most original series of paintings of the immediate postwar period in American art. Yet they were a logical, if unexpectedly ambitious, extension of Pollock's early style. He had merely given his "stream" painting a larger theater; an aerated web of silver and black line, of spattered paint, against a background of delicate color diffusions and stains, replaced the old opaque, resistant pigment. Despite the lyrical sublimation of his more turgid style, something of the original tension of Pollock's feeling remained. In *Cathedral* of 1947 and in the beautiful *Lavender Mist* of 1950, there are congealed puddles of color and blotches of dark tone swimming ominously amid all the elegant rhythmic phrasing like disembodied ghosts of the artist's earlier black moods.

Pollock's predominantly silver monoliths took painting ever closer to a kind of fragile, open-form, continuous-space sculpture. (In a more serene and architectural style, the sculptor Ibram Lassaw has demonstrated that Pollock's methods and intuitions are viable in three-dimensional form.) He made paintings that approached solid relief in texture, and he also simultaneously pulverized the flat, two-dimensional effect that he had in the past been at pains to emphasize, and which was perhaps his strongest link with Cubist tradition. But Pollock's modernity, his mistrust of anything but the immediately given sensation, always asserted itself in the end. Even in his freest inventions he restored the flat, physical reality of the surface by letting his pigment clot or by slapping the unsized edges of the canvas with his paint-dipped palms. Sometimes the synthetic, industrial textures, the moraine of sheer pigment matter, seemed to choke his instinctive grace and lyricism, and a kind of gummy, displeasing effect resulted. At their finest, how-

ever, the great silver paintings from 1948 to 1951 breathe
an easy, natural grandeur that has few parallels in contemporary American art. For the author they arouse primitive
feelings associated with such sonorous phrases as "the deep"
or "the starry firmament," identifying a universe beyond
the human. However, any intelligible, identifiable feeling-
content reveals itself fitfully in the midst of a nameless
chaos, for Pollock's fine lyricism must repeatedly be
wrested free from the anonymous seething of brute pigment
matter. It was one of Pollock's signal accomplishments to
give such magnitude and impressiveness to the act of painting as to make us think of the mysteries of natural creation,
of that "first division of chaos" at the origin of our world.

One cannot live with such an exalted aspiration for long.
Seeking the relief of a more classical dryness, Pollock in
1951 and 1952 reduced his palette to black and white and
returned to the firmer unities of his first style, emphasizing
draftsmanship and making his blacks bite vehemently into
the unsized canvas like an engraver's line. A periodic denial
of color has been a persistent element in Pollock's art from
the beginning. Manet, Lautrec and especially Matisse in his
Cubist phase, gave magisterial blacks and grays a primary
role as if to dramatize the drastic, two-dimensional character of modern painting; by its very nature monochrome
painting is more abstract than color. The repudiation of
color is one way of returning to the fundamentals of structure, as Willem de Kooning, Robert Motherwell, and Franz
Kline have most recently demonstrated. Pollock's "black"
paintings were also curiously enough part of a new search
for order and restraint within a vigorous contemporary
style. The paintings of 1952 had a sobriety and decorum,
even though some of the abstract anatomical imagery of his
earlier period was revived. Among the most impressive,
though least ingratiating, of Pollock's paintings, they left no
doubt as to his power to control large spaces even with the
most radically reduced pictorial means.

In the last four years of his life Pollock alternated in
modes, sometimes drawing in black paint, at other times
creating dramatic displays of refulgent color. He returned
to the "stream" painting of 1948-1951, exploiting a new

device of flooding his canvas with white pigment until only narrow, ragged edges and trickles of dark tone could be discerned, somewhat in the manner of Clyfford Still. He reached no radically new conclusions after 1952 but was intent rather to explore and amplify the many new roads he himself opened in his first ten years of painting.

In these further explorations Pollock's work continued to point up the new set of premises in American painting. He established a new alliance with the spontaneous and the accidental, which was part of a more purposive esthetic than that of the Surrealists. Pollock identified his creative liberties with an unmistakably American atmosphere. His paintings had begun in a fierce mood of nihilism; one has to go back to the late Soutine to find work as raw, direct and careless of the traditional integrity of medium as the early Pollocks. He later also established his connection with Dada's mood of iconoclasm and disgust with society first by his violent imagery, and then by his handling of tarry blacks, his non-esthetic, industrial textures, and by embedding cigarette ends, broken glass and bits of string in his pigment. In the end he subordinated his rancors and romantic individualism to a mood of impersonal idealism, creating finally a new abstract art form of transcendent beauty.

The bold outlines of a vital new idiom were present in Pollock's first show. His energies encompassed forms and methods derived from many sources—Picasso, Miró, Masson and American Indian art—and symbolic references to his own feverish mood of crisis. The outcome was a body of painting with a radical new physiognomy, and stamped with powerfully original feeling. Compared to its more felicitous French counterpart, in the art of Soulages, de Staël or Mathieu, Pollock's Abstract Expressionism was even at its most refined, incomplete, violent, full of astringencies, with a tone harsh and primitive. Yet it helped significantly to create painting modes larger than any Europe had been able to supply for more than two decades. To give personal freedom new and distinctly native artistic outlines was Pollock's great contribution. In the face of the experimental variety of previous twentieth-century European art, it has taken on the character of a major accomplishment.

8

Search for the Absolute

"People seize on painting to cover up their nakedness. . . . They make everything from God to a picture, in their own image. That is why the picture-hook is the ruination of a painting—a painting which has always a certain significance, at least as much as the man who did it. As soon as it is bought and hung on a wall it takes on quite a different kind of significance, and the painting is done for."

—Pablo Picasso, 1935

The history of recent abstract painting in America has been one of assimilation of the devices and esthetic criteria of European modernism, and then a growing independence from them. What began in the thirties as a humble dialogue with the European past, conducted in a spirit of self-education, became in the forties a passionate interrogation of self, unhistorical in character, striking for its pictorial liberties and the development of original expressive forms. When Jackson Pollock, Hans Hofmann, Arshile Gorky and a number of their contemporaries sought in the early years of World War II to emancipate themselves both from the closed world of geometric abstraction and from the image-suggestion of representational and Surrealist art, they suddenly found themselves in an unfamiliar territory, bereft of conventional signposts or prescribed procedures. They had arrived at the unknown somewhat in the spirit of abnegation, but they conferred on their renunciation of the past, positive values of freedom and spontaneity. Free invention became its own justification and the picture plane, the physical reality of surface in all its concreteness, became its own mythology. The function of the image was reversed; it was detached from all objects in the external world, and became instead a vital graph of the artist's own operations; it reflected the self-sufficiency of the creative act. The abstracted image emancipated itself to an ever greater degree, until finally it denied its representational origins and took on an absolute value. Thus Pollock's free inventions may be understood as well as his thematic variations on fantastic Picassoid subject matter in the late thirties, and his arrival in the forties at a form of plastic "writing" which one author has described as "non-representational imagery."

The changes in methods and attitudes, and the events that helped consolidate the *avant-garde* in the early forties, form a great watershed in the evolution of contemporary American painting. While many American writers and the painters themselves have tended to emphasize the independent and native character of these developments, they also represent in the deepest sense the transplantation on American soil of some of the early ideals of European modernism.

In Abstract Expressionism, the artistic statement of the individual personality is subordinate to impersonal, objective principles, commonly held, and to a ceaseless boil of experiment in ever-changing directions. Although the movement already has its masterpieces, its greater and lesser artists, it has also been able to maintain an atmosphere of dynamism, fluidity and change, because its most forceful participants have time and again resisted the temptation to settle into some static or over-individualized idiom. Its productions characteristically bear the mark of the incomplete, of vital approximations, and end with an open question, as if to insure its creators adequate liberty of gesture and to discourage mere mannerism. It is the persistent concern with impersonal plastic problems which has made Abstract Expressionist painting a movement of international significance. Such qualities link it to such early twentieth-century movements as Cubism.

The word "movement," however, has been steadfastly rejected by the artists engaged in a type of painting which in their view is best defined by its climate of vitality and a spontaneous ideal of freedom rather than by any prescribed technical procedures, shared subject matter, program or master-disciple relationships. This is but one among many paradoxes of the new abstraction. Also paradoxical are the facts that the general style shows a deep regard for formal structure while apparently chaotic and indeterminate in appearance; that it focuses squarely on the objective, intrinsic appeal of material medium and yet is romantic in mood; that it is self-abnegating and self-fascinated at once; and that it depends on European precedent, even while it is jealous of its independence and aggressive in its self-determination. Many critics have attempted to relate the idioms of the new painters to decorative wall painting and have seen in the new work a form of monumental decoration. But Robert Motherwell, a significant figure within the group, emphasizes the unique qualities of his work, as one notable example, and he has compared his painting to an "intimate journal." These are two apparently incompatible emotional atmospheres, until we recall that Gauguin's painting, and much subsequent modern art, was simultaneously rationalized on the level of both decoration and subjective symbolism. Perhaps Meyer Schapiro best described the relation of the new abstract painting to decoration when he wrote in connection with Pollock's painting: "A work like Pollock's *Number 1* or his *Autumn Rhythm* is too powerful and earnest to serve as decoration. Only from a distant view, which loses sight of the intimate personal qualities of the surface and execution and all the passion and fantasy within the small areas, can one mistake the ornamental aspect for the essential trait of the whole."

These remarks were made in the course of a Third Programme BBC broadcast, "The Younger American Painters of Today," during the winter of 1956, on the occasion of the Museum of Modern Art's London exhibition, "Modern Art in America." In the same radio talk Dr. Schapiro pointed significantly to a polarity of types in the new American abstract painting. His distinctions will help establish the common sources of a number of apparently dissimilar styles, and will illuminate those features of the new art which make the descriptive term, movement, both legitimate and appropriate. Dr. Schapiro described the painting of Pollock and De Kooning as an art of "impulse and chance" and opposed it to that of Mark Rothko with its emphasis on sensation. "Each," he declared, "seeks an absolute in which the receptive viewer can lose himself, the one in compulsive movement, the other in an all-pervading, as if internalized, sensation of dominant color. The result in both is a painted world with a powerful, immediate impact; in awareness of this goal, the artists have tended to work on a larger and larger scale—canvases as big as mural paintings are common in the shows in New York and indeed are the ones which permit the artists to realize their aims most effectively."

Taking Dr. Schapiro's useful distinction as a point of departure, we may discern other characteristics of the two generic types of abstract painting and draw some conclusions about the differing viewpoints, and human values, supporting each. The headlong, linear styles of Pollock and De Kooning derive from Surrealist automatism, but they embody a dynamic concept of the individual will operating in the here and now, and a faith in the efficacy of action. For these two artists the revelation on canvas of the dynamics of the painting process assumes the character of a significant and *vital* action; the painting becomes a denuded, structural exposure in time and space of the artistic self engaged in a series of critical esthetic episodes, choices and decisions. Because these decisions must be made under the stress of immediate feeling and have been divorced both from traditional artistic values of representation and from reliance on external nature, the artist is driven into a deeper communion with himself as the source of choice and action. It is not too farfetched to say that the renunciation of naturalist illusion and the development of pictorial quality alone as the real content of the work of art have taken on the character of a profound spiritual commitment. The tensions of renunciation have opened up new modes of self-inquiry, wherein passion, disquiet and the individual's sense of existence are identified with the "act" of painting itself.

This does not necessarily mean that the new painting is subjective or "confessional" in character. In fact the strict limits put on the expression of fantasy and psychological content suggest quite the opposite. Rather, the intense concentration on the concrete, material means and on formal values constantly translates all emotion into convincing pictorial sensation. We are left finally with a vivid metaphor for a general dynamism and energy, and with a pictorial reality that is involved like ourselves in a constant and never-finished process of movement, development and change.

In the midst of the formulation of dynamic new spatial concepts and the exaltation of the creative process as an occasion for free and sovereign action, there is nonetheless a sobering strain of desperation and violence in the new work. The paintings of Pollock and De Kooning move toward an extreme of skepticism and rejection. Rarely have the artists turned their backs so violently on conventional taste, seemliness and traditional pictorial accessories even within modern European tradition. Rarely have they so unequivocally sought the raw, the unfinished and the indeterminate. The power of these two artists has been to make their rejections assume positive value and by their own explosive force to impose on us an artistic world so compelling that we no longer miss the familiar, transforming qualities of traditional art.

The extreme liberties, and the spirit of revolt apparent in the paintings of Pollock and De Kooning place these works in a vital relationship to some of the important philosophical problems of our period. The artists have voluntarily accepted new conditions for creating paintings—a series of radical reductions and eliminations in subject matter, image, association and stylistic device, as if to enable themselves to reach certain irreducibles in the work of art and in the self. They have consciously submitted to a severe test; as a result, a sense of crisis and catharsis often pervades their work and may be an important part of its emotional atmosphere. The artist can find little support in the past, even in the immediate, modern past, and must, indeed, rely on little or nothing outside himself and his own actions. This mood need not betray itself in a sense of anguish and violent pictorial expression alone; it can also embrace more pacific attitudes and less vehement pictorial means, depending upon the individual. It is against this background of the drama of the individual revealing himself in the act of painting, and staking his identity on the act of painting itself, that Abstract Expressionism makes its most profound claims to seriousness.

The elevation of the act of painting as a subject matter is a vital reminder that painting is made by the single individual for the single individual. Set in a framework of a problematic present, the artist's decisions on canvas take on the character of both an adventure into the unknown and the expression of his free individuality. No ready-made solutions are admissible; by mutual agreement, the pictorial illusions of the nineteenth century are relegated to the less serious contemporary artists. The essential renunciations of the Abstract Expressionists are transformed to embody new, expressive liberties and a new sense of individual responsibility. The extravagant regard for values of freedom often puts the artists beyond the conventional and at the limits of the permissible in painting, making wide popular interest in their art difficult. The contemporary abstract artists are of an almost religious temper in their sense of dedication, and will themselves into a highly conscious pictorial celibacy in defiance of traditional, nineteenth-centry illusionism. In this latter-day artistic theology without a God, however, the strictness of asceticism has been modified by an ineradicable romantic impulse, by a taste for luxurious sensation and vagrant, distorted memories of the artistic past. Willem de Kooning's paintings in particular suggest that tradition cannot be so easily put aside. The velocity and violence of paint manipulation in his most recent and entirely abstract paintings seem inversely, by the fury of their attack, to pay the ghosts of a representational style their due.

In the painting of Pollock and De Kooning free rein is given to impulse, fancy and a massive flow of material evidence of the untransformed painting process. Such painting suggests an "impure" attitude of mind which accepts chance, change and "action"—an art bound to time and duration. At the opposite pole is the art of such painters as Mark Rothko and Clyfford Still, a type of painting based on more pure and absolute attitudes of consciousness. Originally derived from "symbolist" modes, their art admits "accident" and unpremeditated effects only at the margins and seeks instead a more hieratic style that stands above contingency and chance: a non-temporal, starkly simplified and stable art. These artists play on resonant color sensations and even more radically reduced pictorial content. They make contact with some harmonious sphere of feeling beyond the self. Indeed, their painting threatens to become an instrument of metaphysical knowledge, a mediator between the concrete present and some idealized, mysterious otherness.

Both divergent groups of artists work in very large scale, striving for the impression of a total pictorial environment and for heroic design. More often than not the artist requires a large theater of operations to make his spatial intention clear. The paintings of De Kooning and Pollock continually reassert the individual's struggle with immediate and material facts, no matter how monumental their scale; they are a continuing demonstration of the self engaged in a conflicting pattern of choices and decisions. By contrast, the work of Rothko and Still, with its greater purity, comes to terms with the self more quickly and passes beyond its contending forces. Matter is refined into a luminous suspension which serves as a living sign of some secret inner harmony. The work itself often seems merely a phase of the effort to develop a permanent openness of the spirit to a new and elevated order of truth—a visual poetry of exaltation. Both types of painting, essentially, are records of a moment of consciousness, exploding into restless motor activity on the one hand, or on the other, prolonged into a coloristic reverie.

If the painting of De Kooning and Pollock may be called one of commission, in which the artist doesn't hesitate to reveal himself, that of Still and Rothko is an art of omission, where more is suggested than stated. The first two artists employ emphatic line, and their paintings are energetic, richly complex and dynamic. The last two use color stains or diffusions, or ragged, thickly pigmented drifting shapes; their art is quietist, bare and inert. Where this type of painting intimates and insinuates, that of De Kooning and Pollock insists and perhaps overstates for expressive emphasis. The paintings of Still and Rothko move from the abstract to the concrete. A certain quality of mystery and a residue of vague inwardness suggest the earlier preoccupation of both artists with myth, the primitive, and symbolist abstraction.

Rothko's most recent paintings are built up from a few broad planes of thin color wash arranged in parallel bands, giving the impression of both a polychrome plaque, awesome in scale, and of a luminous color haze. Technically, Rothko's closest affinity is with Matisse's art in the period of the *Blue Window* of 1911 or the *Dance* of the prior year, a time when the French master sought what he described as a scheme of absolute color within the limits of a few simplified planes. Rothko has added his own ardor, purity and monumentality to Matisse's scheme, and, of course, an unprecedented pictorial means. Within the severe limitations he put on the activity of shape, color and pictorial incident, he manages to attain a plenitude of sensation. If Rothko's art sometimes seems too contained in its esthetic strictness, its uncompromising integrity also serves as a reproach to artists willing to settle for more arresting chance effects of handling and texture. At its deep and solemn best, his art is informed by a sense of great tasks, and moves on the heights like that of another modern artist who challenged the absolute, Piet Mondrian.

Rothko's painting style has evolved from a realist mode in the thirties to the grave and monumental inventions of the present day. He showed his first original style in the early forties, under the influence of the international Surrealist movement. He painted then in a nervously linear manner, utilizing a fantastic imagery and a variety of surface textures which seemed at the time related to the paintings of Max Ernst and to the automatic writing of Masson. There was something rather vague and provisional about his acceptance of Surrealism, however; Rothko's fanciful forms seemed to swim even then in a tonal atmosphere which dispersed and muffled their separate identities, and itself became the dominating pictorial impression. During the middle forties he began to work with less explicit forms which resembled waving grasses and submarine vegetal life, and shortly were transformed into a purely abstract scheme of fine line and color diffusions of a Whistlerian delicacy.

Then in 1947 Rothko eliminated recognizable forms defined by lines, building up his surfaces with irregular color stains, high in key, which formed a complex of distinct, segmented areas. The reduced intensities at the edges of these areas served as a unifying transition between the separate, closely juxtaposed and clashing hues. With their softened, rectangular shapes, these zones of color reiterated the horizontal and vertical as emphatic structural accents. The chemical brilliance of Rothko's palette continued into 1949 and 1950, when he began to work in broad, parallel bars of color of varied widths, extending them from the edges of his canvas, or setting solid blocks of tone against a continuous ground of contrasting hue. By giving a thinner consistency and increased luminosity to his rectangular masses at their edges, he preserved a sense of weightless suspension. The rigorous symmetries of his color forms, which are invariably centered in a unified chromatic field, and the massive sense of space enclosure they convey, give Rothko's paintings an extraordinary architectonic power. Beyond purely pictorial values, the basic rationalism of his method and the mood of ideal calm in his paintings have certain moral implications; they seem to embody an underlying ethical belief in the rational principle which governs the world of artistic form and natural life.

Rothko's progress from individualized definition in his earlier work to a larger unity based on freer color rhythms, has been part of a search for a transcendental reality. It is related to and illuminated by Mondrian's concept of "neoplastic" art, although few other points of contact exist between the two artists. Mondrian's injunction, "We must destroy the *particular* form," provided the most radical modern liberation from naturalism and was a step on the path to an art which, as he put it, would "reveal, as far as possible, the universal aspect of life." These aims, it would seem, have found a congenial contemporary application in the paintings of Mark Rothko.

To paraphrase the words of the contemporary theologian, Martin Buber, the meeting with artistic grace can either be "a wrestling bout" or "a light breath." For Rothko it appears, deceptively, a light breath, whereas for Pollock and

De Kooning it is a torment, a desperate wrestling bout or an occasion of orgiastic gaiety. But it should be noted that both Pollock and De Kooning achieve the grace of lightness as they wrest their art free from matter. And while Rothko seems to stand apart from his creations, which achieve an extraordinary impersonality and serenity, his works at the same time are the issue of much personal struggle, revision, and correction. Their material reality as concrete objects of sensation, which is intensely felt at every point in the work, dissociates them from any abstract idealism.

Since 1951 the paintings of Philip Guston have provided a most interesting resolution of the two contrary pulls in contemporary abstraction, of the differences between "action painting" (the useful epithet originated by the poet-critic Harold Rosenberg in his important article, "The American Action Painters") and the more absolutist tendencies of Rothko and Still. Like those of Pollock and De Kooning, Guston's paintings forcefully testify to the creator's active presence in the work of art by the assertive texture and relief of the pigmented surface. However, the working of the surface is less a matter of impulse than of a series of tentative advances toward some more absolute state of being. In this state, the painting detaches itself from its creator and achieves the unity of a single, palpitating sensation, not dissimilar in effect from the saturated colors and splended sonorities of Mark Rothko's paintings.

Guston's paintings have been referred to as "abstract impressionist" because of their high-keyed, warm colors and a fluent brushwork that superficially suggest Monet's late paintings. But they have little to do with the visual in Monet's sense and their emphasis on plane, surface and raw pigment matter are uniquely a part of the general tendency of contemporary American abstraction. Although his handling is direct, positive and vital, Guston, by a process of alternately enriching and impoverishing his surfaces, achieves both an immediate splendor and a weakened echo of it—the direct heat of passion and the cooling, remembered ecstasy.

This particular quality of his lyricism is the persisting

link to his earlier, apparently dissimilar representational style of the forties. It puts one in mind of Keats's discussion of poetry in his letters which begins with the celebrated sentence: "Poetry should surprise by a fine excess . . . and appear almost as a remembrance." Keats continues: "The rise, progress, the setting of the imagery should, like the sun, come natural to him [the reader], shine over him, and set soberly, although in magnificence, leaving him in the luxury of twilight." In the paintings of Guston, too, the spectator is left in the fading "luxury of twilight," but with the memory still of some burning splendor vividly imprinted on his mind. And there clings subtly and tenaciously to many of his paintings an atmosphere of indolent voluptuousness which also points to his romantic sensibility. This vagrant hedonism, however, is strictly supervised, and subordinated to a rigorous formal intention. The luscious pigment celebrates its own occasions, but a sensual estheticism is not invoked for its own sake alone; in fact it only forms the threshold of a further journey, an undertaking whose successful realization has nothing to do with the seductive appeals of medium.

For Guston the act of painting is an onerous task which proceeds painfully from the habitual and customary to the unfamiliar, from old recognitions to new and unforeseen encounters, a complex creative progress toward a more meaningful goal of freedom. The drama of this search is less obviously stated in Guston's work than in some of the more spectacular ventures in contemporary American abstraction, but his canvases shine with their own serene and even light and must be placed in the company of the more grave, impressive work of their period. In terse and suggestive language Guston has described his experience before the evolving picture better than any intermediary could do, and has thus managed to put into words a matter most difficult to express. In a statement to the author he has written:

What is seen and called the picture is what remains —an evidence. Even as one travels in painting towards a state of "unfreedom" where only certain things can happen, unaccountably the unknown and free must appear. Usually I am on a work for a long stretch, until a moment arrives when the air of the arbitrary vanishes and the paint falls into positions that feel destined. The very matter of painting—its pigment and spaces— is so resistant to the will, so disinclined to assert its plane and remain still. Painting seems like an impossibility, with only a sign now and then of its own light. Which must be because of the narrow passage from a diagramming to that other state—a corporeality. In this sense, to paint is a possessing rather than a picturing.

In his work since 1956 Guston has explored a more dramatic palette, identifiable shapes and intensified rhythms. These new paintings are perhaps more aggressive than those of the recent past; for all their apparent surface agitation, however, they do not overpower but continue to insinuate their presence. They are not so much demonstrations of formal principle, non-imagistic though they may appear, as they are signs of privileged moments of consciousness— moments which have their source in great depths, in dreams and in the continuing struggle to achieve artistic certainty without doing violence to that nagging sense of uncertainty and disquiet which assails the most serious modern minds. At times, almost as a relief from the mortification of the act of painting, a dark, sardonic humor will erupt and spread wildly over the surface like an atmospheric disturbance, leaving a wake of tumbled shapes and discordant color accents, and precipitating a whole new chain of formal metamorphoses.

Guston is perhaps most closely allied in spirit to the Surrealists, although his painting means are very different. The goal of Surrealist expression indicated by the French critic Jacques Rivière might well define one aspect of Guston's painting: "To grasp our being before it has yielded to consistency; to seize it in its incoherence, or better, in its primitive coherence, before the idea of contradiction has appeared and compelled it to reduce and construct itself; to replace its logical unity, which can only be acquired, by its absurd unity, which alone is innate."

The formulation of a new ideology on the part of abstract painters and the evolution of new styles occurred within the decade after 1943. The period may generally be divided into two halves; to the years between 1943 and 1948 belong the rediscovery of Surrealism and the new synthesis with abstraction, a revived interest in "myth" and the primitive, and a growing sense of the autonomy of native tendencies. During this period such artists as Jackson Pollock, Hans Hofmann, Robert Motherwell, Adolph Gottlieb, William Baziotes, Mark Rothko and Clyfford Still held their first one-man shows. Willem de Kooning, Franz Kline, Bradley Walker Tomlin, Philip Guston, James Brooks, Jack Tworkov, Esteban Vicente, and a whole new generation of younger painters emerged after 1948. The original band of innovators themselves gradually changed their styles after 1948, working in larger format and substituting, in their varied ways, more abstract qualities for the earlier concern with fantasy and chimerical subject matter. The fantasia of the unconscious gave way to a general dynamism; turgidity, to transparency; and the private obsession was dissolved in the epic, and in monumental designs.

Beginning in 1948 the successive, brilliant one-man shows of Willem de Kooning had an incalculable impact on young painters. They renewed in a refreshing, painterly style the old antagonism to representational manners and doctrinaire abstraction, but also after 1949 they sanctioned the reintroduction of naturalistic imagery. The suppression of color in De Kooning's first one-man show and in paintings of an earlier period by Pollock and Clyfford Still found a favorable response in the commanding black-and-white canvases executed by Robert Motherwell in 1950, beginning with his *Granada* series, and then in the dramatic first one-man show of Franz Kline in 1950. Kline's simplified statements of aggressive, insect-like forms in his first exhibition and his even more drastic black grids in subsequent shows seemed at first glance raw, powerfully magnified enlargements of a section of the calligraphy of Bradley Walker Tomlin. Kline's forms, however, were charged with new velocities and energies, rather brutal energies released at collision point by skidding, ricocheting black bars of paint.

A new spatial dynamism declared itself quite miraculously without the resource of color, depending solely on the weighted brush stroke, the thick or thin, shiny or matte streaks of black and white pigment. With Philip Guston's show of the same year, Kline's exhibition announced the last significant *new* extension of the radical abstract styles of the decade.

Many other painters of the same generation have skillfully refined the innovations of the immediate past with great individual distinction but few have made genuine discoveries of striking originality. The livelier young artists have thus far been intent mainly on assimilation, although a number of distinctly individual temperaments have already appeared on the scene and made their presence felt. A number of younger artists have tried to give a renewed vitality to naturalistic representation, while still retaining the spontaneity of expression and the improvisatory surfaces of Abstract Expressionism. This would seem to be less an index of some positive new painting alternative, however, than a limited, conservative reaction on the part of painters in whom the roots of the new idioms had not struck very deep. The paintings of Pollock and De Kooning on the one hand, and Rothko and Still on the other, continue to define the antipodes of the most vital American painting.

9

Sculpture for an Iron Age

"The age of iron began many centuries ago by producing very beautiful objects, unfortunately for a large part, arms. Today, it provides as well, bridges and railroads. It is time this metal ceased to be a murderer and the simple instrument of a super-mechanical science. Today the door is wide open for this material to be, at last, forged and hammered by the peaceful hands of an artist."

—Julio Gonzalez

Modern American sculpture was until very recently far less adventurous than painting and attracted only a few outstanding personalities. Although it is true that a relatively small number of good sculptors exist even in periods of the most abundant creativity, there was still a marked poverty of first-rate sculptural talent in the first three decades of the century.

During this time the American sculptural evolution paralleled that of painting, beginning with a group of genre sculptors whose work coincided in time and spirit with the Eight. In response perhaps to the social zeal of the naturalist writers and to the general reforming impulse, the Swedish sculptor, Charles Haag, began to model groups of strikers in heroic attitudes shortly after he settled in America in 1903. His impressionistic surfaces, derived from Rodin, his vigorous handling and undisguised working-class sympathies were shared by Mahonri Young, who was doing energetic bronzes of laborers and stevedores in the same period. Later Young, like Luks and George Bellows, turned to prizefighter subjects and became celebrated for the muscular vigor of his athletes in action. The energies of ordinary people, and of children in particular, were the themes of another of the new genre group, the sculptress

Abastenia St. Leger Eberle. In 1914 she took a studio on the Lower East Side from which vantage point she observed at first hand, and did sculptures inspired by, the burgeoning street life of New York's undismayed and vital lower classes.

The naturalism of the Eight had given way before the visual revolution of modernism. But it was renewed with a different accent in the romantic realism of Burchfield and Hopper during the twenties, and then again in regionalist American scene painting, and in the urban realism of Kenneth Hayes Miller and Reginald Marsh of the thirties. Similarly sculpture passed through a period of modified experiment, although by the thirties it was dominated by realistic sentiment and expressionist mannerism once more. The tenacity of representational modes of sculpture in America, so contrary to the European experience during the same period, except perhaps in Germany, paralleled the painting situation. It may be explained by the premature dissolution of any concerted, collective movement toward the experimental, and by the absence of any single master of wide influence who might have found disciples and established the pre-eminence of an uncompromising modern style.

The pioneers in modern American sculpture were affected by radical European art forms, but without exception gave their continental sources a more stylized and decorative character. The Pole, Elie Nadelman, for example, who came to America in 1914, had felt at first hand the influence of the Munich *Jugendstil* and the School of Paris. Between 1907 and 1914 after contact with Paris Cubism, he worked in a more analytical spirit, reducing his figures to a regularized system of curved volumes and their logical spatial echoes. He nonetheless retained a certain tapered elegance of form and never overcame the quality of mannered refinement in his work. Essentially, his style stems from the bloodless and artificial ornament of *Art Nouveau,* despite an apparent commitment to the scrupulous streamlining and drastic geometric simplifications of vital modern forms. He has been rather recklessly described as a precursor of Cubism and a direct influence on Picasso, claims which are contradicted by the actual visual experience of his early work. Nadelman's monotonously repeated, uniform curves, whether in his drawings of 1906 or his sculpture of 1907, fail dismally either to articulate volume in space or to suggest even the rudiments of the new esthetic sensibility. They bear no more profound a relation to the vital plastic inventions of Cubism than does a drafting exercise executed with mechanical-drawing tools.

Nadelman's arbitrary, stylized graces were eminently suitable, however, for the modish and witty statuettes and figures, derived perhaps from popular art traditions, which became his stock-in-trade after he settled in America at the age of thirty-two. It is conceivable that our native art forms, particularly the clean, efficient lines and chaste surfaces of Pennsylvania Dutch folk art, may have influenced him during his residence in this country, thus justifying America's claim to an artist whose mature style was otherwise entirely formed in the great art centers of Europe.

Gaston Lachaise is another artist whose national identity is uncertain at best, but who was assuredly one of the pioneers of modern sculpture in America. Born in Paris in 1882, he came to the United States in 1906. He had already studied at the Académie Nationale des Beaux-Arts, exhibited frequently at the Salon des Artistes Français, and worked for Réné Lalique, the designer of *Art Nouveau* jewelry and objects in glass. In America Lachaise was first an assistant to the academician Henry Hudson Kitson, and then to Paul Manship. In 1913 he showed the first signs of his own distinct style, characterized by fluent articulation of surface, massive, yet weightless, volume, and the masterful control of rhythmic movement. In the twenties and thirties Lachaise's full-blooded female figures grew more distorted and expansive, afflicted by a curiously inflated tropism, until they became grotesquely swollen, like some prehistoric fertility symbol. Lachaise, too, preserved something of the sinuous, flowing line of *Art Nouveau,* but the subtle interplay and resolution of masses in motion gave his sculpture far more expressive power than Elie Nadelman's. Although primarily a modeler, Lachaise was also adept at direct carving, a method which had gone out of style in the first years of this century.

In the hands of William Zorach direct carving became an effective way of expressing a new candor about the nature of the artist's materials, and part of a search for a simple monumentality. Zorach, and his wife Marguerite, had shown paintings influenced by Fauvism in the Forum Exhibition of 1916. That year, however, Zorach turned to sculpture as his principal medium, employing a geometric stylization related to Cubism. His forms underwent a drastic simplification and bent to the rule of the curve and the right angle. Zorach was never a Cubist or a Constructivist sculptor; his aim was the realization of an idealized but consistently representational imagery, and solidly enclosed volumes. Yet the powerful formal organization of his earliest sculpture, his feeling for simplified mass and emphatic plane, owed something to the experience of Cubism; his critics, however, have more often related these elements in his style to the modern classicism of Aristide Maillol.

In the late twenties Zorach began to employ cramped, compact forms. Pressed into unity by the sculptor's forceful will or deliberately imprisoned by the too narrow confines of his stone blocks, these more constricted, angular forms were closer to the spirit of Romanesque relief than they were to the fluent grace and breadth of Maillol. Like so many other American artists of the period, Zorach seemed to be moving toward expressionist distortion.

A controlled Expressionism was also the basis of the style of one of the most interesting stone carvers who emerged in the thirties, John B. Flannagan. Flannagan's earlier work had been Gothic images of suffering, attenuated, free-standing figures in wood handled like bas-relief with affinities both to German Expressionism and primitive Christian art. In the next decade his style broadened, becoming more ample and rounded; in place of expressionist torment, he substituted an effective and personal formal motif: a winding, circular or spiral movement which conveyed a feeling of both enclosure and growth. His subjects were almost exclusively drawn from the animal and insect kingdom, although he executed a number of sensitive portraits and figure compositions. Flannagan's forms emerged from their stones as a chick from her egg, or they were shown in cross-section, usually within a womb-like enclosure. The cyclical movement of emergence, and return to the source, made a modest but convincing allegory of birth and death. Flannagan's characterization of animal life was sometimes poignant and often humorous; it was invariably acute in its observation. The visionary, romantic art of Ryder and Morris Graves, and the microscopic sensibilities of such American poets as Emily Dickinson and Marianne Moore support and confirm the native authenticity of Flannagan's touching, creatural realism.

He had very little influence on his contemporaries, although his intuitive sense that a somewhat abstract figuration could stimulate emotional as well as intellectual reactions may have done something to loosen the grip of the derivative, stylized modernism which dominated American sculpture. Flannagan's feeling, too, for the inherent expressive qualities of the sculptor's materials may have anticipated a later generation. "Often there is an occult attraction in the very shape of a rock as sheer abstract form," he wrote. "It fascinates with a queer atavistic nostalgia, as either a remote memory or a stirring impulse from the depth of the unconscious." Even in the forties, when America's most impressive sculptors were abstractionists and welders in metal, who expressed their deepest commitment to modernism in terms of radical new techniques, Flannagan's search for sculptural symbols that would coordinate a vital abstract manner of expression with intensely individual emotion remained meaningful.

His essentially romantic art was, nevertheless, too narrow and restricting to provide a substantial basis for a general style. Flannagan was essentially a provincial temperament, although an intense one, only capable of a partial assimilation of the vital form-language of his time.

That curious conflict in American art between an authentic but limited native expression, and the attainment of a contemporary sophistication was never so acute as it was in the decade of the thirties. To put caution aside and seek mastery of European modes put the American artist in danger of eclecticism and an empty mannerism. The lesson of modernism had been, on the whole, that the influence of contemporary European art forms tended to compromise the American artist's own peculiar angle of vision. On the other hand, those artists who ignored Europe were equally in danger from the pressures of provincialism, from the regionalist, social-realist or expressionist themes of the period which put a premium on sentimental anecdote, making painting and sculpture a matter of melodramatic feeling rather than artistic style.

A spirit of aggressive self-determination has been one of the characteristic features of much recent American art, and while it has often been a vital factor in our originality, it has also cut off many of our artists from the most generative influences of modern art. Henry James provided a valuable corrective to the general view of national artistic identity when he described the American artist as one, in effect, who is sufficiently cultivated to be a European but *chooses* to be an American. Some of our outstanding artists have undoubtedly been sincerely naïve—so absorbed by their own romantic innocence that they could remain blissfully ignorant of Europe with impunity. But surely our most satisfying creative personalities have been the products of a completed assimilation of international styles, who then applied themselves, in an act of deliberate choice, to the American experience.

Prominent in this category of moderns, Alexander Calder has been for many years a sculptor unique for his urbanity and stylistic sophistication. An apostle of modern abstract idioms, in the critical period between the Armory Show and contemporary abstraction, Calder played a role similar to that of Stuart Davis. During the discouraging decade of the thirties he was one of the few American sculptors to work in the experimental spirit; he gave the important Constructivist ideal in sculpture a continuing vitality and meaning without sacrificing his own distinctly native qualities. These qualties were a wry humor, a playful fantasy and a wonderfully resourceful inventiveness. Most important, too, was Calder's sensitive commitment to metals, which comprised a candid admission on the part of the artist that he was inextricably a part of, and had therefore better make some relevant artistic use of, the Iron Age. The basic conception of his art became, as he put it, "the idea of detached bodies floating in space, of different sizes and densities . . . some at rest while others move in peculiar manners. . . . Symmetry and order do not make a composition. It is the apparent accident to regularity which makes or mars a work." Calder's organized formal accidents, taking place among moving ensembles of standardized metal shapes, which in themselves would have given supreme pleasure to the most austere modern engineer, took the sting off mechanization. Using almost uniform shapes, if not sizes, cut out of sheet steel, Calder gave to modern machine civilization a new lyricism and artistic expression.

His deceptively simple and irresistible constructions have often been described disapprovingly, in our solemn age, as esthetic playthings. Neither Klee nor Miró would consider the term a reproach. Calder, indeed, won his first recognition as a maker of animated toys; his famous miniature circus, with its expressive wire and wood marionettes of big-top performers, delighted Joan Miró and attracted the enthusiastic interest of a wide circle of international artists in Paris between 1927 and 1930. During the thirties Calder continued his work in three-dimensional construction, living in Paris most of the year with occasional visits to America. Direct contact with Mondrian and Miró were important factors in the evolution of his style. By 1932 he had put aside his representational sculpture in wire for the first ventures in those free-standing, mechanically driven structures, "stabiles," and somewhat later, the wind-propelled "mobiles" on which his major reputation is based.

Mondrian's strict, geometric schemes first turned Calder away from his representational interests to abstract compositions, giving him what he later described as "the necessary shock." Calder has recalled in an interview the excitement and the sense of discovery in his first visit to Mondrian's studio, with its scrupulously clean, white walls to which the artist had tacked removable paper rectangles of red, blue and yellow. "I thought at the time," Calder later declared, "how fine it would be if everything there moved, though Mondrian himself did not approve of this idea at all. I went home and tried to paint. But wire, or something to twist or tear or bend is an easier medium for me to think in." From Miró's free forms and flattened kidney shapes Calder may have derived his basic vocabulary of shape, and perhaps found stimulation for his delightful eruptions of humor. He digested the influence of both artists thoroughly, however, and in a very short time the American sculptor arrived at his own thoroughly original idiom.

It is impossible now to think of Calder's inventions apart from the Amercan experience, even as we grant that he is among the most international and urbane of our contemporary artists. His flower-like constructions often seem a witty and tactful commentary on the national passion for the mechanical gadget. The mobile brings mechanism into contact with a world of tenuous natural growth and achieves an organic-esthetic life of its own. Its exquisite movements and varied spatial configurations seem to obey a rhythmic principle which we associate with nature. Jean-Paul Sartre has written that Calder's sculptures "are at once lyrical inventions, technical combinations almost mathematical and, at the same time, the sensible symbol of Nature—this great vague Nature, which throws pollen about lavishly and will produce brusquely the flight of a thousand butterflies. . . ." In Calder's inventive schemes there is something fresh, youthful, gay. Pragmatic procedures and an unapologetic materialism, in the service of an ideal of grace, and tempered by irony, might best define the qualities of his exquisite art.

The distance between Calder and our most interesting contemporary sculptors is enormous. It is quite as great as that which separates Stuart Davis from Pollock, De Kooning and Rothko. Perhaps the most profound inspiration of the newer sculptors has been the rugged metal constructions of the Spaniard, Julio Gonzalez, although no contemporary American can be said to be directly derivative. Many aspects of European modernism including Constructivism, Surrealism and Expressionism, actually have been fused in the new sculpture. These influences have been assimilated and charged with vital new meanings in the expressive forms developed by such artists as David Smith, Herbert Ferber, Seymour Lipton, Theodore Roszak, David Hare and Ibram Lassaw. In their varied ways all these sculptors repudiate traditional conceptions of sculpture as an art of volume and monolithic mass in favor of a more dynamic esthetic of open, linear forms, held in subtle spatial tension. During the forties, an idiom of fluid metal construction first emerged as the most compelling tendency in advanced American sculpture, and it has been the dominating direction ever since, with a wide influence in the younger generation.

Like the Abstract Expressionist painters of the forties, the new sculptors have made a personal synthesis of stylistic elements derived from both a formal, architectonic tradition and from Surrealism. Under the aegis of Surrealism they have sought an explosive release of feeling and new creative liberties that would leave room for impulse and fantasy; and they have often relied on accidental and highly emotive effects in the handling of their materials. In sculpture as in painting the artist's need to experience fully, even extravagantly, his own free individuality has driven him away from the more rigid, geometric conventions of doctrinaire abstraction.

While the new sculptor still accepts the framework of international idioms, he also strains against their restrictions, against any forms of containment and against "finish." Out of the simultaneous acceptance and renunciation of European authority the American sculptor has begun to create a new artistic reality and to find a new identity, within the bold outlines of a more elemental style. He repudiates the traditional beguilements of surface and mass, and even any air of studio professionalism, in favor of immediacy and spontaneity; he rejects vehemently the shapely and the stylized for chance effects; he finds non-artistic, industrial textures more vital than rubbed and polished surfaces. He often challenges the limitations of his materials and medium, creating rude structures that are all perforation and movement, closely allied to the Abstract Expressionist paintings of Pollock and De Kooning.

Whatever individual variations the new sculptors may play on the theme of themselves, they all enjoy a new sense of decisiveness and freedom, and share a certain moral energy, for they have come to see their art as an elementary expression of belief in their own romantic individualism and in creation as a *vital* action. The rawness and nakedness of their forms, their contempt for seductive surface, may be taken as a sign of the independence and fertility of the artistic act. By the deliberate emphasis on powerful rudimentary structures, the sculptor expresses his faith in the inherent value of artistic liberty and gives a special weight to creation itself as the main spiritual activity of the artist, rather than some traditional ideal of imitation.

If the American artist sets forth such attitudes and feelings in his work under conditions of greater intensity than he has done heretofore, it is a measure of his heightened awareness of the mounting tensions of contemporary life. He lives in an intensely commercial culture which puts small value on the creative individual and forces the artist to assert himself by increasingly violent expressive gestures, simply to make himself felt and to be inwardly convinced that the spiritual life has some point after all. Despite these and other serious difficulties that have separated the modern artist from his audience, and from common experience, many sculptors have devised novel contemporary strategies to put themselves in contact again with the currents of modern life. Far more than the general public, who complain so readily of art's cerebral quality, or its sterility, the artist has been aware of the need to inject genuine emotion into his work and to guard himself against empty formalism.

With all its violent social conditioning, the new movement in metal sculpture is not merely a product of exasperation and strident feeling; on the contrary, it admits many variations in mood, from dramatic emotionalism to a calm and measured lyricism. For Ibram Lassaw, sculpture is an art of contemplation and rich, refined sensation, quietist and serene. David Smith shows more aggression and a deliberate coarseness in his inventive, architectonic schemes, and on occasion a quality of baroque excess. But more often than not, he has succeeded in subordinating his taste for the immoderate to the discipline of his materials. Seymour Lipton establishes a relation with the organic, vegetal forms of nature. Herbert Ferber's art is thorny, barbed, unwelcoming, and full of delicate grace, by turns. David Hare feels the pull of primitive cultures and of Dada's discontinuities; he consults the unconscious, more than any of his contemporaries. Yet the mysterious psychological resonances of his forms are achieved in the act of execution and through the manipulation of his material. Theodore Roszak seeks potent new sculptural symbols and poetry at some level of feeling which underlies the more rational formulations of language. While these artists are not formally associated in a school, and would reject the notion of a common style, their work is the issue of much fertile intercommunication and shows a community of purpose.

David Smith was the first American sculptor to work consistently in welded metals. In 1933, shortly after he had been deeply impressed by an issue of *Cahiers d'Art* devoted to the iron constructions of Picasso and Gonzalez, Smith borrowed welding equipment and did his first metal sculpture. He had already studied painting with the modernist, Jan Matulka, at the Art Students League, and had begun to break away from painting into a form of painted wooden construction, related somewhat to Picasso's Constructivist collages of 1914. Explaining his own development, Smith has written:

> While my technical liberation came from Picasso's friend and countryman, Gonzalez, my esthetics were influenced by Kandinsky, Mondrian and Cubism. My student period was involved only with painting. The painting developed into raised levels from the canvas. Gradually the canvas became the base and the painting was a sculpture. I have never recognized any separation between media except one element of dimension. The first painting of cave men was both curved line and color, a natural reaction and a total statement.

My first steel sculpture was made in the summer of 1933, with borrowed equipment. The same year I started to accumulate equipment and moved into the Terminal Iron Works on the Brooklyn waterfront. My work of 1934-36 was often referred to as line sculpture, but to me it was as complete a statement about form and color as I could make. The majority of work in my first show at the East River Gallery in 1937 was painted. I do not recognize the limits where painting ends and sculpture begins.

Smith has followed an unenviable, lonely course in American sculpture in that he has worked directly in iron and steel without a surfacing of bronze, brass or nickel silver. His rugged architectonic schemes are both more closely related to Constructivism, and more laden with symbolic references, than the comparable welded sculpture of Lipton, Ferber, Roszak or Lassaw. For Smith steel has striking natural attributes and certain positive values. "The metal," he has written, "possesses little art history. What associations it possesses are those of this century: power, structure, movement, progress, suspension, destruction, brutality."

Iron and steel are both malleable and of a stubborn refractoriness: they may be easily cut, forged and shaped by the oxyacetylene torch, and they also powerfully assert their permanency, and arouse sensations directly related to our industrial age. Thus the medium combines the advantages of contemporary painting or the painted collage, with the enduring, intrinsic appeal of the sculpture medium as structure and space enclosure. Smith has always made a point, even a fetish, of dramatic content, loading his structures with a wealth of symbolic references; in the early and middle forties, he was characterized rather appropriately as a "social Surrealist." His artistic strength, however, derives from a remarkable mastery of structure, rhythmic movement and a varied play of sculptural silhouettes. At the same time the artist insists quite properly on the importance of his dramatic content as a necessary spur for plastic inventions. If his imagery has been decidedly anecdotal at times, his symbolism is also the very source of his expressive individuality and a measure of his range as an artist.

Smith has often been compared with Gonzalez, and their similarities are both acknowledged and obvious. There are, however, distinct and radical differences. Unlike the Spaniard, Smith shows more candor about his materials and emphasizes their raw, untransformed qualities. His forms are harsh, physical and to a degree resist conventional esthetic criteria. Obliquely they reflect mistrust of "beauty" and the more cultivated uses of the medium. Gonzalez, on the other hand, was sometimes trapped by seductive surface, by patinated texture and by the operation of his own civilizing sensibilities. He let his harsh materials assert themselves, but only as a co-ordinated ambiguity which would add force to an essentially contemplative, refining formalism. Even his most violent or Surrealist inventions are relatively restrained. Smith's elementary force and assertive materialism go beyond the limits of the permissible in art, as defined by modern European tradition. But his work at its best also has the power to show us the expressive limitations of a civilized hedonism which must reduce all experience to the sensuous alone, and at all costs avoid unmannerly extravagance.

Certainly a large part of Smith's public appeal has been his very personal frame of allusion. His own analysis of the sculpture *Cathedral* of 1950, as related to the artist-critic Elaine de Kooning and ably transcribed by her in the June 1, 1950, number of *Art News,* may amaze us by the degree to which the artist encourages a specific reading of his abstract imagery. The work in question is an open metal cage, with appended plaques and a varied ensemble of structural elements. At the center is a vertical form in the shape of a fork supported by a fluted column, and gripping with its tines a number of sagging, turnip-like objects reclining in vegetal quietude on a stepped base. One of the upright plaques has been cut away at the center to make an empty silhouette resembling the human form, and it is bisected by a curving metal spine; on an iron ring to one side rests a vaguely skeletal, ribbed figure. These forms have been interpreted by the artist as a social drama of predatory violence, in which the main fork-like member represents a cathedral which is in turn "a symbol of power— the state, the church or any individual's private mansion built at the expense of others." The prone forms held in the twisted tines are to be read as a "symbol of sacrifice," "a man subjugated." Themes of sacrifice and brutality are carried further by the skeleton on the metal ring, which is an "altar table," and by the metal spine of the empty silhouette with which Smith wished to suggest the stitching on a medieval winding sheet.

In the mid-forties Smith had been even more preoccupied with symbolic meaning, and didactic social content. At that time he cast in bronze a sculpture called *The Rape* which showed an outstretched female figure menaced by a cannon on wheels; the ambiguity of the cannon as an instrument of both war and sex was inescapable. In an interesting appreciation, Stanley Meltzoff interpreted the violent sculptural pun as a reflection of Smith's interest in Joyce's *Finnegans Wake*. "Using adjectives found in the first chapter of *Finnegans Wake*," Meltzoff conjectured, "Smith's cannon is 'sexcaliber' and 'camiballistic.' The cannon, like Joyce's Sir Tristram, is a '*violer d'amores*,' an amoral musical amorist, part viola and part violater."

There is some question whether Smith's abstract imagery communicated exactly the meanings desired when his symbols surrendered their naturalistic guise, in *Cathedral* for example. Rather they suggested a general Surrealist apparatus and some of those conventional stage properties useful to convey apprehension which have been developed by Picasso and particularly by Alberto Giacometti. Although the imagery of *Cathedral* is reminiscent of Giacometti's *Palace at Four AM*, the impact of the forms is, needless to say, quite unrelated. There is a refreshing colloquialism and robust humor to Smith's adaptations, more of the "tall tale" and native burlesque than the Surrealist horror theater. Despite his continuing social preoccupations and use of Surrealist devices, Smith is primarily a constructor of plastic forms which are most rewarding when considered in their architectonic aspect. In this light *Cathedral* would seem to be a highly successful resolution of disparate and conflicting formal elements held in dynamic spatial tension. It effectively deals with a modern structural problem in open, platform sculpture, and is full of unexpected and original invention which far outweighs the entirely legitimate borrowings from contemporary Surrealist imagery.

Over the past five years Smith has been less concerned with symbolism. There still remain residual ties to Surrealism in his "found" objects, those parts of actual machinery or their convincing facsimiles which he incorporates into his work, and in the suggestions of aggressive, predatory life in the forms themselves. He has worked at times during this period in a bare, linear style which depends largely on sustained, rhythmic invention and a balance of dynamic movements springing from a single fulcrum. *Australia* (Plate 29) and many sculptures in the *Agricola* series are among his most successfully realized ventures in this idiom. Smith has also created monumental standing figures, curiously suggesting primitive totems, in which large steel cusps and trough-like lengths of metal are disposed in a system of weights and counter-weights, rising from a tripod or single metal column. These *Tank Totems* (so-called because the disk forms are actual ready-made plating used in boiler construction) must surely rank with the most grave and monumental contemporary sculpture in America. Recently Smith experimented with flat, attenuated steel bars and slabs of irregular contour which rise to great heights, like totems that have been denuded of their imagery and symbolism. But his temper is too restive to endure for long such simplified forms, and he has already shown signs of zestful new departures in more inventive and complex schemes.

In the mid-forties, a number of other significant American sculptors reached a decisive point in their development. They had begun to explore the new resources of welded metals; their styles were based, as Smith's had been, on a synthesis of Constructivist and Expressionist, or in some cases, Surrealist, devices. This critical phase of self-discovery and of growing stylistic certainty coincided with a similar, dramatic moment in painting, although painting then seemed more advanced and adventurous. It was only after 1945 that the new converts to metal sculpture acquired sufficient confidence in the independent powers of their medium to make significantly original ventures. David Smith had been first on the scene in welded sculpture, but to artists like Lipton and Ferber his idiom of found and forged shapes, and his almost exclusive interest in iron and steel, were restricting. In their own distinctive styles they began to enlarge the possibilities of contemporary sculpture within a more fluid idiom which utilized metal alloys. They fashioned their surfaces by burning and welding, by flowing molten metals over hammered metal forms which served as rough drafts for their finished structures. Such methods afforded them multiple advantages, to be exploited according to the dictates of their individual temperaments and technical ingenuity. Accessible to them was a freedom comparable to that of the modeler who builds up form progressively from a core; but they also encountered the fruitful resistance of direct cutting without its constraints, since welding and the use of molten metal allowed wide revision and supplementary invention.

Self-taught, Lipton began the independent study of sculpture in 1932 and by the end of the decade was carving wood figures, violent in their distortions and charged with didactic social content. From 1940 to 1942 he completed such pieces as *Refugee* and *Breadline*, in stone and wood respectively, and had carried his expressive language to a point of near-abstraction. Writing of this period, Lipton has described his growing preoccupation with themes of struggle, first in society and then in universal nature:

In the late thirties I made wooden pieces based on social problems, the formal mood stemming from such things as Gothic bestiary, Hieronymous Bosch, German Expressionism and primitive sculpture. The prevailing feeling was one of fierceness. I soon found wood and social problems too limiting for my creative freedom. I went to metal casting. Leaving the human figure in 1942, I began using skeletal forms, horns, pelvis, first in bronze and then in lead construction, etc., to convey the basic struggles in nature on a broader biological level. Aeschylus had always been for me a guiding force of tragic, poetic catharsis.

Gradually the sense of the dark inside, the evil of things, the hidden areas of struggle became for me a part of the cyclic story of living things. The inside and outside became one in the struggle of growth, death and rebirth in the cyclic renewal process. I sought to make a sculpture as an evolving entity, to make a thing suggesting a process. But this development was also intensified by my search for new sculptural ideas. Everyone had used solid forms, pierced forms, prefabricated open forms, etc. I felt the rightness of curved, convoluted forms, outgrowing but not fully spread, as a new sculptural phraseology for what I was doing, a concern with internal and external anatomy.

Fierceness underneath and within, but with strength, beauty and positiveness in tensional balanced integration.

It was in 1945 that Lipton first began to work in sheet lead, evolving the basic techniques and the abstract imagery which became the core of his style. Such pieces as *Moloch, Number 3, Dissonance* and *Wild Earth Mother,* dating from this period and shown in his first exhibition of metal sculpture in 1948, were composed in aggressive shapes of crushing power. These somber, weighty forms, with their angular contours and heaving surfaces, in which gaping holes were torn or ragged troughs scored, seemed like grotesque primordial shapes reborn in the Age of the Machine. While there was some lyrical relief in the handling of sinuous surface and in a quality of free inventiveness, the artist rarely yielded to "softness." He seemed to wish to inveigh against life and to proclaim what a poet has called all its "bloody hypotheses," in a dolorous spring ritual of birth and death. For all Lipton's indulgence of his more violent instincts, he nevertheless achieved an expression not merely of elemental savagery but also one marked by disciplined craftsmanship and formal certainty.

Although the artist later attained a more coherent power of expression, he has never surpassed the thrusting impact of this earlier work.

About 1950 Lipton's sculptures relinquished something of their obdurate quality and violent romanticism; his emotions became more objective, and his work lighter in spirit. In place of the chunky, pyramidal and pelvic shapes, he substituted thin, curving shells of sheet steel, which he covered with varying deposits of bronze, or nickel silver, to enhance both textural interest and structural strength. Andrew Ritchie has recently explained the change in mood and methods in an excellent appreciation: "Reflecting a new-found faith in the regenerative processes of nature the artist leaves the human figure, with all its recent connotations of hate and death, and looks instead to plant forms, in bud and expanding under pressure of the life-force. And it is to such biological imagery that his sculpture has become devoted until today."

In such recent pieces as *Earth Mother* of 1951 and *Sanctuary* and *Storm Bird,* both completed in 1953, the qualities of passion, intensity and invention of Lipton's earlier art reached a new fulfillment with greater clarity and precision of expression. These sculptures synthesize machine forms and movements with associations of natural growth. Indeed, it is Lipton's signal power to be able to combine effectively an imagery derived from two such far-removed spheres, those of mechanical movement and organic nature. The artist's double-sidedness, his synthesis of the biomorphic and the mechanical, represents a further expansion of modern sensibility and a conquest by artistic metaphor of another area of contemporary experience.

If his recent forms seem to represent a more optimistic outlook by comparison with his work immediately after the war, they also continue to reveal the artist's preoccupation with the elemental, dark forces at the mysterious heart of nature. Lipton's rhetoric, whether verbal or visual, carries an authentic prophetic accent. In 1947 he published a statement which still serves to define his abiding sense of moral purpose; it prepares us for the emotional atmosphere of his work:

The bud, the core, the spring, the darkness of earth, the deep animal fountainhead of man's forces are what interest me most as the main genesis of artistic substance. . . . The tensions in man as an individual and social being, the blind energies and sudden momentary clairvoyances—all struggle along to achieve a fruition, some balance, some steady vision. These harsh tensions, dramatic or lyrical, are a basic reality in man. This is the realism that I am trying to get at in sculptural language.

Over the last five years Lipton has executed three important sculpture commissions, two for the architect Percival Goodman's Temple Israel, Tulsa, Oklahoma (1954) and Temple Beth-El, Gary, Indiana (1955); and one for Skidmore, Owings and Merrill's Inland Steel Building in Chicago (1956). The *Menorah* for the Tulsa temple and other even more recent pieces such as *Pioneer,* of 1957, are monumental in scale and feeling, with a breadth of generalization unique in Lipton's work. These sculptures give us a glimpse of a new mood that is Augustan, positive, logical, proof against even the most contentious play of emotion. They promise a further movement toward stability and calm, indicating a growing sympathy for the classical spirit.

Following the course of many of the artists of his generation, Herbert Ferber had been influenced by the social preoccupations of the depression years and by the general movement of Expressionism. After study at New York's Beaux-Arts Institute of Design between 1927 and 1930, Ferber began to carve in wood and stone massive, full-blown nudes of a restrained sensuality, with affinities to the sculpture of both Maillol and Zorach. In 1928 he traveled in Europe, where he discovered Barlach and German Expressionism, saw Negro sculpture in the *Musée de l'Homme* in Paris, and came to love the naïve imagery and powerful, compact forms of Romanesque sculpture. Upon his return Ferber turned to themes of individual figures and groups carved in straining attitudes and contorted movement which served to underscore their symbolic character as vehicles of social protest. The emphatic frontal-

SCULPTURE FOR AN IRON AGE   181

ity of his forms, their simple compactness and a figurative
convention that approached grotesque caricature linked
them to monumental Romanesque sculpture. By the early
forties Ferber's increasingly violent distortions had nearly
dispensed with recognizable subject matter, and his figures
were reduced to an effective formula of near-abstract curvilinear forms. And then early in 1945 he broke completely
with representation, and for a time with sculpture. For a
number of months he did no carving at all but instead executed countless drawings, conceived under the combined
influence of the English sculptor Henry Moore, and of
Picasso's fantastic abstract anatomies.

Between 1945 and 1947 Ferber experimented in wax
and cement, lead and other metals, exploring the relationship of materials to forms and developing his own characteristic expressive effects. *Hazardous Encounter* and *Apoc-
alyptic Rider* of 1947, both executed in plaster and cast in
bronze, dramatized the search for vehement expression,
surging movement and disquieting imagery that was apparent in the contemporary sculpture of Roszak, Lipton and a
number of other Americans. His shapes suggested claws,
rows of teeth, thorns, a violently uprooted tree. There were
shapes which would have made ideal stage properties in the
threatening imaginary landscapes of Picasso or Miró, in an
artistic world where the animate might trade roles at any
moment with the inanimate.

By 1949 Ferber's style had reached full power as he
boldly juxtaposed spiky forms, thin twists of metal, and
bulging tubular frames. These alternately delicate and
massive creations solidly displaced and pierced space, and
often conveyed a quality of biting emotion. *Horned Sculpture* of 1949 is an excellent example; its stark, bone-like,
vertical trunk vaguely suggests both a primitive idol and
some destitute but obstinate oak, riven by lightning, denuded of most of its leaves but still bravely contesting the
elements. A network of small rods and an even finer complex of criss-crossing metal slivers bind the shapes and
varied spatial silhouettes into a unity, and create a rhythm
of minor accents contrapuntal to the main movement.

Ferber proceeds by stages, from a line or wash drawing

to a small, working model, and then attacks the final large-scale sculpture as an independent structure, often discarding or elaborating on some of the features of his model. He cuts with automatic shears from sheet copper or brass appropriately shaped strips. The flat strips are joined by welding to form long, narrow v-shaped troughs and sharply angular zigzags, or they are bent and hammered into a variety of curved shapes. These individual elements are then welded together into an open construction of geometric and organic forms. In the process Ferber continues to cut, perforate or build out his surfaces with the torch in irregular bosses and protuberances. In this way, he can simultaneously introduce new structural tensions and provide himself with occasions for the invention of interesting new shapes and rhythms, which may either reassert his original forms or actively oppose them. Such a method of working requires a special alertness, since the sculptor is tempted to yield to his more enthusiastic impulses as he follows his model. A mere enlargement is liable to monotony if the artist passively accepts his original plan and methodically reproduces it. The change in scale, however, in itself creates unforeseen formal opportunities.

From 1949 to 1954 Ferber continued to work in open, linear forms. He sometimes rotated a number of varied structural elements around a rising column of metal, emphasizing a more conventional Constructivist esthetic, as in *Flame* of 1949. Alternately, he expressed rhythmic, curving growth in organic shapes derived from nature. One of the most commanding sculptures of these years, *He Is Not a Man* (1950), was unusual for its Surrealist atmosphere. In 1951 came the first and perhaps the most ambitious of a number of architectural commissions, a large project for the façade of the Synagogue in Millburn, New Jersey, measuring nearly eight by thirteen feet. An armature of plumbing pipe was enclosed in light shells of copper, soldered together and then brazed with lead. The freely twisting, spatulate and scythe-like forms, suggesting flickering tongues of flame, were pierced and delicately connected by bundles of thin copper rod. This device served to float the heavier forms and gave the whole massive structure an air of weightless suspension, providing a notably successful solution to the problem of vital architectural sculpture.

Recently Ferber has sought greater simplicity in his forms, although he has put them through more complex rhythmic gyrations. One of his most interesting experiments has been with roofed sculpture in which long, twisting leaf forms are suspended from a rectilinear plate above, parallel with the sculpture's base, or cantilevered from a shield set at an oblique angle to the base. The result is an even more daring, anti-gravitational effect and a new expressive freedom in the pure springing movement of form in space. These golden shapes, set boldly at liberty from their structural frame, seem to write themselves in the air like a moving finger of light. They approximate in three dimensions something of the split-second spontaneity of gesture found in the more dramatic, contemporary Abstract Expressionist painting. In other work Ferber has continued a form of transparent metal collage, using indeterminate wafer-thin shapes which resemble torn papers and function almost as painterly accents against an irregular mesh network.

While sculptors using welded metals have dominated the American scene, there has also been vigorous creative work with more traditional materials. The Japanese-American, Isamu Noguchi, at one time an apprentice helper to Brancusi, worked during the forties in a variety of polished stones. He demonstrated a suave and fluent mastery of abstract idioms, with Surrealist overtones, deftly creating interlocking systems of flattened biomorphic forms derived from Arp or Miró. More recently he has made free-standing terracottas in rounded, doll-like shapes, or he has ingeniously grouped on a vertical post varied *kasama* forms, the durable earthenware that has for centuries been used in Japan to make kitchen vessels. The tension between the naïve conventions of popular art forms and a sophisticated modernity has given these playful inventions a distinct individuality. Another artist working quite independently is Raoul Hague, one of a few contemporaries who continue to carve directly in wood. His massive, rounded abstract forms show great decisiveness and an impressive power.

Among the most individual and delightful of contemporary constructions are the Abstract-Surrealist boxes of Joseph Cornell whose work combines the devices of Constructivism with painting and collage techniques. His rectilinear enclosures are as geometrical, ascetic and also as subtly articulated as an excellent *de Stijl* painting. But these strict, unadorned structures house the most unexpected romantic bric-a-brac: pasted fragments of nostalgic photographs, scenes from a Victorian "grand tour," heraldic inventions or snatches of a counterfeit but somehow touching modern mythology culled from astrological illustrations. The curious fusion, at poetic intensity, of precious sentiment, bizarre imagery and a stern formal rectitude give Cornell's constructions a quality entirely their own. If these boxes are so compelling, it is because they have a quality of authentic experience. They consecrate the monkish life of art, a life more often than not of renunciation and crushing isolation which finds its creative meaning in the assiduous cultivation of childhood memories, fantasy and images of desire.

In sculpture as in painting, the past decade has been for the American *avant-garde* a period of exciting ventures and new beginnings. For the first time since the period of the Armory Show and in a far more decisive manner, American sculpture has collectively found an atmosphere and a tongue. It is now contributing significantly to the international art of our time, and its innovations are slowly achieving world-wide recognition. "How many people know," an English critic recently commented on an American exhibition in London, "that Britain's recent iron age of sculpture was anticipated in America? The sculpture at the Tate Gallery in *Modern Art in the United States* is a reminder that Butler, Chadwick and Clarke were preceded by David Smith (by more than ten years) and by Herbert Ferber, Seymour Lipton, Theodore Roszak and Ibram Lassaw (with smaller priorities). They formulated a common answer to the problem (later resolved here in much the same way): how to make iron sculpture without being a Constructivist."

Nearly a hundred years ago Henry James spoke of the "terrible burden" imposed on the American artist by his provincial condition, his isolation from and continuing dependence on Europe. The American artist had to test himself by continental esthetic criteria for they represented the highest standards of contemporary civilization; he also had to fight "against a superstitious valuation of Europe." The basis of his independent strength—a detachment from his continental sources—was the very cause of a deep sense of inhibition. But James looked to the future hopefully. The American, he wrote, has to deal "more or less, even if only by implication, with Europe; whereas no European is obliged to deal in the least with America. No one dreams of calling him less complete for not doing so. . . . The painter of manners who neglects America is not thereby incomplete as yet; but a hundred years hence—fifty years hence perhaps—he will doubtless be accounted so."

American painters and sculptors may point with justifiable pride to the virtual fulfillment in the visual arts of James's literary prophecy. Their innovations have now become a shaping force in world art, and their vitality has been refreshing and salutary, helping to dispel the thickening mists of artistic caution, complacency and fatigue. The real test of our contemporary art will only come in the next decade or two, however, for only time will tell how deep or enduring is the present commitment to modern forms. In the meantime the resourcefulness of American artists has proved once more the amazing variety, durability and capacity for renewal of that collective visual revolution which we call modern art, and has restored fresh meaning to a principle of creative liberty. Against the background of a period in which individual freedom is severely threatened, and at a time when a genuine internationalism has become an imperative of modern life—a condition, indeed, of survival—such an accomplishment has far-reaching social as well as artistic implications.

Glossary

Abstract Art

Painting or sculpture without representational intentions, having little or no resemblance to natural appearances. Kandinsky from 1910 and Mondrian after 1917 developed the purest abstract styles in modern painting, but the term is often used to refer to work by the Cubists, Miró and others even when there are some evocations of nature. The two main modes of twentieth-century abstraction derive from the rational, structural style of Cézanne and from the emotionally charged color and free, curvilinear design of Gauguin and Van Gogh. Cézanne's painting leads to Cubism and geometric abstraction; Gauguin's and Van Gogh's to the Fauves, Kandinsky and the automatic writing or biomorphic forms of abstract-surrealist art.

Abstract Expressionism

A term first applied to Kandinsky's non-objective paintings after 1910. In recent years critics have most commonly used it in reference to a varied body of abstract painting which emerged in America during and after World War II and whose main exponents in this country have been the painters Gorky, Pollock, Motherwell, Rothko, Still, De Kooning, Kline, Guston and others. A wide and diversified movement rather than a single monolithic style, Abstract Expressionism synthesizes the liberties of Surrealism with either the emotional force of Expressionism, or more recently, the hedonistic refinements of late Impressionist painting. Although most of its productions are apparently anti-formalistic, the movement could only have developed in an artistic climate which drew strength from the examples of Picasso, Mondrian, Miró and Matisse. The new painters have also been called "Action" painters and are better known in Europe by that epithet. Abstract Expressionism, or Action painting, has now become a broad international tendency, and can claim its pioneers on both sides of the Atlantic.

The Armory Show

America's first comprehensive international exhibition of modern art, held in New York at the Sixty-Ninth Regiment Armory on Twenty-Sixth Street from February 17 to March 15, 1913. The show was subsequently also seen in Chicago and Boston. Originally intended as a large "independents" show of American artists, the exhibition radically changed its character under the leadership of Arthur B. Davies, President of an organizing committee of twenty-five artists, who called themselves the Association of American Painters and Sculptors. The composition of the show was left largely in the hands of Davies, Walt Kuhn, Secretary of the Association, and Walter Pach. Some 1,600 items were in the exhibition, covering a period in European art from Ingres and Delacroix to the Cubists and including a selection of contemporary American art made by William Glackens.

Art Nouveau

Also called the *Jugendstil* in Germany. An international style of architecture, architectural decoration and objects of everyday use based on curvilinear forms. It originated in Belgium in the early nineties under the leadership of Henry van de Velde. Its stylistic vocabulary was derived from the paintings of the French Post-Impressionists.

The Blue Rider (Der Blaue Reiter)

The name of an exhibition, a volume of esthetic studies and a movement, all organized in Munich in 1911 by the Russian expatriate, Wassily Kandinsky, and Franz Marc. They were joined in their first exhibition by August Mäcke, Heinrich Campendonk and Gabriele Münter, and the following year by Paul Klee. Their work was influenced by the intense, spec-

trum colors of Delaunay and the Fauves, and by the
geometric schemes of Cubism as well. To these sources
they added their own Teutonic brand of vehement
emotion. Marsden Hartley was close to the Blue
Rider in style during his first period of European travel
and, at the invitation of Franz Marc, showed with
them at the first German Autumn Salon of 1913 held
in Berlin.

The Bridge (Die Brücke)

A painting movement organized in Dresden in 1905
by Kirchner, Schmidt-Rottluff and Heckel; they were
joined in 1906 by Pechstein and Nolde, and in 1910
by Otto Mueller. The Bridge members worked under
the combined influence of Munch, the *Jugendstil* and
folk and primitive art forms. Their brilliant palette
and free handling very closely resembled the Fauves',
although they seem to have arrived at their styles independently. After 1910, these painters moved to
Berlin where their art acquired a progressively more
violent Expressionist character.

Cubism

A movement in painting originated in 1908 by Picasso and Braque which transposed natural forms into
abstract arrangements of overlapping or transparent
planes. It was based on Cézanne's late work and came
as a more formal, architectonic reaction to the free
color and loose structure of the Fauvist painters.
Among the many modern American artists affected
by Cubism directly at some time in their career have
been Marin, Weber, Hartley, Demuth, Sheeler, Spencer, Davis and, more indirectly, almost all of the present group of Abstract Expressionists.

Dada

An experimental movement in literature and painting originating in Zurich in 1916 under the leadership
of Tristan Tzara, Hugo Ball, Richard Hülsenbeck and

Hans Arp, and growing out of wartime disillusionment. Its fantasy, "shock" tactics and use of normally non-artistic material anticipated Surrealism. Dada was a modern form of protest against the sacred cows of art tradition. Out of its exasperations, disparagements and perversity flowed many entertaining and in some cases permanently significant works of art. In New York, Picabia, Duchamp and Man Ray had as early as 1915 begun to work in a proto-Dada style; such literary reviews as Alfred Stieglitz's *291* of that same year and Duchamp's *The blind man* and *Wrong-wrong* of 1917 anticipated later Dada publications. A number of early American moderns, including Man Ray, Dasburg and Demuth, were influenced by Dada art, but only Man Ray became intimately involved in the movement.

The Eight

Also known as the "revolutionary gang," and in later years, as the "ash-can school." A group of artists of divergent tendency, but realists mainly, who joined forces in a single exhibition as an expression of protest against the conservative exhibition policies of the National Academy. Led by Robert Henri they opened their exhibition at the Macbeth Gallery in New York on February 3, 1908. Other members were Sloan, Shinn, Glackens, Luks, Lawson, Prendergast and Davies.

Expressionism

Modern art emphasizing subjective feeling of a confessional character and violently expressive handling of medium. It describes much of twentieth-century German art, including the painting of Nolde (after 1910, when the term first came into use), Beckmann, the Austrian-born Kokoschka, but also some aspects of Picasso and of French painting of the School of Paris. Its spiritual fathers in the late-nineteenth century were Van Gogh, Ensor and Munch. It has had a wide influence in American art, particularly during the thirties.

Fauvism

Led by Henri Matisse in 1905, the Fauve painters freely distorted form and invented a vivid, spontaneous color expression in the effort to liberate themselves from more traditional painting procedures. Matisse, Derain, Braque, Vlaminck, Rouault, Dufy and others exhibited together as Fauves. The movement lasted only three years, but its influence has been international and of lasting significance.

The Forum Exhibition

The Forum Exhibition of Modern American Painters was organized by the critic, Willard Huntington Wright, in 1916. It was conceived as a sobering counter-exhibition to the Armory Show which Wright felt had inadequately represented American painting and identified modern art with sensationalism in the public mind. Christian Brinton, Alfred Stieglitz and Robert Henri were among the sponsors; some of the seventeen painters who exhibited work were Benton, Dasburg, Dove, Hartley, S. Macdonald-Wright, Marin, Maurer, Russell, Sheeler, Marguerite and William Zorach.

Futurism

An Italian painting movement, beginning in 1910 and related in its geometric forms to Cubism, which attempted to capture movement and show the dynamism of the modern world. Its leaders were Boccioni (a fine sculptor as well as a painter), Balla, Carrà, Russolo and Severini.

The Immaculates

Sometimes called the Precisionists, a number of artists just before and after 1920 began to apply principles of abstract design and a feeling for mechanical functionalism to the subject matter of the American industrial scene. Their work was characterized in varying degrees by sharp, clean contours, smooth, meticulous technique and large areas of flat, unmodulated color. Charles Sheeler's and Preston Dickinson's paintings are notable examples with their schematic, purified realism. They were anticipated by Charles Demuth, who was, however, more concerned with formal structure for its own sake rather than descriptive content. Georgia O'Keeffe was technically related to them although her subjects were mainly natural objects, which she transformed into romantic symbols.

Impressionism

A method of pigment application, utilizing small, vibrant dabs of pure color which were mixed optically by the eye. By this technique the Impressionists could better show the movement and scintillation of light in nature, and the spontaneity of their own feelings. Monet, Renoir, Pissarro, Sisley and Berthe Morisot, particularly, painted in this manner after 1874, the year of the first Impressionist group exhibition in Paris. In America Impressionism belatedly enjoyed its first vogue around 1900, with the paintings of Childe Hassam and John Twachtman.

Independents Exhibitions

Any open, non-jury exhibition, usually established to challenge an academy or other official art institution which has closed the doors of its exhibitions to progressive artists. The first show of this character in modern times was the celebrated *Salon des Indépendants* held in Paris in 1884. Arnold Friedman, Glenn Coleman and Julius Golz organized a so-called Original Independent Show of 1908, in New York, but they consciously restricted their selection. Actually the first large "open" show of American art was the Exhibition of Independent Artists, initiated by Sloan, Henri, Davies, Kuhn and Bellows and held in 1910. Established in 1917, the Society of Independent Artists was the most celebrated new group of progressive artists, and their early shows, the most striking. The first exhibition was hung at the Grand Central Palace, New York, and consisted of 2,500 works by 1,300 artists, including the Europeans: Picasso, Gleizes, Duchamp-Villon, Brancusi and Metzinger, among others. From the French Independents of 1884 was adopted the slogan, "No Jury—No Prizes." (The 1917 show of the Society of Independent Artists has since become equally celebrated for the single item to which it refused house room, a urinal entitled *The Fountain* submitted by Marcel Duchamp.) Other non-jury annuals were held in Baltimore and Chicago as well as New York during the twenties. Later the movement all but vanished as museums, exhibition societies and private galleries grew in number, and liberalized their exhibition policies.

Magic Realism

An extremely meticulous naturalism which is intense in mood and has existed since the period of the New Objectivity in Germany. Among recent Americans, Ben Shahn, Andrew Wyeth and Henry Koerner have worked in this genre, combining careful craftsmanship often with bizarre and violent fantasy. Most artists of this tendency, however, seem to prefer the realistic to the magical in their painting equation, and rarely surrender their hold on visual facts, which they reproduce in clinical detail.

The Nabis

Sérusier, Denis, Valloton, Bonnard and Vuillard were among the members of this French painters' group inspired by Gauguin's Pont-Aven painting; they took their name from the Hebrew word "prophet." Active between 1890 and 1900, the Nabis adhered to Gauguin's practice of using suggestive, or "symbolic," color and strongly outlined surface patterns but varied widely in style and choice of subject matter. Bonnard and Vuillard applied the new theories of decoration to everyday subjects, giving to these themes special qualities of intimacy and mystery; esthetically, these two were the most significant painters of the group.

Naturalism

A broad literary and artistic movement in the middle and latter half of the nineteenth century, the aim of which was to depict life by a documentary realism, and to show the heroic energies of the lower classes. The reforming zeal and social aims of the naturalist writers, whether in France or America, were not shared to any great extent by such painters as Courbet and Eakins, who are roughly comparable; nor were they given an important place by the group of insurgent American realists of 1908, who mainly comprised the Eight. For all these artists naturalism was a matter merely of establishing a heightened sense of natural reality by the accurate transcription of objective visual facts.

In painting the term naturalism also is applied to any style of any period based on natural appearances, whether or not the painter directs his art toward social criticism.

Neo-Impressionism

A movement founded by Seurat and Signac about 1885 in an effort to make Impressionism systematic and scientific. These artists employed the primary and intermediate colors in contrasting dots, giving their surfaces a confetti-like appearance; their color researches were based on the optical theories and demonstrations of Chevreul, Rood and other scientists.

The New Objectivity (Die Neue Sachlichkeit)

A phrase invented by a German museum director, G. F. Hartlaub, in 1924 to describe the general return to realism in his country after the more experimental prewar modes of painting. It has been associated with the excruciatingly detailed portraits of George Grosz; Otto Dix's semi-surrealist illusionism; Max Beckmann's intensely realistic, if violently distorted, figure compositions of the early twenties. The term has also been extended to include the return to the object in the paintings of Picasso, Matisse, Braque and many other European artists after the first World War. In America a reaction in favor of more conventional styles was apparent during the same period in the art of Max Weber, the Immaculates, and the romantic realists, Hopper and Burchfield.

Pointillism

The Neo-Impressionist technique of painting in little contrasting dots of pure color, which a critic of the period once ungraciously described as "colored fleas." A modified, low-keyed pointillism was used by some of the Cubists and Futurists to achieve interesting surface textures.

Post-Impressionism

The collective but diversified reaction by a number of painters to the Impressionists' emphasis on the literal truth of their visual sensations and to their formless compositions. Cézanne, Seurat, Gauguin, Van Gogh and Lautrec, in their varied and distinct styles, would all be considered Post-Impressionists.

Primitivism

An outgrowth of the encyclopedic and ethnographic museums of the late nineteenth century, and of the artist's discovery of vital new esthetic values in the objects of these collections. Gauguin became perhaps the first, and most dramatic, modern primitive when he tried to paint "like children," with a deliberate

crudeness and ingenuousness, during his Pont-Aven
period. In the art of Munch and then of the members
of the Bridge group in Germany, primitivism was an
important force, as it was for the Fauves, and for Picasso around 1907. Many modern artists who are self-
taught and apparently innocent of a stereotyped art
school training, from Henri Rousseau to Grandma
Moses, have been labeled primitives.

Social Realism

An American term popular particularly during the
depression years, applied to painting and sculpture of
social protest. Many of the artists of that time, whose
work was directed at the abuses in our political and
economic life, worked stylistically under the influence
of contemporary Mexican painting or of the German
Expressionists.

The Style (de Stijl)

A movement founded in Leyden, Holland, in 1917
by Mondrian, Vantongerloo, and other artists, design-
ers and architects. It was dedicated to applying principles of abstract, geometrical design to the fine and
applied arts.

Surrealism

A movement in literature and art founded officially
by the poet-painter, André Breton, in Paris in 1924.
The Surrealist painters emphasized "the omnipotence
of the dream" and chance associations of the sub-
conscious mind. They were indebted to Dada and to
the "metaphysical" paintings of De Chirico. Masson,
Miró and Max Ernst for a time adopted idioms in
which nervous sensibility and automatism were the es-
sence of the work; Dali, Tanguy and later Surrealists
painted fantastic and hallucinatory images in works
which were described as "hand-painted dream photographs."

Synchromism

A movement founded by Stanton Macdonald-Wright and Morgan Russell in 1913, the year they first showed their abstract paintings at the Carroll Gallery in New York; later associated with them were Patrick Bruce and Arthur Burdett Frost, Jr. The Synchromists painted in spectrum colors of graduated intensities, creating rhythmic abstract compositions which were most probably derived from the very similar style of Delaunay and Kupka.

291 Gallery

The name by which Alfred Stieglitz's Little Gallery of the Photo-Secession at 291 Fifth Avenue became known. Between 1908 and 1917, especially, 291 showed much of the best advanced modern European art of its time, as well as the painting of the Americans Marin, Maurer, Carles, Walkowitz, Hartley, Dove, Nadelman, O'Keeffe, Bluemner and S. Macdonald-Wright. The works of Picasso, Matisse, Manolo, Rousseau, Picabia, Brancusi and African Negro sculpture were seen for the first time in this country under 291's auspices. This famous street number also became the name of an occasional magazine published by Stieglitz for a short time from 1915; Marius de Zayas, Picabia and Marcel Duchamp played a leading part in giving the New York review a proto-Dada character at least a year before the official birth of the movement in Zurich.

Biographies of
Selected Painters and Sculptors

by Charles McCurdy
Head, Art Reference Department, Pratt Institute, Brooklyn

Baziotes, William

Born, Pittsburgh, Pa., 1912. Studied: National Academy of Design, 1933-36. Worked on WPA Federal Art Project, New York, 1936-41. Taught: Brooklyn Museum Art School; New York University; People's Art Center, the Museum of Modern Art, New York. One-man shows: Art of This Century, 1944; Kootz Gallery, New York, regularly from 1946. Included in *15 Americans* exhibition, Museum of Modern Art, New York, 1952. Lives in New York. In the collections of Addison Gallery of American Art, Andover, Mass.; Art Institute of Chicago; Baltimore Museum of Art; Fogg Art Museum, Harvard University, Cambridge, Mass.; Los Angeles County Museum; Minneapolis Institute of Arts; Metropolitan Museum of Art, Museum of Modern Art, and Whitney Museum of American Art, all of New York; University of Illinois, Urbana; Washington University, St. Louis, and others. Dealer: Kootz Gallery, New York.

Bellows, George Wesley

Born, Columbus, Ohio, 1882. Attended Ohio State University. To New York in 1904. Studied with Henri, K. H. Miller and H. G. Maratta. Associated with early American realists. First prize for landscape, National Academy of Design, 1908. Taught: Art Students League, 1910; Art Institute of Chicago. Exhibited in the Armory Show, 1913. Began to work in lithography in 1916. Died, 1925. In the collections of Art Institute of Chicago; Boston Public Library; Buffalo Fine Arts Academy; Phillips Gallery, Washington, D. C.; Brooklyn Museum and others.

Benton, Thomas Hart

Born, Neosho, Mo., 1889. Studied: Art Institute of
Chicago. To Paris in 1913. Served with the Navy in
World War I. Showed in Forum Exhibition of 1916.
Became a leading exponent of regionalist American
scene painting in the late twenties, early thirties.
Murals depicting rural American life for the New
School for Social Research, New York, 1930, and the
old Whitney Museum of American Art Library, 1931.
Author of *An Artist in America.* Now lives in Kansas
City, Mo. In the collections of the Museum of Modern
Art, and Whitney Museum of American Art, New
York; Brooklyn Museum, and others. Dealer: Asso-
ciated American Artists, New York.

Bloom, Hyman

Born Lithuania, 1913. To the U. S. in 1920. Studied:
Boston Museum School. Worked on the WPA Federal
Arts Project. Included in group exhibition, *Americans
1942,* Museum of Modern Art, New York. One-man
shows: Stuart Art Gallery, Boston, 1945; Durlacher
Bros., New York, regularly from 1948; Boris Mirski
Art Gallery, Boston, 1949. Retrospectives: Albright
Art Gallery, Buffalo, 1954; Whitney Museum of
American Art, New York, 1955. Lives in Boston. In
the collections of Museum of Modern Art, Whitney
Museum of American Art, New York, and others.
Dealer: Durlacher Brothers, New York.

Burchfield, Charles

Born, Ashtabula Harbor, Ohio, 1893. Studied: Cleveland School of Art, 1912. Awarded scholarship to the
National Academy of Design, 1916, where he attended
one class. Served with Camouflage Section of the U.S.
Army in World War I. Taught: University of Minnesota; Art Institute of Buffalo, 1949; Ohio University,
1950 and 1953; Buffalo Fine Arts Academy, 1951-52.
One-man shows: Cleveland School of Art, 1916; Art
Institute of Chicago, 1923; Rehn Gallery, New York,

regularly from 1931 through 1954. Retrospectives:
Museum of Modern Art, New York, 1932; Carnegie
Institute, Pittsburgh, 1941; Albright Art Gallery, Buffalo, 1944; Cleveland Museum of Art, 1953 (drawings); Whitney Museum of American Art, New York,
1956. Lives in Gardenville, New York. In the collections of Cleveland Museum of Art; Metropolitan Museum of Art, and Whitney Museum of American Art,
New York; City Art Museum of St. Louis; Fogg Art
Museum, Cambridge, Mass.; Munson-Proctor-Williams
Institute, Utica; Syracuse Museum of Fine Arts; Pennsylvania Academy of Fine Arts; Albright Art Gallery,
Buffalo, and others. Dealer: Rehn Gallery, New York.

Calder, Alexander

Born, Philadelphia, Pa., 1898, son of sculptor, Stirling
Calder. Graduated from Stevens Institute, Hoboken,
N.J., 1919. Studied: Art Students League, New York,
1923-26. To Paris, 1926, and frequent trips to
Paris until 1934. First abstract constructions in
Paris, 1931, where he became member of the "Ab-
straction-Creation" group. First wind-driven mobiles
exhibited in 1932. Setting for Martha Graham's dance
work *Panorama*, Bennington, Vt., 1935; setting for
Erik Satie's *Socrate*, Hartford, Conn., 1936; *Mercury
Fountain*, Spanish Pavilion, Paris Exposition, 1937;
Water Ballet, New York World's Fair, 1939; illustrations for *Three Young Rats*, 1944. One-man shows:
Weyhe Gallery, New York, 1928; Julien Levy Gallery, New York, 1932; Pierre Matisse Gallery, from
1934; San Francisco Museum of Art, 1942; Museum
of Modern Art, New York, 1943; exhibitions in Ma-
drid, Barcelona, Honolulu, Rome, Hamburg, Milan,
London, Berlin. Lives in Roxbury, Conn. In the collections of Addison Gallery of American Art,
Andover, Mass; Wadsworth Atheneum, Hartford;
Honolulu Academy of Art; Smith College, Northampton, Mass.; Pennsylvania Museum of Art, Philadelphia; City Art Museum of St. Louis; Phillips Gallery,

200   MODERN AMERICAN PAINTING AND SCULPTURE

Washington, D. C.; Museum of Modern Art, and Whitney Museum of American Art, New York, and others. Dealer: Perls Galleries, New York.

Davies, Arthur B.

Born, Utica, N. Y., 1862. Studied: Chicago Academy of Design, 1878; Art Institute of Chicago, 1882; Art Students League, New York, 1886. European trip, 1893. President of the Association of American Painters and Sculptors which was responsible for the organization of the Armory Show, 1913. Murals for the home of Lillie P. Bliss and the Detroit Institute of Arts. Died, 1928. In the collections of Brooklyn Museum; Addison Gallery of American Art, Andover, Mass.; Toledo Museum of Fine Arts; Phillips Gallery, Washington, D. C.; Art Institute of Chicago; Metropolitan Museum of Art, New York, and others.

Davis, Stuart

Born, Philadelphia, Pa., 1894. Left East Orange, N. J., High School in 1910 to study in New York with Robert Henri whom he met through his father, Edward Wyatt Davis, art editor of the *Philadelphia Press.* Covers and drawings for the old *Masses,* 1913-16; cartoonist for *Harper's Weekly,* 1913. Exhibited five water colors in the Armory Show, 1913. Taught: Art Students League, New York, 1931; New School for Social Research since 1940. Mural for Radio City Music Hall, New York, 1932; WPA Federal Art Project, 1933; mural for New York World's Fair, 1939; murals for Drake University, Des Moines; WNYC, New York. One-man shows: Sheridan Square Gallery, New York, 1917; Newark Museum, 1925; Downtown Gallery, New York, 1927, 1930, 1932 and 1943; Whitney Studio Galleries, New York, 1929. Retrospectives: Cincinnati Modern Art Society and Indiana University, 1941; Museum of Modern Art, New York, 1945. Lives in New York. In the collections of Whitney Museum of American Art, Museum of Modern Art, and Solomon R. Guggenheim Museum, all of New York; Pennsylvania Academy of Fine Arts, Philadelphia; Washington University, St. Louis; Philadelphia Museum of Art and others. Dealer: Downtown Gallery, New York.

De Kooning, Willem

Born, Rotterdam, 1904. Studied: Rotterdam Academy of Fine Arts. To the U. S. in 1926. One-man shows: Egan Gallery, New York, 1948; Sidney Janis Gallery, New York, 1953 to present; Venice *Biennale*, 1954. Retrospective: School of the Boston Museum of Fine Arts, 1953. Taught: Black Mountain College, N. C., 1948; Yale University School of Fine Arts, New Haven, Conn., 1950-51. Lives in New York. In the collections of Museum of Modern Art, and Whitney Museum of American Art, New York; Art Institute of Chicago; St. Louis Museum. Dealer: Sidney Janis Gallery, New York.

Demuth, Charles

Born, Lancaster, Pa., 1883. Studied: Franklin and Marshall Academy, 1899; Drexel Institute, Philadelphia, 1901; Pennsylvania Academy of Fine Arts, 1905. Trip to Paris, London and Berlin, 1907. Returned to the Pennsylvania Academy, 1908; second trip to Paris, and studied at the Académie Moderne, Académie Julien and the Académie Colarossi, 1912. First one-man show, Daniel Gallery, New York, 1915. In group exhibition at the Anderson Galleries, New York, arranged by Stieglitz, 1925. One-man shows: Stieglitz's Intimate Gallery, 1929; An American Place, New York, 1931; Downtown Gallery, New York, 1950. Retrospective: Museum of Modern Art, New York, 1950. Died, 1935. In the collections of Museum of Modern Art, Whitney Museum of American Art, and Metropolitan Museum of Art, all of New York; Detroit Institute of Arts; Columbus Gallery of Fine Arts, Columbus, Ohio;

Philadelphia Museum of Art; Art Institute of Chicago and others. Dealer: Downtown Gallery, New York.

Dove, Arthur G.

Born, Canandaigua, N. Y., 1880. Illustrated for *McClure's, Judge* and other magazines, 1904-08. Studied in France and Italy, 1908-10. First exhibited at 291 Gallery, 1910; Forum Exhibition, 1916; Anderson Galleries, New York, 1927, 1929; An American Place, New York, regularly from 1930 to 1945; Phillips Gallery, Washington, D. C., 1947; Downtown Gallery, New York, from 1949. Retrospective: White Art Museum, Cornell University, Ithaca, New York, 1954. Died, 1946. In the collections of Baltimore Museum of Art; Art Institute of Chicago; Detroit Institute of Arts; University of Minnesota; Smith College Museum, Northampton, Mass.; Whitney Museum of American Art, and Museum of Modern Art, New York; Carnegie Institute, Pittsburgh; Philadelphia Museum of Art; Phillips Gallery, Washington, D. C., and others. Dealer: Downtown Gallery, New York.

Ferber, Herbert

Born, New York, 1906. Studied: College of the City of New York; Columbia University; Beaux-Arts Institute of Design, New York. Tiffany Foundation Fellowship. First sculpture exhibition Midtown Gallery, New York, 1937; other one-man shows: Betty Parsons Gallery, 1947, 1950; Kootz Gallery, 1955. Group shows: *Abstract Painting and Sculpture in America* exhibition, 1951; *15 Americans,* 1952; *Sculpture of the 20th Century,* 1953, all at the Museum of Modern Art, New York. Lives in New York. In the collections of Museum of Modern Art, Whitney Museum of American Art, and Metropolitan Museum of Art, all of New York; Albright Art Gallery, Buffalo, and others. Dealer: Kootz Gallery, New York.

Flannagan, John B.

Born, Fargo, N. D., 1895. Studied: Minneapolis Institute of Arts, 1914-17. Guggenheim Fellowship, 1932; trip to Ireland. Exhibitions: Weyhe Gallery, New York, from 1927 to 1938; Buchholz Gallery, New York, 1942; Museum of Modern Art, New York, 1942; Virginia Museum of Fine Arts, Richmond, 1946. Died, 1942. In the collections of Whitney Museum of American Art, and Museum of Modern Art, New York, and others.

Glackens, William J.

Born, Philadelphia, Pa., 1870. Studied: Pennsylvania Academy of Fine Arts, 1895. Illustrator for the *Philadelphia Press, New York World, New York Herald, McClure's, Scribner's* and *Saturday Evening Post.* Showed as member of the Eight, 1908. Helped organize the Armory Show and made selection of American section, 1913. Elected to the National Academy, 1933. Exhibitions: The Eight, Macbeth Gallery, New York, 1908; Independents Exhibition, New York, 1910. Died, 1938. Retrospectives: Whitney Museum of American Art, New York, 1939; Carnegie Institute, Pittsburgh, 1939. In the collections of Addison Gallery of American Art, Andover, Mass.; Albright Art Gallery, Buffalo; Barnes Foundation, Merion, Pa.; Museum of Fine Arts, Boston; Detroit Institute of Arts; Metropolitan Museum of Art, and Whitney Museum of American Art, New York; the Phillips Gallery, Washington, D. C., and others. Dealer: Kraushaar Galleries, New York.

Gorky, Arshile

Born, Hayotz Dzore, Armenia, 1904. Studied: Polytechnic Institute, Tiflis, 1916-18. To the U. S. 1920. Studied engineering, Brown University. To New York 1925. Died, 1948. Exhibitions: Mellon Galleries, Philadelphia, 1934; Julien Levy Gallery, New York, 1946, 1947, 1948; Kootz Gallery, New York, 1950; Whit-

ney Museum of American Art, New York, 1951; Paul
Kantor Gallery, Los Angeles, 1952; Martha Jackson
Gallery, New York, 1954; Sidney Janis Gallery, New
York, 1955. In the collections of Whitney Museum of
American Art, and Museum of Modern Art, New
York; Albright Art Gallery, Buffalo, and others.
Dealer: Sidney Janis Gallery, New York.

Gottlieb, Adolph

Born, New York, 1903. Studied: Art Students League,
New York, and in Europe. One-man shows: Artists
Gallery, New York, 1940, 1943; 67 Gallery, New
York, 1945; Kootz Gallery, New York, 1947; Jacques
Seligmann Galleries, New York, 1949; Kootz Gallery,
New York, 1950, 1951, 1953; Arts Club of Chicago,
1953; Bennington College, Bennington, Vt.; Williams
College, Williamstown, Mass., 1954. Lives in Brook-
lyn. In the collections of Whitney Museum of Ameri-
can Art, and Museum of Modern Art, New York; De-
troit Institute of Fine Arts; University of Illinois, Ur-
bana; University of Miami, Miami, Florida, and others.
Dealer: French and Company, New York.

Graves, Morris

Born, Fox Valley, Ore., 1910. Trip to the Orient,
1928-30. Won first prize for painting, Northwest Annual, Seattle Art Museum, 1933. Worked for WPA
Arts Project, 1937. Various trips throughout U. S.
until 1942 when inducted into U. S. Army. Awarded
Guggenheim Fellowship, 1946. Trip to Europe, 1938-
39; Mexico, 1950 and to Ireland and Japan, 1956.
Exhibitions: Seattle Art Museum, 1936; *Americans
1942* exhibition and *Romantic Painting in America*,
Museum of Modern Art, New York, 1943; Arts Club
of Chicago, 1943; Detroit Institute of Arts, 1943;
California Palace of the Legion of Honor, San Fran-
cisco, 1948; Los Angeles County Museum, 1948; Oslo
Kunstforening, Oslo, 1955; Whitney Museum of
American Art, New York, 1956; Art Galleries, Uni-

versity of California, Los Angeles, 1956. Lives in Seattle, Washington. In the collections of Albright Art Gallery, Buffalo; Art Institute of Chicago; Baltimore Museum of Art; Cleveland Museum of Art; Detroit Institute of Arts; Museum of Fine Arts, Boston; Phillips Gallery, Washington, D. C.; San Francisco Museum of Art; Seattle Art Museum; Metropolitan Museum of Art, Museum of Modern Art, and Whitney Museum of American Art, all of New York, and others. Dealer: Willard Gallery, New York.

Guston, Philip

Born, Montreal, 1913. Taught: State University of Iowa, 1941-45; St. Louis School of Fine Arts, 1945-47; Munson-Williams-Proctor Institute, Utica, N. Y., 1947; Art Students League, New York, 1948; New York University, New York, from 1950 to the present. Received 1st prize, Carnegie International, 1945; Guggenheim Fellow, 1948; Prix de Rome, 1949. One-man shows: Midtown Gallery, New York, 1945; Boston Museum of Fine Arts, 1946; Peridot Gallery, New York, 1952; Egan Gallery, New York, 1953; Sidney Janis Gallery, New York, 1956. Group shows: Whitney Museum of American Art Annuals, New York, 1941-55; Guggenheim Museum of Art, New York, 1954; *12 Americans* exhibition, Museum of Modern Art, New York, 1956; V São Paulo *Bienal,* Brazil, 1959; and in Europe. Lives in New York. In the collections of Museum of Modern Art, and Whitney Museum of American Art, New York; State University of Iowa, Iowa City, Iowa; Munson-Williams-Proctor Institute, Utica, New York; Albright Art Gallery, Buffalo, and others. Dealer: Sidney Janis Gallery, New York.

Hare, David

Born, New York, 1917. Exhibitions of color photography: Julien Levy Gallery, New York, 1940; Weyhe Gallery, New York, 1941. Sculpture exhibitions: Art of This Century, New York, 1944, 1946; Julien Levy Gallery, New York, 1949; Kootz Gallery, New York, 1948-56. Included in São Paulo *Bienal*, Brazil, 1957. Lives in New York. In the collections of Museum of Modern Art, and Whitney Museum of American Art, New York; Wadsworth Atheneum, Hartford, Conn.; San Francisco Museum of Art; Washington University, St. Louis, and others. Dealer: Kootz Gallery, New York.

Hartley, Marsden

Born, Lewiston, Me., 1877. Studied: Chase School and National Academy of Design, New York, 1898-1900. First one-man show at Stieglitz's 291 Gallery, New York, 1909. Exhibited with the Blue Rider Group in First Autumn Salon, Berlin, and the Armory Show, New York, 1913. One-man show: Berlin, 1914. Trips to Europe, Mexico and Canada. Awarded Guggenheim fellowship in 1931. Retrospective: Museum of Modern Art, New York, 1944. Died 1943. In the collections of Museum of Fine Arts, Boston; Brooklyn Museum of Art; Cleveland Museum of Art; Detroit Institute of Arts; Metropolitan Museum of Art, Museum of Modern Art, and Whitney Museum of American Art, all of New York; Portland Museum of Art; Phillips Collection, Washington, D. C.; Worcester Art Museum, and others. Dealers: Downtown Gallery, Paul Rosenberg Gallery, Bertha Schaefer Gallery, all New York.

Henri, Robert

Born, Cincinnati, Ohio, 1865. Studied: Pennsylvania Academy of Fine Arts, Philadelphia; Ecole des Beaux-Arts and Académie Julien, Paris. Showed with the Eight at Macbeth Gallery, New York, 1908. Helped organize the Independents Exhibition, 1910. Awarded numerous medals including the Gold Medal, Art Club of Philadelphia, 1909; Silver Medal, Buenos Aires, 1910; Temple Gold Medal, Pennsylvania Academy of

Fine Arts, 1929. Memorial exhibition: Metropolitan Museum of Art, New York, 1931. Died, 1929. In the collections of Buffalo Fine Arts Academy; Art Institute of Chicago; Detroit Institute of Arts; Milwaukee Art Institute; Minneapolis Institute of Arts; Brooklyn Museum; Newark Museum; City Art Museum of St. Louis; Whitney Museum of American Art, and Museum of Modern Art, New York, and others. Dealer: Kraushaar Galleries, New York.

Hofmann, Hans

Born, Weissenberg, Germany, 1880. Studied in Munich. Paris, 1904-14. Conducted own school, Munich, 1915-32. Opened school in New York, 1934, two years after arriving in U. S. Teacher of Carl Holty, Vaclav Vytlacil, Giorgio Cavallon, George McNeil and Larry Rivers. One-man shows: California Palace of the Legion of Honor, San Francisco, 1931; Art of This Century, New York, 1944; Betty Parsons Gallery, New York, 1946, 1947; Kootz Gallery, New York, 1947, 1949, 1950-55. Included in exhibition, *Abstract Painting and Sculpture in America,* Museum of Modern Art, New York, 1952. Retrospectives: Whitney Museum of American Art, New York; San Francisco Museum of Art; Walker Art Center, Minneapolis; Munson-Williams-Proctor Institute, Utica, New York, all in 1957. Lives in New York. In the collections of Whitney Museum of American Art, Museum of Modern Art, and Metropolitan Museum of Art, all of New York, and others. Dealer: Kootz Gallery, New York.

Hopper, Edward

Born, Nyack, N. Y., 1882. Studied: Chase School, New York, 1900-05. Trip to Paris, 1906-07. Exhibited in the Armory Show, 1913. Has won many awards including the Gold Medal from the National Institute of Arts and Letters. Received honorary degree from Rutgers University, 1953. One-man shows: Whitney Studio Club, New York, 1919; Rehn Gallery, New York, 1924;

Museum of Modern Art, New York (retrospective), 1933; other exhibitions at Whitney Museum of American Art, New York (retrospective), 1950; Boston Museum of Fine Arts, 1950; Detroit Institute of Art, 1950; and Venice *Biennale*, 1952. Lives in New York. In the collections of Wadsworth Atheneum, Hartford, Conn.; Walker Art Center, Minneapolis; Museum of Modern Art, New York; Carnegie Institute, Pittsburgh, and others. Dealer: Rehn Gallery, New York.

Kline, Franz

Born, Wilkes-Barre, Pa., 1910. Studied: School of Fine and Applied Art, Boston University, 1931-35; Heatherly's Art School, London, 1937-38. To New York in 1938. One-man shows: Egan Gallery, New York, 1950, 1951, 1954; Margaret Brown Gallery, Boston, 1952; Sidney Janis Gallery, New York, 1956. Exhibited: National Academy, New York; Institute of Design, Chicago; *12 Americans,* Museum of Modern Art, 1956. Received National Academy Award, 1943-44. Taught: Black Mountain College, 1952; Pratt Institute, 1953-54; Philadelphia Museum School of Art, 1954. In the collections of Albright Art Gallery, Buffalo; Museum of Modern Art, and Solomon R. Guggenheim Museum, New York; Carnegie Institute, Pittsburgh; Munson-Williams-Proctor Institute, Utica, N. Y., and others. Dealer: Sidney Janis Gallery. New York.

Lachaise, Gaston

Born, Paris, 1882. Studied: Ecole Bernard Palissy, 1895; Atelier Gabriel Jules Thomas, Académie Nationale des Beaux-Arts, 1898-1903. Arrived in U. S., 1906. Exhibited in the Armory Show, 1913. One-man shows: Bourgeois Galleries, New York, 1918; Stieglitz Gallery, New York, 1927; Knoedler Gallery, New York, 1947; Weyhe Gallery, New York, 1956; Margaret Brown Gallery, Boston, 1957. Retrospectives:

Museum of Modern Art, New York, 1935; Whitney Museum of American Art, New York, 1937. Executed reliefs for RCA Building, Rockefeller Center, New York, 1931; International Building, Rockefeller Center, New York, 1934. Sculpture commission for Fairmount Park, Philadelphia, 1935. Died, 1935. In the collections of Cleveland Museum of Art; Whitney Museum of American Art, and Museum of Modern Art, New York; Smith College Museum, Northampton, Mass., and others.

Lassaw, Ibram

Born, Alexandria, Egypt, 1913. Studied: Clay Club, 1927-32; Beaux-Arts Institute of Design, New York, 1930-31. Exhibitions: American Abstract Artists from 1937; the Venice *Biennale*, 1954; *12 Americans* exhibition, Museum of Modern Art, New York, 1956. One-man shows: Kootz Gallery, New York, 1951, 1952, 1954, 1955. Lives in New York. In the collections of Museum of Modern Art, and Whitney Museum of American Art, New York; Carnegie Institute, Pittsburgh, and others. Dealer: Kootz Gallery, New York.

Lippold, Richard

Born, Milwaukee, Wis., 1915. Studied: University of Chicago and the Art Institute of Chicago, 1933-37. First one-man exhibition: Willard Gallery, New York, 1947. Exhibited in *Abstract Painting and Sculpture in America* Exhibition, Museum of Modern Art, New York, 1951; *15 Americans,* Museum of Modern Art, New York, 1952; Whitney Museum of American Art, New York; Metropolitan Museum of Art, New York. Lives in New York. In the collections of Museum of Modern Art, Whitney Museum of American Art, and Metropolitan Museum of Art, all of New York; Detroit Institute of Arts; Munson-Williams-Proctor Institute, Utica, New York, and others. Dealer: Willard Gallery, New York.

Lipton, Seymour

> Born, New York, 1903. Self-taught. Instructor at New
> School for Social Research, New York; New Jersey
> State Teachers College; Cooper Union. Contributor to
> *Magazine of Art,* 1947, and *College Art Journal,* 1951.
> One-man shows in New York: Galerie St. Etienne,
> 1943; Betty Parsons Gallery, 1948 to present. Exhib-
> ited in *12 Americans,* Museum of Modern Art, New
> York; Whitney Museum of American Art, New York;
> Yale University, New Haven, Conn.; Baltimore Mu-
> seum; San Francisco Museum of Art, and others. One-
> man show, XXIX Venice *Biennale,* Venice, Italy, 1958.
> In the collections of Whitney Museum of American
> Art, and Museum of Modern Art, New York, and
> others. Dealer: Betty Parsons Gallery, New York.

Luks, George B.

> Born, Williamsport, Pa., 1867. Studied: Pennsylvania
> Academy of Fine Arts and in Düsseldorf, Paris and
> London. Illustrations for *Philadelphia Bulletin, New
> York Herald* and *New York World.* Exhibited with
> the Eight, 1908. Taught at the Art Students League
> and founded his own school in the Lincoln Arcade,
> New York. Received many awards including the Hud-
> nut Water Color Prize, 1916; the Logan Medal, Art
> Institute of Chicago, 1920 and 1926; and the Cor-
> coran Gold Medal, 1932. Died, 1933. Retrospective:
> Newark Museum of Art, 1934. In the collections of
> Metropolitan Museum of Art, and Whitney Museum
> of American Art, New York; the Albright Art Gallery,
> Buffalo; the Phillips Gallery, Washington, D. C. and
> others. Dealer: Kraushaar Galleries, New York.

Macdonald-Wright, Stanton

> Born, Charlottesville, Va., 1890. To France in 1907.
> Studied: Ecole des Beaux-Arts, Académie Julien and
> the Sorbonne. Exhibited in the Armory Show of 1913.
> Returned to the U. S. in 1916. One-man show at Stieg-
> litz's 291 Gallery, New York, 1917; New York Inde-

pendents exhibition, 1917. One-man show at Rose
Fried Gallery, 1955. Taught: University of California
at Los Angeles. Author of *A Treatise on Color,* and
contributor to many art magazines. Lives in Los Angeles. In the collections of Museum of Modern Art,
and Whitney Museum of American Art, New York;
Newark Museum; Denver Art Museum; Grand Rapids
Art Gallery, and others. Dealer: Rose Fried Gallery,
New York.

Marin, John

Born, Rutherford, N. J., 1870. Studied: Pennsylvania
Academy of Art, 1899; Art Students League, New
York, 1901-03. To Paris in 1905. In Europe until
1909; returned to New York, 1909; painted in the
Tyrol, Austria, 1910; back in America permanently,
1911. Exhibited in Independents of 1909 and held
first one-man show at Stieglitz's 291 Gallery, New
York; Armory Exhibition, 1913; Forum Exhibition,
1916. Other one-man shows: 291 Gallery, New York,
1913, 1915; Daniel Gallery, New York (retrospective),
1920; Brooklyn Museum, 1922; Intimate Gallery,
1925, 1928; An American Place, New York, 1929-50;
Downtown Gallery, New York, 1939-54. Retrospectives: Museum of Modern Art, New York, 1936; Institute of Contemporary Art, Boston; Phillips Gallery,
Washington, D. C.; Walker Art Center, Minneapolis,
all in 1947; Los Angeles County Museum, 1949; Venice *Biennale,* 1950; John Marin Memorial Exhibition,
University of California Art Galleries, Los Angeles,
1955. Died, 1953. In the collections of Columbus Gallery of Fine Arts, Columbus, Ohio; Whitney Museum
of Art, Museum of Modern Art and Metropolitan Museum of Art, all of New York; Art Institute of Chicago; Museum of Fine Arts, Boston; San Francisco
Museum of Art; Brooklyn Museum of Art; Wadsworth
Atheneum, Hartford, Conn.; City Art Museum, St.
Louis, and others. Dealer: Downtown Gallery, New
York.

Motherwell, Robert

Born, Aberdeen, Wash., 1915. Studied: Stanford University, 1933-37; Harvard, 1937-38; Columbia University, 1940-41. Self-taught painter. Contributor to many art magazines including *Dyn*, 1944, and *VVV*, 1942; editor of *Modern Artists in America*, 1952; *The Dada Painters and Poets*, 1952. One-man shows: Art of This Century, New York, 1944; Kootz Gallery, 1946 to 1952; San Francisco Museum of Art, 1946; Sidney Janis Gallery, 1957. In group show, *14 Americans*, Museum of Modern Art, 1946. Lives in New York. In the collections of Museum of Modern Art, and Whitney Museum of American Art, New York, and others. Dealer: Sidney Janis Gallery, New York.

Noguchi, Isamu

Born, Los Angeles, 1904. Lived in Japan during childhood and returned to U. S. in 1918. Studied with Gutzon Borglum, 1922; assistant to Brancusi in Paris, 1927-28. Returned to U. S. in 1929. Has traveled extensively throughout Europe and the Far East. Relief for façade of the Associated Press Bldg., Rockefeller Center, New York, and commissioned to design a fountain for the New York World's Fair, 1939. One-man show: Schoen Gallery, New York, 1929. Exhibited in *14 Americans*, Museum of Modern Art, New York, 1946; San Francisco Museum of Art, 1942. Lives in New York. In the collections of Albright Art Gallery, Buffalo; Museum of Modern Art, Whitney Museum of American Art, and Metropolitan Museum of Art, all of New York; Toronto Art Gallery, and others. Dealer: Stable Gallery, New York.

O'Keeffe, Georgia

Born, Sun Prairie, Wis., 1887. Graduated from Chatham Episcopal Institute, Va. Studied: School of Art Institute of Chicago, 1904-05; Art Students League,

New York, where she won still-life prize, 1907-08.
Supervisor art, public schools, Amarillo, Tex., 1912-14;
teacher of art in other schools. To New Mexico in
1917. Married Alfred Stieglitz, 1924. Trips to Canada,
Bermuda, 1932, 1934. Honorary Ph.D. in Fine Arts,
William and Mary College, 1939; Litt.D., University
of Wisconsin, 1942. Moved to Abiguiu, New Mexico,
1949. In Stieglitz's 291 Gallery group show, 1916.
First one-man show, 291 Gallery, New York, 1917.
Exhibited at Intimate Gallery, 1926-29; An American
Place, 1930-46; Downtown Gallery, New York, 1937,
1952, 1955. Retrospectives: Art Institute of Chicago,
1940; Museum of Modern Art, New York, 1946. In
the collections of Cleveland Museum of Art; Whitney
Museum of American Art, Museum of Modern Art,
and Metropolitan Museum of Art, all of New York;
Art Institute of Chicago; Boston Museum of Fine
Arts; Philadelphia Museum of Art, and others. Dealer:
Downtown Gallery, New York.

Pollock, Jackson

Born, Cody, Wyoming, 1912. Grew up Arizona and
California, 1915-29. Studied with Thomas Hart
Benton, Art Students League, New York, 1929-31.
Worked on WPA Federal Art Project, New York,
1938-42. Lived in Long Island from 1946 until his
death, August 11, 1956. One-man shows: Art of This
Century, New York, 1943-47; Arts Club of Chicago,
1945, 1951; San Francisco Museum of Art, 1945;
Betty Parsons Gallery, 1948-51. Exhibited in Peggy
Guggenheim's Art of This Century collection, Venice
and Milan, Italy, 1950; Venice *Biennale*, 1950; Mu-
seum of Modern Art, *15 Americans*, 1952; Galerie
Michel Tapié, Studio Paul Facchetti, Paris, 1952; Williams College, 1952; Kunsthaus, Zurich, 1953; Sidney
Janis Gallery, 1952, 1954 and 1955. Retrospective:
Museum of Modern Art, New York, 1956; IV São
Paulo *Bienal*, Brazil, 1957. In the collections of Balti-
more Museum of Art; Albright Gallery, Buffalo; Art

Institute of Chicago; Dallas Museum of Fine Arts; Solomon R. Guggenheim Museum, and Metropolitan Museum of Art, New York; Museum of Modern Art, New York; Carnegie Institute, Pittsburgh; San Francisco Museum of Art; Munson-Williams-Proctor Institute, Utica, and others.

Prendergast, Maurice

Born, St. Johns, Newfoundland, 1859. Studied: Académie Julien, Paris, 1886; Académie Colarossi. Trips to Europe in 1898, 1912 and 1914. Won $2,000 prize at the Corcoran Biennial, 1923. Died, 1924. Exhibited at Kraushaar and Milch Galleries, New York. Retrospective: Addison Gallery of American Art, Andover, Mass., 1938. In the collections of Phillips Gallery, Washington, D. C.; Museum of Modern Art and Whitney Museum of American Art, New York; Barnes Foundation, Merion, Pa., and others. Dealer: Kraushaar Galleries, New York.

Roszak, Theodore J.

Born, Poznan, Poland, 1907. Studied: Columbia University, 1926; National Academy of Design, 1926; Art Institute of Chicago, 1925 and 1927. Trip to Europe, 1929-31. Taught: Art Institute of Chicago, 1928; Design Laboratory, New York, 1938; Sarah Lawrence College, Bronxville, N. Y., 1941- . First one-man show, Allerton Gallery, Chicago, 1928. Awarded American Traveling Fellowship, 1928. Included in *Abstract Painting and Sculpture in America* exhibition, Museum of Modern Art, New York, 1951. Retrospectives: Whitney Museum of American Art, New York, 1956; Walker Art Center, Minneapolis, 1957; Los Angeles County Museum, 1957; San Francisco Museum of Art, 1957; Seattle Art Museum, 1957. Lives in New York. In the collections of Museum of Modern Art, and Whitney Museum of American Art, New York; Smith College, Northampton, Mass., and others. Dealer: Pierre Matisse Gallery, New York.

Rothko, Mark

Born, Dwinsk, Russia, 1903. To U. S., 1913. Grew up in Portland, Oregon. Student at Yale University, 1921-23; studied painting with Max Weber, 1926. One-man shows: Portland (Oregon) Art Museum, 1933 (water colors and drawings); Contemporary Arts Gallery, New York, 1933; Art of This Century, New York, 1945; Betty Parsons Gallery, New York, annually 1946-1949, 1951; Sidney Janis Gallery, New York, 1955, 1958. Exhibited at San Francisco Museum of Art, 1946; *15 Americans,* Museum of Modern Art, New York, 1952; XXIX Venice *Biennale,* Venice, Italy, 1958. Lives in New York. In the collections of Whitney Museum of American Art, and Museum of Modern Art, New York; Art Institute of Chicago, and others. Dealer: Sidney Janis Gallery, New York.

Shahn, Ben

Born, Kaunas, Russia, 1898. To U. S., 1906. Studied: New York University; City College of New York; National Academy of Design. Trips to Europe, 1925 and 1927. Many illustrations for books; series of 10 water colors illustrating the Sacco-Vanzetti trial, 1931-32. Assisted Diego Rivera on the Rockefeller Center frescoes, 1932-33. Worked on WPA Federal Art Project, 1933-34. Has received many government commissions for murals, including Bronx Central Annex post office, New York; Jamaica, Long Island, Post Office; Federal Security Building, Washington, D. C. First one-man show, Downtown Gallery, New York, 1930; subsequent one-man shows: Downtown Gallery, New York, 1932, 1933, 1944, 1949, 1951, 1952, 1955. Retrospectives: Museum of Modern Art, New York, 1947; Venice *Biennale,* 1954. Included in Venice *Biennale,* 1956. Lives in Roosevelt, New Jersey. In the collections of Museum of Modern Art, and Whitney Museum of American Art, New York; Walker Art Center, Minneapolis; Phillips Gallery, Washington, D. C.; and others. Dealer: Downtown Gallery, New York.

Sheeler, Charles

Born, Philadelphia, 1883. Studied: Philadelphia School of Industrial Art, 1900-03; Pennsylvania Academy of the Fine Arts, Philadelphia, 1903-06. Trips to Europe, 1904, 1905, 1909. Exhibited in the Armory Show, 1913. One-man shows (painting and photography): De Zayas Gallery, New York, 1920; Whitney Studio Club, New York, 1924; Downtown Gallery, 1931, 1940, 1946, 1949, 1951, 1956. Retrospectives: Museum of Modern Art, New York, 1939; Art Galleries, University of California, Los Angeles, 1955. Artist in Residence, Phillips Academy, Andover, Mass., 1946. Lives in Irvington-on-Hudson, New York. In the collections of Columbus Gallery of Fine Arts, Columbus, Ohio; Museum of Modern Art, and Whitney Museum of American Art, New York; California Palace of the Legion of Honor, San Francisco; Fogg Art Museum, Harvard University, Cambridge, Mass.; the Worcester Art Museum, and others. Dealer: Downtown Gallery, New York.

Shinn, Everett

Born, Woodtown, N. J., 1876. Studied: Pennsylvania Academy of Fine Arts, Philadelphia. Illustrations in *Philadelphia Press* and other newspapers and magazines. Member of the Eight. Died, 1953. Retrospective: Ferargil Galleries, New York, 1943. In the collections of Whitney Museum of American Art, New York; Albright Art Gallery, Buffalo; Art Institute of Chicago; Phillips Gallery, Washington, D. C., and others. Dealer: Kraushaar Galleries, New York.

Sloan, John

Born, Lock Haven, Pa., 1871. Studied at the Pennsylvania Academy of Fine Arts. Staff artist for the *Philadelphia Press* and *Enquirer;* contributor to New York magazines. Member of the Eight. Taught at the Art Students League, New York. One of the founders of the Society of Independent Artists, New York, 1917.

Received many awards including the Honorable Mention, Carnegie Institute, 1905; Gold Medal, the Sesqui-Centennial Exposition, Philadelphia, 1926. Retrospectives: Addison Gallery of American Art, Andover, Mass., 1938; Whitney Museum of American Art, New York; Corcoran Gallery of Art, Washington, D. C.; Toledo Museum of Art, all in 1952. Died, 1951. In the collections of Art Institute of Chicago; Brooklyn Museum; Detroit Institute of Arts; Rochester Museum; Phillips Gallery, Washington, D. C.; Wadsworth Atheneum, Hartford; Whitney Museum of American Art, New York, and others. Dealer: Kraushaar Galleries, New York.

Smith, David

Born, Decatur, Ind., 1906. Studied briefly Ohio University, Notre Dame University; student of painting at the Art Students League, New York, under Jan Matulka, 1927-32. First one-man show, East River Gallery, New York, 1938. Recipient of Guggenheim Fellowship, 1950, 1951. Taught: Sarah Lawrence College, University of Arkansas, University of Indiana, University of Mississippi. Exhibited nationally and internationally, including group shows in Zurich and Paris, 1953. Retrospectives: Buchholz Gallery, New York, 1946; Willard Gallery, New York, 1946; Walker Art Center, Minneapolis, 1952; Cincinnati Museum, 1954; Museum of Modern Art, New York, 1957; XXIX Venice *Biennale*, Venice, Italy, 1958; V São Paulo *Bienal*, Brazil, 1959. Lives in Bolton Landing, New York. In the collections of Detroit Institute of Arts; Whitney Museum of American Art, and Museum of Modern Art, New York; Carnegie Institute, Pittsburgh; Munson-Williams-Proctor Institute, Utica, New York, and others.

Spencer, Niles

Born, Pawtucket, R. I., 1893. Studied: Rhode Island School of Design; Art Students League, New York;

and with Henri and Bellows. Trips to Europe, 1921, 1928. Received Honorable Mention, Carnegie Institute, Pittsburgh, 1930. First one-man show, Daniel Gallery, New York, 1925. Frequent exhibitions at Downtown Gallery, New York. Memorial exhibitions at Akron Art Institute and Museum of Modern Art, New York, 1954. Died, 1953. In the collections of Museum of Modern Art, Whitney Museum of American Art, and Metropolitan Museum of Art, all of New York, and others. Dealer: Downtown Gallery, New York.

Stella, Joseph

Born, Muro-Lucano, Italy, 1880. To U. S., 1900. First exhibited as an Italian belonging to the Futurist group. Studied: New York School of Art. Exhibited in Armory Show of 1913 and with the Society of Independent Artists, New York, 1917. Died, 1946. In the collections of *Société Anonyme*, Yale University; Newark Museum; Museum of Modern Art, Whitney Museum of American Art, New York, and others.

Still, Clyfford

Born, Grandin, N. D., 1904. Studied: Spokane University, Washington State College. Taught: Washington State University, 1933-41; California School of Fine Arts, 1946-50; Hunter College and Brooklyn College, New York. One-man shows: San Francisco Museum of Art, 1941; Art of This Century, 1946; Betty Parsons Gallery, New York, 1947, 1950, 1951. Exhibited in *15 Americans*, Museum of Modern Art, New York, 1952. Lives in New York. In the collections of Museum of Modern Art, New York; San Francisco Museum of Art, and others.

Tobey, Mark

Born, Centerville, Wis., 1890. Self-taught artist. First exhibited at Knoedler Gallery, New York, 1917. Traveled throughout the world. Studied later with Kenneth

Hayes Miller. Exhibited nationally and internationally, including Venice *Biennale*, 1948, 1956, 1958. Winner of grand prize, XXIX, Venice *Biennale*, Venice, Italy, 1958. Exhibited in *14 Americans*, Museum of Modern Art, New York, 1946. Retrospective: Whitney Museum of American Art, New York, 1951. Lives in Seattle, Washington. In the collections of Museum of Modern Art, and Whitney Museum of American Art, New York; Munson-Williams-Proctor Institute, Utica, N. Y.; San Francisco Museum of Art, and others. Dealer: Willard Gallery, New York.

Tomlin, Bradley Walker

Born, Syracuse, N. Y., 1899. Studied: Syracuse University. Trips to Europe. Taught: Sarah Lawrence College, Bronxville, N. Y. One-man shows: Montross Gallery, New York, 1924, 1927; Rehn Gallery, New York, 1931-42, 1944; Betty Parsons Gallery, New York, 1950, 1953. Exhibited in *Abstract Painting and Sculpture in America*, 1951, and *15 Americans*, 1952, both at the Museum of Art, New York. Retrospective: Whitney Museum of American Art, New York, 1957. Died, 1953. In the collections of Addison Gallery of American Art, Andover, Mass.; Brooklyn Museum; Metropolitan Museum of Art, Whitney Museum of American Art, and Museum of Modern Art, all of New York; Phillips Gallery, Washington, D. C.; University of Iowa, and others. Dealer: Betty Parsons Gallery, New York.

Weber, Max

Born, Byelostok, Russia, 1881. To U. S., 1891. Studied: Pratt Institute, Brooklyn, New York, 1898-1900; European academies. Trip to Europe, 1905-08. Studied with Henry Matisse. Exhibited nationally and internationally. First one-man show, Hass Gallery, New York, 1909. Showed at Stieglitz's 291 Gallery, New York, 1911. Retrospective: Whitney Museum of American Art, New York, 1949. Recipient of many awards including Gold Medal, Art Institute of Chicago, 1928; Corcoran Bronze Medal, 1941. Author of *Cubist Poems,* London, 1914, and *Primitives,* 1926. Lives in New York. In the collections of Brooklyn Museum; Museum of Modern Art, and Whitney Museum of American Art, New York; Wichita Museum; Santa Barbara Museum; Walker Art Center, Minneapolis, and others. Dealer: Paul Rosenberg Gallery, New York.

Zorach, William

Born, Eurburick-Kovno, Russia, 1887. To U. S., 1891. Studied: Cleveland School of Design; National Academy of Design, New York. One-man shows (sculpture and water colors): the Downtown Gallery, 1931-33, 1936, 1943-44, 1947-48, 1951, 1955. Contributor to art magazines and author of book, *Zorach Explains Sculpture.* Lives in Brooklyn, New York. In the collections of Museum of Modern Art, Whitney Museum of American Art, and Metropolitan Museum of Art, all of New York; Los Angeles Museum of Art; Munson-Williams-Proctor Institute, Utica, N. Y., and others. Dealer: Downtown Gallery, New York.

Selected References on
American Painting and Sculpture

by Bernard Karpel

Librarian, Museum of Modern Art, New York

MODERN ART

BARR, ALFRED H., JR., editor. *Cubism and Abstract Art*. New York Museum of Modern Art, 1936.

—— *Fantastic Art, Dada, Surrealism,* New York, Museum of Modern Art, 1937.

GOLDWATER, ROBERT. *Primitivism in Modern Painting.* New York, Harper, 1938.

HUNTER, SAM. *Modern French Painting.* New York, Dell, 1956.

ART SINCE 1945, by Will Grohmann, Herbert Read, Carlo Argan, J. P. Hodin, Marcel Brion, Sam Hunter and others. New York, Harry N. Abrams, 1958.

LAKE, CARLTON AND MAILLARD, ROBERT, editors. *Dictionary of Modern Painting.* New York, Paris Book Center, 1955.

MOTHERWELL, ROBERT, editor. *The Dada Painters and Poets.* New York, Wittenborn, Schultz, 1951.

RITCHIE, ANDREW. *Sculpture of the Twentieth Century.* New York, Museum of Modern Art, 1952.

SOBY, JAMES T. *After Picasso.* Hartford, Mitchell; New York, Dodd, Mead, 1935.

—— *Contemporary Painters.* New York, Museum of Modern art, 1948.

—— *Modern Art and the New Past.* Norman, University of Oklahoma, 1957.

SWEENEY, JAMES J. *Plastic Redirections in Twentieth Century Painting.* Chicago, University of Chicago, 1934.

AMERICAN ART AND CULTURE

AARON, DANIEL, editor. *America in Crisis.* New York, Knopf, 1952. Chapter 9, "Rebellion in Art," by Meyer

Schapiro, is on the Armory Show and its influence.

AMERICA AND ALFRED STIEGLITZ. Edited by W. Frank, L. Mumford, D. Norman, P. Rosenfeld, H. Rugg. Garden City, Doubleday, Doran, 1934.

BAUR, JOHN I. H. *Revolution and Tradition in Modern American Art*. Cambridge, Harvard University, 1951. The Library of Congress Series in American Civilization.

BOAS, GEORGE, editor. *Romanticism in America*. Baltimore, Johns Hopkins Press, 1940.

CAHILL, HOLGER AND BARR, ALFRED H. JR. *Art in America in Modern Times*. New York, Reynal and Hitchcock, 1934.

——— *Art in America: a Complete Survey*. New York, Reynal and Hitchcock, 1935.

COMMAGER, HENRY S. *The American Mind*. New Haven, Yale University Press, 1950.

FRANK, WALDO. *The Rediscovery of America*. New York and London, Scribners, 1929.

GOODRICH, LLOYD AND MORE, HERMAN. *Juliana Force and American Art*. New York, Whitney Museum of American Art, 1949.
"Survey of American art, 1909-1948."

GRACE, GEORGE C. AND WALLACE, DAVID H. *Dictionary of Artists in America, 1564-1860*. New York, Yale University, 1957.

HARVARD GUIDE TO AMERICAN HISTORY. Cambridge, Harvard University, 1954.
Sections on cultural and intellectual trends.

HOFFMANN, FREDERICK J., ALLEN, CHARLES AND ULRICH, CAROLYN F. *The Little Magazine*. Charles Allen, Princeton, N. J. Princeton Univ. Press, 1946. The literary, cultural and experimental periodical in America.

INDEX OF TWENTIETH CENTURY ARTISTS. New York, College Art Association, 1933-1937.
A bibliography on American artists.

KEPPEL, FREDERICK P. AND DUFFUS, R. L. *The Arts in American Life*. New York and London, McGraw-Hill, 1933. Recent social trends monographs.

KOUWENHOVEN, JOHN A. *Made in America: the Arts in Modern Civilization*. Garden City, Doubleday, 1948.

KUHN, WALT. *The Story of the Armory Show*. New York, the Author, 1938. Supplemented by a similar article in the *Art News Annual*, 1939.

LANDGREN, MARCHAL E. *Years of Art: the Story of the Art Students' League of New York*. New York, McBride, 1940.

LARKIN, OLIVER W. *Art and Life in America*. New York, Rinehart, 1949. Recipient of the Pulitzer Prize in History.

LYNES, RUSSELL. *The Tastemakers*. New York, Harper, 1954.

MC CAUSLAND, ELIZABETH. "A Selected Bibliography on American Painting and Sculpture." In *Who's Who in American Art*, v. 4, pp. 611-653. Washington, D. C., American Federation of Arts, 1947.
A chronological list "from colonial times to the present," this bibliography originally appeared in the *Magazine of Art*, v. 39, pp. 329-349, Nov. 1946.

MATHER, FRANK J. JR. *The American Spirit in Art*, by F. J. Mather, C. R. Morey, W. J. Henderson. New Haven, Yale University, 1927.
Vol. 12 of *The Pageant of America*.

MELLQUIST, JEROME. *The Emergence of an American Art*. New York, Scribner's, 1942.

MUMFORD, LEWIS. *The Brown Decades, 1865-1895*. 2nd rev. ed. New York, Dover, 1955 (c1931).

PACH, WALTER. *The Art Museum in America*. New York, Pantheon, 1948.

—— *Queer Thing, Painting: Forty Years in the World of Art*. New York and London, Harper, 1938.

RICHMAN, ROBERT, editor. *The Arts at Mid-Century*. New York, Horizon, 1954.

ROURKE, CONSTANCE. *The Roots of American Culture and Other Essays*. New York, Harcourt, Brace, 1942.

—— *American Humor*. 1931.

SAYLER, OLIVER M. *Revolt in the Arts*. New York, Brentano's, 1930. "Survey of the creation, distribution, and appreciation of art in America."

TOCQUEVILLE, ALEXIS DE. *Democracy in America.* London, 1835; 2 v. ed. New York, Knopf, 1942; abridged ed. New York, Oxford, 1947.

WHO'S WHO IN AMERICAN ART. Washington, D. C., American Federation of Arts, 1935-1947; New York, R. R. Bowker, 1953-current.

CRITICISM AND HISTORY IN AMERICA

BARKER, VIRGIL. *A Critical Introduction to American Painting.* New York, Whitney Museum of American Art, 1931.

BARNES, ALBERT C. *The Art in Painting.* New York, Harcourt, Brace, 1925.

BLESH, RUDI. *Modern Art U.S.A.: Men, Rebellion, Conquest 1900-1956.* New York, Knopf, 1956.

CAFFIN, CHARLES H. *How to Study Pictures.* New York, Century, 1905.

CHENEY, MARTHA C. *Modern Art in America.* New York and London, McGraw-Hill, 1939.

CHENEY, SHELDON. *A Primer of Modern Art.* New York, Boni and Liveright, 1924.

—— *The Story of Modern Art.* New York, Viking, 1941.

CORTISSOZ, ROYAL. *American Artists.* New York and London, Scribner's, 1923.

CRAVEN, THOMAS. *Modern Art—the Men, the Movements, the Meaning.* New York, Simon and Schuster, 1934.

DREIER, KATHERINE S. *Western Art and the New Era.* New York, Brentano, 1923.

EDDY, ARTHUR J. *Cubists and Post-Impressionists.* Chicago, McClurg, 1914; revised ed. 1919.

GALLATIN, ALBERT E. *American Water-Colourists.* New York, Dutton, 1922.

—— *Certain Contemporaries, a Set of Notes in Art Criticism.* New York, Lane, 1916.

HARTLEY, MARSDEN. *Adventures in the Arts.* New York, Boni & Liveright, 1921.

HARTMANN, SADAKICHI. *A History of American Art.* 2 vol. rev. ed. Boston, Page, 1932.

HENRI, ROBERT. *The Art Spirit.* Philadelphia, Lippincott, 1923; rev. ed. 1939.

JARVES, JAMES J. *Art-Hints*. New York, Harper, 1855.

—— *The Art-Idea*. New York, 1864.

—— *Art Thoughts*. New York, Hurd and Houghton, 1869.

JEWELL, EDWARD A. *Have We an American Art?* New York, Longmans, Green, 1939.

LA FOLLETTE, SUZANNE. *Art in America*. New York and London, Harper, 1929.

MATHER, FRANK J. *Modern Painting, a Study of Tendencies*. New York, Holt, 1927.

—— *Estimates in Art, Series II*. New York, Holt, 1931.

MOTHERWELL, ROBERT AND REINHARDT, AD, editors. *Modern Artists in America: First Series*. New York, Wittenborn, Schultz [1951].
Documentation by Bernard Karpel.

PACH, WALTER. *Modern Art in America*. New York, Kraushaar Art Galleries, 1928.

PAINTERS AND SCULPTORS OF MODERN AMERICA. New York, Crowell, 1942.
Introduction by M. Wheeler to articles from the "Magazine of Art."

SAN FRANCISCO ART ASSOCIATION. *The Western Round Table on Modern Art*. Edited by D. MacAgy. San Francisco, The Association, 1949.
Also abridged in Motherwell *Modern Artists in America* (1951).

SULLIVAN, LOUIS H. *Kindergarten Chats* (Revised 1918) *and Other Writings*. New York, Wittenborn, Schultz, 1947.

ZAYAS, MARIUS DE AND HAVILAND, PAUL B. *A Study of the Modern Evolution of Plastic Expression*. New York, "291" [Gallery], 1913.

LITERARY AND BIOGRAPHICAL WORKS

ADAMS, HENRY. *The Education of Henry Adams*. Washington, D. C. [Privately Printed], 1907. Other editions: Cambridge, Mass., Riverside Press, 1918; New York, Modern Library, 1931.

ANDERSON, SHERWOOD. *Sherwood Anderson's Memoirs*. New York, Harcourt Brace, 1942.

BEER, THOMAS. *The Mauve Decade*. Garden City, N. Y., Garden City Pub. Co., 1926; London, Knopf, 1926.

BOURNE, RANDOLPH S. *The History of a Literary Radical*. New York, Huebsch, 1920.

BROOKS, VAN WYCK. *America's Coming of Age*. New York, Huebsch, 1914.

CANBY, HENRY S. *The Age of Confidence*. New York, Farrar and Rinehart, 1934.

COWLEY, MALCOLM. *Exile's Return: a Narrative of Ideas*. New York, Norton, 1934.

DREISER, THEODORE. *The Genius*. New York, Lane, 1915.

HAPGOOD, HUTCHINS. *A Victorian in the Modern World*. New York, Harcourt, Brace, 1939.

HOFSTADTER, RICHARD. *The Age of Reform*. New York, Knopf, 1955.

HUNEKER, JAMES G. *Steeplejack*. New York, Scribner's, 1920.

JAMES, HENRY. *The American Scene*. New York, Harper, 1907; New York, Scribner's, 1946.

JOSEPHSON, MATTHEW. *Portrait of the Artist as American*. New York, Harcourt, Brace, 1930.

KAZIN, ALFRED. *On Native Grounds: an Interpretation of Modern American Prose Literature*. New York, Reynal and Hitchcock, 1942.

LAWRENCE, DAVID H. *Studies in Classic American Literature*. New York, Seltzer, 1923.

LUHAN, MABEL D. *Intimate Memoirs*, v. 3: *Movers and Shakers*. New York, Harcourt, Brace [1933-37].

MATTHIESSEN, FRANCIS O. *The American Renaissance*. London and New York, Oxford University Press, 1941.

MENCKEN, HENRY L. *Prejudices: Second Series*. New York, Knopf, 1923.

MILLER, HENRY. *Tropic of Cancer*. Paris, Obelisk, `1935. Published 1934; also 1939 edition.

PARRINGTON, VERNON L. *Main Currents in American Thought*. 3 v. New York, Harcourt, Brace, 1927-30.

ROSENFELD, PAUL. *Port of New York: Essays on Fourteen American Moderns*. New York, Harcourt, Brace, 1924.

SANTAYANA, GEORGE. *Character and Opinion in the United States*. New York, Scribner's, 1920.

STEIN, GERTRUDE. *The Autobiography of Alice B. Toklas.* New York, Literary Guild, 1933.

PERIODICALS AND SPECIAL NUMBERS

ART D'AUJOURD'HUI. Paris, June 1951.
"La Peinture aux États-Unis," edited by Michel Seuphor.

ART IN AMERICA. Cannondale, Conn., 1913-current.
Most valuable in its recent "New Series" quarterly, devoted to the Younger Americans, e.g., v. 46, no. 1, Feb. 1956: "New Talent in the U.S.A."

CAMERA WORK. Nos. 1-50. New York, 1902-1917.
Edited by Alfred Stieglitz. Includes 3 special numbers: 1906, 1912, 1913.

DIAL. New York, 1920-1929.
Vols. 68-86 edited by Marianne Moore and S. Thayer.

DYN. Nos. 1-6. Mexico, 1942-1944.
Edited by Wolfgang Paalen

EIDOS. Nos. 1-3. London, 1950.
"A Journal of Painting, Sculpture and Design."

MAGAZINE OF ART. Washington, D. C. and New York, 1916-1953.
Originally the *American Magazine of Art* (1916ff). Special March 1949 issue: "A Symposium—the State of American Art."

PERSPECTIVES. Nos. 1-16. New York, 1952-56.
Published by Intercultural Publications under a grant of the Ford Foundation.

PLASTIQUE. No. 3. Paris and New York, 1938.
American number, ed. by S. H. Taeuber-Arp, A. E. Gallatin, G. L. K. Morris.

POSSIBILITIES. No. 1, Winter 1947-48. New York, Wittenborn, Schultz, 1948. One issue, edited by R. Motherwell and others. Statements by artists of the New York School.

QUADRUM. Nos. 1-2. Brussels, Association pour la Diffusion Artistique et Culturelle, 1956-current.
International survey; foreign and English texts; American distributor: Wittenborn and Co., N. Y.

TIGER'S EYE. Nos. 1-9. Westport, Conn. 1947-1949.

Edited by R. and J. Stephan. Includes articles by B. B. Newman (no. 1, Oct. 1947; no. 3, Mar. 1948) and others; section on "The Ides of Art" (no. 2, Dec. 1947, no. 4, June 1948; no. 6 Dec. 1948); numerous illustrations.

"291." Nos. 1-12. New York, 1915-1916.

Edited by Alfred Stieglitz.

VVV. Nos. 1-4. New York, 1924-1944.

Edited by David S. Hare. Editorial advisers: A. Breton, M. Duchamp, M. Ernst.

ARTICLES

BALDINGER, W. S. "Formal Change in Recent American Painting." *Art Bulletin,* v. 19, pp. 580-591, Dec. 1937.

BOLANDER, K. S. "Ferdinand Howald and His Collection." *Bulletin of the Columbus Gallery of Fine Arts,* v. 1, pp. 7-12, Jan. 1931.

Additional Howald article, May 1934.

CAHILL, HOLGER. "Twentieth Century Art in the United States." *Marg* (Bombay), v. 10, no. 1, pp. 46-62, Dec. 1956.

"Sculpture," pp. 63-67.

COX, KENYON. "The Modern Spirit in Art" [at the Armory]. *Harper's Weekly,* v. 57, p. 10, Mar. 15, 1913.

DASBURG, ANDREW. "Cubism—Its Rise and Influence." *Arts,* v. 4, pp. 279-284, Nov. 1923.

DAVIES, ARTHUR B. "Explanatory Statement: the aim of the A. A. P. S." *Arts and Decoration,* v. 3, p. 149, Mar. 1913.

The Armory Association.

DE CASSERES, BENJAMIN. "American Indifference." *Camera Work,* no. 27, p. 24, 1909.

—— "The Unconscious in Art." *Camera Work,* no. 36, p. 17, 1911.

—— "Modernity and the Decadence." *Camera Work,* no. 37, p. 17, 1912.

—— "Insincerity: a New Vice." *Camera Work,* no. 42, p. 17, 1913.

GREENBERG, CLEMENT. "American-Type Painting." *Partisan Review*, v. 22, no. 2, pp. 179-196, Spring 1955.

—— "The Present Prospects of American Painting and Sculpture." *Horizon,* nos. 93-94, pp. 20-30, Oct. 1947.

—— [Reviews]. For references in *The Nation* and *Partisan Review* see listing in Goodall (below, p. 235).

HESS, THOMAS B. "U. S. Painting: Some Recent Directions." *Art News Annual,* v. 25, pp. 76-98, 174-180, 199, 1956.

HUNTER, SAM. "Painting by Another Name." *Art in America,* v. 42, pp. 291-295, Dec. 1954.

—— "The Eight—Insurgent Realists." *Art in America,* v. 44, pp. 20-22, 56-58, Fall 1956.

"IRASCIBLE EIGHTEEN." *New York Herald-Tribune,* p. 18, May 23, 1950. Editorial on artists' protest to the Metropolitan Museum.

KRAMER, HILTON. "The New American Painting." *Partisan Review,* v. 20, pp. 421-427, July—Aug. 1953.

LAFFAN, W. MACKAY. "The Material of American Landscape Painting." *American Art Review,* v. 1, p. 23, 1880.

LARKIN, OLIVER. "Alfred Stieglitz and '291.' " *Magazine of Art,* v. 40, pp. 179-183, May 1947.

LEWISOHN, SAM A. "Is There an American Art Tradition?" *Formes,* v. 21, pp. 204-205, Jan. 1932.

MC BRIDE, HENRY. "Modern Art." *Dial,* v. 81, pp. 86-88, July 1926.

Also numerous reviews on the New York scene in the *Dial.*

MATHER, FRANK J. "The Forum Exhibition." *The Nation,* v. 102, p. 340, Mar. 23, 1916.

—— "Old and New Art" [at the Armory]. *The Nation,* v. 96, pp. 240-243, Mar. 6, 1913.

—— "Some American Realists." *Arts and Decoration,* v. 7, pp. 13-16, Nov. 1916.

MELLQUIST, JEROME. "The Armory Show 30 Years Later." *Magazine of Art,* v. 36, pp. 298-301, Dec. 1943.

MELVILLE, ROBERT. "Action Painting, New York—Paris—London." *Ark,* no. 18, pp. 30-33, Nov. 1956.

MOTHERWELL, ROBERT. "The Painter and His Audience." *Perspectives USA,* no. 9, pp. 107-112, 1954.

—— "The Rise and Continuity of Abstract Art." *Arts and Architecture,* v. 68, pp. 20-21, Sept. 1951.

PACH, WALTER. "The Eight Then and Now." *Art News,* v. 42, pp. 25, 31, Jan. 1, 1944.

PECKHAM, MORSE. "The Triumph of Romanticism." *Magazine of Art,* v. 45, pp. 291-299, Nov. 1952.

ROOSEVELT, THEODORE. "A Layman's View of an Art Exhibition." *Outlook,* v. 103, pp. 718-720, Mar. 29, 1913.

ROSENBERG, HAROLD. "The American Action Painters." *Art News,* v. 51, pp. 22-23, 48-50, Dec. 1952.

ROSENBLUM, ROBERT. "The New Decade" [at the Whitney and the Museum of Modern Art]. *Arts Digest,* v. 29, pp. 20-23, May 15, 1955.

ROSENFELD, PAUL. "American Painting." *Dial,* v. 71, pp. 649-670, Dec. 1921.

SCHAPIRO, MEYER. "The Younger American Painters of Today" [at the Tate Gallery]. *The Listener,* no. 1404, pp. 146-147, Jan. 26, 1956.

—— "The Nature of Abstract Art." *Marxist Quarterly* (N. Y.), no. 1, pp. 77-98, Jan.-Mar. 1937.

SCHMALENBACH, FRITZ. "American Scene" [eine neue Malereiströmung in der Vereinigten Staaten]. *Werk,* v. 29, no. 1, pp. 25-31, Jan. 1942.

SEITZ, WILLIAM. "Spirit, Time and Abstract Expressionism." *Magazine of Art,* v. 46, pp. 80-87, Feb. 1953.

STEIN, LEO. "Panic in Art" [the Armory Show]. *New Republic,* v. 1, pp. 20-21, Nov. 7, 1914.

STEINBERG, LEO. "The Eye Is a Part of the Mind." *Partisan Review,* v. 20, pp. 194-212, Mar.-Apr. 1953.

SUTTON, DENYS. "The Challenge of American Art." *Horizon,* no. 118, pp. 268-284, Oct. 1949.

TANNENBAUM, LIBBY. "Notes of Mid-Century." *Magazine of Art,* v. 48, pp. 289-292, Dec. 1950.

SWEENEY, JAMES J. "Five American Painters." *Harper's Bazaar,* v. 78, pp. 76-77, Apr. 1944.

"WHAT ABSTRACT ART MEANS TO ME." *Bulletin of the Museum of Modern Art,* v. 18, no. 3, Spring 1951. Statements by A. Calder, S. Davis, W. de Kooning, F. Glarner, G. L. K. Morris, R. Motherwell.

WRIGHT, WILLARD H. "Forum Exhibition at the Anderson Galleries." *Forum*, v. 55, pp. 457-471, Apr. 1916.

"YOUNGER AMERICAN EXTREMISTS." *Life Magazine*, v. 25, no. 15, pp. 62-64, Oct. 11, 1948.

ZAYAS, MARIUS DE. "The Sun Has Set." *Camera Work*, Special Number, p. 57, June 1913.

CATALOGS, EXHIBITIONS, GROUPS

ALBRIGHT ART GALLERY. 50th Annual Exhibition: "50 Paintings, 1905-13," Buffalo, 1955.
Catalog introduction by Robert Goldwater. Includes discussion of the Armory Show and American taste.

AMERICAN ARSTRACT ARTISTS. New York, Ram Press and Wittenborn, Schultz, 1946.
Directory-Yearbook also issued 1938. Latest anthology issued 1957 by Wittenborn and Co.: *World of Abstract Art*.

ART OF THIS CENTURY. "Art of This Century—1910 to 1942." Edited by Peggy Guggenheim. New York [The Gallery], 1942.
Supplemented by her biography: *Out of This Century* (New York, Dial, 1946).

ASSOCIATION OF AMERICAN PAINTERS AND SCULPTORS. "International Exhibition of Modern Art." New York, The Association, 1913.
The "Armory Show" catalog; variant catalogs for Boston and Chicago exhibition. Preface by F. J. Gregg, statement by A. B. Davies.

BROOKLYN MUSEUM. "The Eight." Foreword by J. I. H. Haur. Brooklyn Institute of Arts and Sciences, 1943.
Shown Nov. 1943–Jan. 1944. Recollections by E. Shinn. Biographical notes.

CALIFORNIA PALACE OF THE LEGION OF HONOR. "4th Annual Exhibition of Contemporary American Painting." San Francisco, 1950.
Text by T. C. Have, J. MacAgy, F. S. Bartlett. Also "3rd Annual Exhibition of Painting, 1948-49" (Text by J. MacAgy).

CARNEGIE INSTITUTE, DEPARTMENT OF FINE ARTS. "Survey of American Painting." Introduction by Homer St.-Gaudens. Pittsburgh, 1940.

CENTURY ASSOCIATION. "Robert Henri and His Pupils." Essays by H. A. Read. New York, The Association, 1946.

CHICAGO ART INSTITUTE. "Abstract and Surrealist Art: 58th American Annual." Chicago, 1947.

THE FORUM. "Forum Exhibition of Modern Painters . . . on view at the Anderson Galleries, New York," Kennerly, 1916.
Foreword by Alfred Stieglitz.

GUGGENHEIM, SOLOMON R., MUSEUM. "Younger American Painters: a Selection." Introduction by J. J. Sweeney. New York, The Museum, 1954.

MINNEAPOLIS. UNIVERSITY OF MINNESOTA GALLERY. "40 American Painters, 1940-1950." Minneapolis, 1951.
Biographical notes.

NEW YORK METROPOLITAN MUSEUM OF ART. "100 American Painters of the 20th Century." Introduction by Robert B. Hale. New York, The Museum, 1950.

NEW YORK MUSEUM OF MODERN ART. [American Exhibitions]. New York, The Museum, 1930-1956.
For a detailed list see *Museum Bulletin*, no. 1, Nov. 1940. Selected exhibitions include: "Paintings by Nineteen Living Americans" (1930).

—— "American Painting and Sculpture, 1862-1932." Text by H. Cahill (1932).

—— "Americans 1942." Edited by D. C. Miller (1942).

—— "Romantic Painting in America." Edited by J. T. Soby and D. C. Miller (1943).

—— "American Realists and Magic Realists." Text by A. H. Barr, D. C. Miller, L. Kirstein and the artists (1943).

—— "Fourteen Americans." Edited by D. C. Miller, texts by the artists (1946).

"Abstract Painting and Sculpture in America." Edited by A. C. Ritchie (1951).

—— "15 Americans." Edited by D. C. Miller, texts by the artists (1952).

—— "12 Americans." Edited by D. C. Miller, texts by the artists (1956).

NEW YORK UNIVERSITY. "Museum of Living Art: A. E. Gallatin Collection." New York, The University, 1940.
Collection now in the Philadelphia Museum of Art, with current catalogue.

PHILADELPHIA MUSEUM OF ART. "Artists of the Philadelphia Press: William Glackens, George Luks, Everett Shinn, John Sloan." Philadelphia, The Museum, 1945.
Also article in the *Museum Bulletin*, Nov. 1945.

PHILLIPS COLLECTION. "The Phillips Collection, a Museum of Modern Art and Its Sources": Catalogue. Washington, D. C., 1952.
Supplemented by: "A Collection in the Making" (New York, 1926).

—— "Bulletin of the Phillips Collection, 1927-1932" (issued 1929-30 as "Art and Understanding").

—— "The Artist Sees Differently" (2 v., 1931).

—— "American Paintings of the Phillips Collection" (1944).

SAO PAULO, V. BIENAL. Catalogue: Guston, Smith, Francis, Frankenthaler, Goldberg, Kadish, Kohn, Leslie, Marca-Relli, Metcalf, Mitchell, Rauschenberg. Minneapolis, The Minneapolis Institute of Arts, 1959. Text by Sam Hunter.

SOCIETY OF INDEPENDENT ARTISTS. "Catalogue of the First Annual Exhibition, Grand Central Palace, April 10 to May 6." New York, 1917.

TATE GALLERY. "Modern Art in the United States: A Selection from the Collection of the Museum of Modern Art." London, 1956.
Organized by the International Circulating Exhibitions division of the Museum of Modern Art. Introduction by Cahill also published in *Marg* (Dec. 1956).

URBANA, UNIVERSITY OF ILLINOIS. "Contemporary American Painting." Urbana, Ill., The University, 1948—current.
Annuals issued 1948, 1950, 1951, 1953, 1955, 1957, including prefaces by A. S. Weller. Sculpture included in 1953, 1957.

VENICE, XXIX BIENNALE. "Lipton, Rothko, Smith, Tobey."

Catalogue, New York, Museum of Modern Art, 1958. Texts by Sam Hunter and Frank O'Hara.

VENICE, XXV BIENNALE. "Catalogo." Pp. 374-386. Venezia, Alfieri, 1950. Included American section of seven artists; texts by D. Phillips, A. H. Frankfurter, A. H. Barr, Jr.

VENICE, XXVII BIENNALE, AMERICAN PAVILION. "2 Pittori: De Kooning, Shahn." "3 Scultori: Lachaise, Lassaw, Smith." New York, Museum of Modern Art, 1954. Exhibition organized by the Museum of Modern Art. Texts and artist's statements in Italian and English.

VIRGINIA MUSEUM OF FINE ARTS. "American Painting 1950." Foreword by J. J. Sweeney. Richmond, Va., 1950.

WALKER ART CENTER. "Contemporary American Painting." Minneapolis, 1950. Foreword to 5th Biennial by H. H. Arnason.

WHITNEY MUSEUM OF AMERICAN ART. [American Exhibitions]. New York, 1935-1955. These have included, in part, the following: "Abstract Painting in America" (1935).

—— "New York Realists, 1900-1914." Text by A. H. Read (1937).

—— "20th Century Artists . . . from the Permanent Collections" (1939).

—— "Pioneers of Modern Art in America." Text by L. Goodrich (1946).

—— "The New Decade: 35 American Painters and Sculptors." Text by J. I. H. Baur (1955).

YALE UNIVERSITY ART GALLERY. "Collection of the Société Anonyme: Museum of Modern Art 1920." New Haven, Conn., Associates in Fine Arts, 1950. K. S. Dreier and M. Duchamp, trustees; G. H. Hamilton, editor; notes and bibliographies.

PAINTING IN THE U.S.

BARKER, VIRGIL. *American Painting—History and Interpretation*. New York, Macmillan, 1950.

BAUR, JOHN I. H., editor. *American Painting in the 19th Century*. New York, Praeger, 1953.

BAUR, JOHN I. H., editor. *New Art in America: 50 American Painters in the 20th Century.* New York Graphic Society and F. A. Praeger, 1957.

Texts also by L. Goodrich, D. C. Miller, J. T. Soby, F. S. Wight.

BOSWELL, PEYTON JR. *Modern American Painting.* New York, Dodd, Mead, 1939.

BROWN, MILTON. *American Painting from the Armory Show to the Depression.* Princeton, N. J., Princeton University Press, 1955.

Extensive bibliography.

BRUCE, EDWARD AND WATSON, FORBES. *Art in Federal Buildings.* Vol. 1: "Mural Designs, 1934-36." Washington, D. C., Art in Federal Buildings, Inc., 1936.

CAFFIN, CHARLES H. *The Story of American Painting.* New York, Stokes, 1907.

FLEXNER, JOHN T. *A Short History of American Painting.* Boston, Houghton Mifflin, 1950.

GOODALL, DONALD B. AND KASANIN, MARC C. *Partial Bibliography of American Abstract-Expressive Painting, 1943-1956.* University of S. California. Department of Fine Arts, 1956.

HESS, THOMAS B. *Abstract Painting—Background and American Phase.* New York, Viking, 1950.

ISHAM, SAMUEL. *The History of American Painting.* New York, Macmillan, 1927. Revised edition, 1936, with supplement by Royal Cortissoz.

JANIS, SIDNEY. *Abstract and Surrealist Art in America.* New York, Reynal and Hitchcock, 1944.

KOOTZ, SAMUEL. *Modern American Painters.* New York, Brewer and Warren, 1930.

—— *New Frontiers in American Painting.* New York, Hastings House, 1943.

MORRIS, KYLE, editor. ["Contemporary Slides, a Visual and Documentary Report on the New York Exhibition Scene"]. New York, Contemporary Slides, 1954—current.

Mimeograph notes accompany a series of color slides. Issued in parts with cumulated index.

POHL, LA VERA ANN. *Die Entwicklung der Malerei in Amerika von 1913-1938*. Bonn, J. F. Carthaus, 1939. Dissertation for Bonn University. Bibliography.

RICHARDSON, EDGAR P. *American Romantic Painting*. New York, Weyhe, 1944.
Painting in America: the Story of 450 Years. New York, Crowell, 1956. Bibliography.

SUTTON, DENYS. *American Painting*. London, Avalon, 1948; New York, Transatlantic Arts, 1949.

WALKER, JOHN AND MAGGILL, JAMES. *Great American Paintings from Smibert to Bellows, 1729-1924*. New York, London, Toronto: Oxford University Press, 1943.

WATSON, FORBES. *American Painting Today*. Washington, D. C., American Federation of Arts, 1939.

WIGHT, FREDERICK S. *Milestones of American Painting in Our Century*. Boston, Institute of Contemporary Art; New York, Chanticleer, 1949.

WRIGHT, WILLARD H. *Modern Painting: Its Tendency and Meaning*. New York and London, Lane, 1915.

AMERICAN PAINTERS

BAZIOTES

15 AMERICANS. Pp. 12-14. New York, Museum of Modern Art, 1952.

BELLOWS

CHICAGO ART INSTITUTE. "George Bellows: Paintings, Drawings and Prints." Chicago, The Institute, 1946.
Supplemented by essay by D. C. Rich: "Bellows Revalued." *Magazine of Art*, v. 39, pp. 139-142, Apr. 1946.

EGGERS, GEORGE W. "George Bellows." New York, Whitney Museum of American Art, 1931.

BENTON

BENTON, THOMAS H. *An Artist in America*. New York, McBride, 1937.

BLOOM

FREEDBERG, SYDNEY. "Hyman Bloom." *Perspectives USA*, No. 6, pp. 45-54, Winter 1954.

WIGHT, FREDERICK. "Hyman Bloom." Boston, Institute of Contemporary Art, [1954].
Catalog for exhibit at Whitney Museum and elsewhere.

BLUME

BLUME, PETER. "After Superrealism." *New Republic,* v. 80, pp. 338-340, Oct. 3, 1934.

SOBY, JAMES T. "History of a Picture: *South of Scranton.*" *Saturday Review of Literature,* v. 30, pp. 30-32, Apr. 26, 1943.

—— "Peter Blume's Eternal City." *Museum of Modern Art Bulletin,* v. 10, pp. 1-6, Apr. 1943.

BROOKS

JAMES BROOKS. *Magazine of Art* v. 46, pp. 24-25, Jan. 1953.

TWELVE AMERICANS. Pp. 14-20, New York, Museum of Modern Art, 1956.

BURCHFIELD

ALBRIGHT ART GALLERY. "Charles Burchfield: Retrospective Exhibition of Water Colors and Oils, 1916-1943." Buffalo, Buffalo Fine Arts Academy, 1944.

WHITNEY MUSEUM OF AMERICAN ART. "Charles Burchfield." New York, 1956.
Also exhibited at Baltimore, Boston, etc. Text by J. I. H. Baur.

CHASE

ART ASSOCIATION OF INDIANAPOLIS. "Chase Memorial Exhibition." Indianapolis, John Herron Art Institute, 1949.

ROOF, KATHERINE M. *The Life and Art of William Merritt Chase.* New York, Scribner's, 1917.

COLEMAN

GLASSGOLD, C. A. "Glenn O. Coleman." New York, Whitney Museum of American Art, 1932.
Supplemented by "Glenn O. Coleman Memorial Exhibition" (Whitney Museum, 1932).

CORNELL

LEVY, JULIEN. *Surrealism.* Pp. 77-88, New York, Black Sun, 1936.

CURRY

SCHMECKEBIER, LAURENCE E. *John Steuart Curry's Pageant*

of America. New York, American Artists Group, 1943.

DAVIES

CORTISSOZ, ROYAL. "Arthur B. Davies." New York, Whitney Museum of American Art, 1931.

WATSON, FORBES. "Arthur Bowen Davies." *Magazine of Art,* v. 45, pp. 362-368, Dec. 1952.

DAVIS

SWEENEY, JAMES J. "Stuart Davis." New York, Museum of Modern Art, 1945.

WALKER ART CENTER [Stuart Davis]. Minneapolis, The Museum, 1957.
    Exhibition catalog also issued by the Whitney Museum.

DE KOONING

DE KOONING, WILLEM. "What Abstract Art Means to Me." *Museum of Modern Art Bulletin,* v. 18, no. 3, pp. 4-8, 1951.

HESS, THOMAS B. "De Kooning Paints a Picture: Woman." *Art News,* v. 52, pp. 30-33, 64-67, Mar. 1953.

DEMUTH

FAISON, S. L. JR. "Fact and Art in Charles Demuth." *Magazine of Art,* v. 43, pp. 123-128, Apr. 1950.

RITCHIE, ANDREW C. "Charles Demuth." New York, Museum of Modern Art, 1950.

DOVE

CORNELL UNIVERSITY, WHITE MUSEUM OF ART. "Arthur G. Dove, a Retrospective Exhibition." Ithaca, N. Y., Cornell Univ., 1954.
    Text by D. Phillips, A. R. Solomon.

GOLDWATER, ROBERT. "Arthur Dove." *Perspectives USA,* No. 2, pp. 78-88, Winter 1952.

DU BOIS

DU BOIS, GUY PÈNE. *Artists Say the Silliest Things.* New York, American Artists Group and Duell, Sloan and Pearce, 1940.

DUVENECK

HEERMANN, NORBERT. *Frank Duveneck.* Boston, Houghton Mifflin, 1918.

EAKINS

GOODRICH, LLOYD. "Thomas Eakins, His Life and Works."
New York, Whitney Museum of American Art, 1933.

EILSHEMIUS

SCHACK, WILLIAM. *And He Sat Among the Ashes.* New
York, American Artists Group, 1939.

FRIEDMAN

HESS, THOMAS B. "Friedman's Tragedy and Triumph." *Art
News,* v. 48, pp. 26-27, Feb. 1950.

SCHACK, W. "Ordeal of Arnold Friedman." *Commentary,*
v. 9, pp. 40-46, Jan. 1950.

GLACKENS

DU BOIS, GUY PÈNE. "William Glackens." New York, Whitney Museum of American Art, 1931.
    Also "Memorial Exhibition Catalog," Dec. 1939–Jan.
    1939.

GORKY

DE KOONING, ELAINE. "Gorky, Painter of His Own Legend."
Art News, v. 49, pp. 38-41, 63-66, Jan. 1951.
    Also note preface by André Breton to Julien Levy Gal-
    lery catalog (1945): "The Eye of Spring, Arshile
    Gorky."

SCHWABACHER, ETHEL. "Arshile Gorky: Memorial Exhibition." New York, Whitney Museum of American Art,
1951.
    Also shown at Minneapolis, San Francisco.

GOTTLIEB

FITZSIMMONS, JAMES. "Adolph Gottlieb" *Everyday Art
Quarterly* (Minneapolis), no. 25, pp. 1-4, 1953.

GOTTLIEB, ADOLPH. "My Paintings." *Arts and Architecture,*
v. 68, pp. 20-21, Sept. 1951.

GRAVES

REXROTH, KENNETH. "The Visionary Painting of Morris
Graves." *Perspectives USA,* no. 10, pp. 58-66, Winter
1955.

WIGHT, FREDERICK S. *Morris Graves.* Berkeley and Los Angeles, Univ. of California Press, 1956.
    Exhibition also shown at Whitney Museum, N. Y.

GUSTON

JANSON, H. W. "Philip Guston." *Magazine of Art,* v. 40, pp. 54-58, Feb. 1947.

TWELVE AMERICANS. Pp. 36-43, New York, Museum of Modern Art, 1956.
Supplemented by Leo Steinberg review, *Arts,* v. 30, pp. 42-45, June 1956.

HARTIGAN

TWELVE AMERICANS. Pp. 52-57, New York, Museum of Modern Art, 1956.

HARTLEY

MC CAUSLAND, ELIZABETH. Marsden Hartley. Minneapolis, University of Minnesota, 1952.

WHEELER, MONROE. "Marsden Hartley." in "Lyonel Feininger—Marsden Hartley." New York, Museum of Modern Art, 1944.
With statement by the artist.

HASSAM

ADAMS, ADELINE V. *Childe Hassam.* New York, American Academy of Arts and Letters, 1938.

POUSETTE-DART, NATHANIEL, compiler. *Childe Hassam.* New York, Stokes, 1922.

HENRI

READ, HELEN A. "Robert Henri." New York, Whitney Museum of American Art, 1931.

YARROW, W. AND BOUCHE, L., editors. *Robert Henri, His Life and Works.* New York, Boni and Liveright, 1921.

HOFMANN

HOFMANN, HANS. "Search for the Real, and Other Essays." Andover, Mass., Addison Gallery of American Art, 1948.

WIGHT, FREDERICK S. "Hans Hofmann." New York, Whitney Museum of American Art, 1957.

HOMER

GOODRICH, LLOYD. "Winslow Homer." New York, Whitney Museum of American Art, 1944.

HOPPER

BARR, ALFRED H. JR. "Edward Hopper, Retrospective Exhibition." New York, Museum of Modern Art, 1933.

GOODRICH, LLOYD. "Edward Hopper, Retrospective Exhibition." New York, Whitney Museum of American Art, 1950.

KLINE

GOODNOUGH, ROBERT. "Kline Paints a Picture: Abstract Painting." *Art News,* v. 51, pp. 36-39, Dec. 1952.

TWELVE AMERICANS. Pp. 58-63, New York, Museum of Modern Art, 1956.
Supplemented by Leo Steinberg review ["Kline at the Janis Gallery"],
Arts, v. 30, pp. 42-44, Apr. 1956.

KUNIYOSHI

GOODRICH, LLOYD. "Yasuo Kuniyoshi, Retrospective Exhibition." New York, Whitney Museum of American Art, 1948.

YASUO KUNIYOSHI. New York, American Artists Group, 1945.

LAWSON

DU BOIS, GUY PÈNE. "Ernest Lawson." New York, Whitney Museum of American Art, 1932.

LEVINE

WIGHT, FREDERICK S. "Jack Levine." Boston, Institute of Contemporary Art, 1952.
Exhibited also at the Whitney Museum, N. Y., and elsewhere.

LUKS

CARY, ELIZABETH L. "George Luks." New York, Whitney Museum of American Art, 1931.

MACDONALD-WRIGHT

LOS ANGELES COUNTY MUSEUM. "Retrospective Showing of the Work of Stanton Macdonald-Wright." Los Angeles, 1956.
Introduction by R. F. Brown.

MAC IVER

BAUR, JOHN I. H. "Loren MacIver—I. Rice Pereira, Retrospective Exhibition." New York, Whitney Museum of American Art, 1953.

MARIN

HELM, MAC KINLEY. *John Marin.* Boston, Pellegrini and Cudahy and Institute of Contemporary Art, 1948.

LOS ANGELES, UNIVERSITY OF CALIFORNIA ART GALLERY. "John Marin Memorial Exhibition." Los Angeles, Cal., University of California, 1955.
Texts by D. Phillips, W. C. Williams, D. Norman. Also shown at Cleveland, Boston, Washington, San Francisco.

NORMAN, DOROTHY, editor. *Selected Writings of John Marin.* New York, Pellegrini and Cudahy, 1949.

SOBY, JAMES T. "The Paintings of John Marin." *Perspectives USA,* no. 11, pp. 48-53, Spring 1955.

MAURER

MC CAUSLAND, ELIZABETH. *Alfred Maurer.* New York, A. A. Wyn, 1951. Also catalog jointly issued by Whitney Museum, N. Y., and Walker Art Center, Minneapolis (1949).

MOTHERWELL

DOCUMENTS OF MODERN ART. "Director: Robert Motherwell." New York, Wittenborn, Schultz, 1946-1955.

KEES, WELDON. "Robert Motherwell." *Magazine of Art,* v. 41, pp. 86-88, Mar. 1948.

MOTHERWELL, ROBERT. "The Modern Painter's World." *Dyn,* v. 6, p. 14, Nov. 1944.

—— "Painter's objects." *Partisan Review,* v. 11, pp. 93-97, Winter 1944.

—— "What Abstract Art Means to Me." *Museum of Modern Art Bulletin,* v. 18, no. 3, 1951.

MYERS

MYERS, JEROME. "The Artist in Manhattan." New York, American Artists Group, 1940.

O'KEEFFE

RICH, DANIEL C. "Georgia O'Keeffe." Chicago, Art Institute of Chicago, 1943.

POLLOCK

GREENBERG, CLEMENT. [Art Reviews]. *The Nation,* Nov. 27, 1943; Apr. 7, 1945; Apr. 13, 1946; Dec. 28, 1946;

Feb. 1, 1947; Jan. 24, 1948. *Partisan Review*, no. 1, Jan.-Feb. 1952. *Harper's Bazaar*, Feb. 1952.

HUNTER, SAM. "Jackson Pollock." *Museum of Modern Art Bulletin*, v. 24, no. 2, 1956-57.
Includes catalog of exhibition and bibliography.

NEW WORLD WRITING: "9th Mentor Selection." Pp. 174-192, New York, New American Library, 1956.
Includes "Jackson Pollock: The Maze and the Minotaur" by Sam Hunter.

PRENDERGAST

ADDISON GALLERY OF AMERICAN ART. "The Prendergasts: Retrospective Exhibition of the Work of Maurice and Charles Prendergast." Andover, Mass., Phillips Academy, 1938.

BREUNING, MARGARET. "Maurice Prendergast." New York, Whitney Museum of American Art, 1931.

ROTHKO

COLLIER, OSCAR. "Mark Rothko." *Iconograph* (N. Y.), pp. 40-44, Fall 1947.

MAC AGY, DOUGLAS. "Mark Rothko." *Magazine of Art*, v. 42, pp. 20-21, Jan. 1949.

ROTHKO, MARK. "The Romantics Were Prompted." *Possibilities* (N. Y.), no. 1, pp. 84-93, Winter 1947-48.

RUSSELL

ROSE FRIED GALLERY. "Morgan Russell, 1884-1953: an Exhibition in Memoriam." New York, 1953.
Catalog includes homage by Holger Cahill; statement by artist (1913). Same gallery also issued, 1953, folder for "The Synchromists: Morgan Russell, S. Macdonald-Wright, Patrick Henry Bruce."

MAURSTED, BETTY. "Morgan Russell." *Walker Art Center Calendar*, pp. [3-4], Apr. 1954.

RYDER

PRICE, FREDERIC N. *Ryder, 1847-1917*. New York, Rudge, 1932.

SHAHN

RODMAN, SELDEN. *Portrait of the Artist as American*. New York, Harper, 1951.

SOBY, JAMES T. *Ben Shahn.* West Drayton, Middlesex, Penguin Books and New York, Museum of Modern Art, 1947.
Supplemented by *Bulletin of the Museum of Modern Art,* nos. 4-5, 1947.

SHEELER

ROURKE, CONSTANCE. *Charles Sheeler.* New York, Harcourt, Brace, 1938.

WILLIAMS, WILLIAM C. "Charles Sheeler." New York, Museum of Modern Art, 1939.

SHINN

CANDEE, M., editor. "Everett Shinn." *Current Biography* (N.Y.), v. 12, no. 5, pp. 49-51, May 1951.

KENT, N. "The Versatile Art of Everett Shinn." *American Artist,* v. 9, pp. 8-13, 35-37, Oct. 1945.

SLOAN

BROOKS, VAN WYCK. *John Sloan: A Painter's Life.* New York, Dutton, 1955.

GOODRICH, LLOYD. "John Sloan: Retrospective Exhibition." New York, Whitney Museum of American Art, 1952.

SLOAN, JOHN. "Gist of Art." New York, American Artists Group, 1939.

SPENCER

CAHILL, HOLGER. "Niles Spencer." *Magazine of Art,* v. 45, pp. 313-315, Nov. 1952.

WATSON, FORBES. "A note on Niles Spencer." *The Arts* (N.Y.), v. 8, pp. 166-169, Sept. 1925.
Supplemented by his "Niles Spencer: "Interview," *American Artist,* v. 8, pp. 14-17, Oct. 1944.

STILL

15 AMERICANS. Pp. 21-23, New York, Museum of Modern Art, 1952.
Includes letter by the artist.

TOBEY

FLANNER, JANET. "Tobey, Mystique Errant." *L'Oeil,* v. 1, no. 6, pp. 26-31, June 15, 1955.

PORTLAND ART MUSEUM. "Paintings by Mark Tobey." Portland, 1945.

Also exhibited at Detroit and San Francisco. Supplemented by "Mark Tobey Retrospective Exhibition," New York, Whitney Museum of American Art, 1951.

TOMLIN

BAUR, JOHN I. H. ["Bradley Walker Tomlin"]. New York, Whitney Museum of American Art, 1957.

15 AMERICANS. Pp. 24-26, New York, Museum of Modern Art, 1952.

TWACHTMAN

CLARK, ELIOT C. *John Twachtman.* New York [Privately printed], 1924.
American Artists Series.

TWORKOV

PORTER, FAIRFIELD. "Tworkov Paints a Picture." *Art News,* v. 52, pp. 30-33, May 1953.

TWORKOV, JACK ["Statement on His Work"]. *Baltimore Museum News,* v. 12, p. 4, Nov. 1948.

WEBER

CAHILL, HOLGER. "Max Weber." New York, Downtown Gallery, 1930.
Supplemented by "Max Weber: Retrospective Exhibition," New York, Museum of Modern Art, 1930.

GOODRICH, LLOYD. "Max Weber Retrospective Exhibition." New York, Macmillan Co., for the Whitney Museum of American Art, 1949.

WOOD

GARWOOD, DARRELL. *Artist in Iowa: a Life of Grant Wood.* New York, Norton, 1944.

SCULPTURE IN AMERICA

BRUMMÉ, C. LUDWIG. *Contemporary American Sculpture.* New York, Crown, 1948.
Foreword by William Zorach. Bibliography.

GIEDION-WELCKER, CAROLA. *Contemporary Sculpture: an Evolution in Volume and Space.* New York, Wittenborn, 1955.
Biographical and bibliographical notes on Calder, Ferber, Hare, Lassaw, Lippold, Lipton, Smith.

GREENBERG, CLEMENT. "The Present Prospects of American Painting and Sculpture." *Horizon*, nos. 93-94, pp. 20-30, Oct. 1947.

—— "The New Sculpture." *Partisan Review*, v. 16, pp. 637-642, June 1949.

IDES OF ART: "14 sculptors write." *Tiger's Eye*, no. 4, pp. 73-84, June 1948.

MILLER, DOROTHY C., editor. "Fourteen Americans." New York, Museum of Modern Art, 1946.
Includes Hare, Noguchi, Roszak "with statements."

—— editor. "15 Americans." New York, Museum of Modern Art, 1952.
Includes Ferber, Lippold, "with statements."

—— editor. "12 Americans." New York, Museum of Modern Art, 1956.
Includes Hague, Lassaw, Lipton, de Rivera "with statements."

MUNRO, ELEANOR. "Explorations in Form: a View of Some Recent American Sculpture." *Perspectives USA*, no. 16, pp. 160-172, Summer 1956.

NEW YORK, MUSEUM OF MODERN ART. "American Painting and Sculpture, 1862-1932." New York, 1932.
Essay by Holger Cahill.

NEW YORK, MUSEUM OF MODERN ART. "The New Sculpture: a Symposium." New York, 1952.
Unpublished typescript report of meeting. Speakers: Smith, Roszak, Ferber, Lippold. Moderator: A. C. Ritchie.

RITCHIE, ANDREW C. "Abstract Painting and Sculpture in America." New York, Museum of Modern Art, 1951.
Bibliography on American art and sculpture.

SCHNIER, JACQUES. *Sculpture in Modern America*. Berkeley and Los Angeles, Univ. of California, 1948.

SEYMOUR, CHARLES JR. *Tradition and Experiment in Modern Sculpture*. Washington, D. C., American University Press, 1949.

STONE, WARREN R. "The Contemporary Movement in American Sculpture." *Art*, no. 15, pp. 6-7, June 9, 1955.

TAFT, LORADO. "Modern Tendencies in Sculpture." Chicago, Art Institute of Chicago, 1921.

SCULPTORS

CALDER

CALDER, ALEXANDER. "Mobiles." In M. Evans, editor, *The Painter's Object*, pp. 63-68, London, Howe, 1937.

SARTRE, JEAN-PAUL. "Existentialist on Mobilist." *Art News*, v. 46, no. 10, pp. 22-23, 55-56, Dec. 1947.

SWEENEY, JAMES J. "Alexander Calder." 2nd edition. New York, Museum of Modern Art, 1951.

CORNELL

JOSEPH CORNELL. *Design Quarterly*, no. 30, p. 12, 1954.

DE CREEFT

CAMPOS, JULES. "José de Creeft." New York, Herrmann, 1945.

FERBER

FERBER, HERBERT. "On Sculpture and Painting." *Tiger's Eye*, no. 4, pp. 75-76, June 1948.

—— "On Sculpture." *Art in America*, v. 42, pp. 262-265, Dec. 1954.

GOODNOUGH, ROBERT. "Ferber Makes a Sculpture." *Art News*, v. 51, pp. 40-43, 66, Nov. 1952.

FLANNAGAN

FLANNAGAN, JOHN B. *Letters . . . with an Introduction by W. R. Valentiner*. New York, Curt Valentin, 1942.

MILLER, DOROTHY C., editor. "Sculpture of John B. Flannagan." New York, Museum of Modern Art, 1942.

GROSS

LOMBARDO, JOSEF V. *Chaim Gross, Sculptor*. New York, Dalton House, 1949.

HAGUE

HESS, THOMAS B. "Introducing the Sculpture of Raoul Hague." *Art News*, v. 53, pp. 19-21, Jan. 1955.

HARE

GOLDWATER, ROBERT. "David Hare." *Art in America*, v. 44, pp. 18-20, Winter 1956

HARE, DAVID. "The Spaces of the Mind." *Magazine of Art*, v. 43, pp. 48-53, Feb. 1950.

SARTRE, JEAN-PAUL. "N-Dimensional Sculpture." In Samuel Kootz Gallery, "Women, a Collaboration . . . ," pp. [33-35], New York, Kootz Editions, 1948.

LACHAISE

GALLATIN, ALBERT E. *Gaston Lachaise*. New York, Dutton, 1924.

KIRSTEIN, LINCOLN. "Gaston Lachaise: Retrospective Exhibition." New York, Museum of Modern Art, 1935. Supplemented by "Gaston Lachaise [Exhibition]," New York, Knoedler, 1947.

LASSAW

CAMPBELL, L. "Lassaw Makes a Sculpture: Clouds of Magellan." *Art News*, v. 53, pp. 24-27, 66-67, Mar. 1954.

SAWIN, MARTICA. "Ibram Lassaw." *Arts*, v. 30, pp. 22-26, Dec. 1955.

LIPPOLD

CAMPBELL, LAWRENCE. "Lippold Makes a Construction." *Art News*, v. 55, pp. 30-33, Oct. 1956.

LIPPOLD, RICHARD. "Sculpture?" *Magazine of Art*, v. 44, pp. 315-319, Dec. 1951. Additional texts in *Tiger's Eye*, June 1948; *Arts and Architecture*, Aug. 1947, May 1950; *Art in America*, Winter 1956.

LIPTON

LIPTON, SEYMOUR. "Some Notes on My Work." *Magazine of Art*, v. 40, pp. 264-265, Nov. 1947.

—— Experience and Sculptural Form." *College Art Journal*, v. 9, pp. 52-54, 1949.

RITCHIE, ANDREW C. "Seymour Lipton." *Art in America*, v. 44, pp. 14-17, Winter 1956.

MALDARELLI

MODERN CLASSICIST. *Life*, no. 12, pp. 137-140, Mar. 24, 1947.

WATSON, E. W. *"Oronzio Malderelli"* [interview] *American Artist*, v. 12, pp. 35-39, Mar. 1948.

NADELMAN

KIRSTEIN, LINCOLN. "Sculpture of Elie Nadelman." New York, Museum of Modern Art, 1948.

MURRELL, WILLIAM. *Elie Nadelman.* Woodstock, N. Y., Fisher, 1924.

SMITH

DE KOONING, ELAINE. "David Smith Makes a Sculpture." *Art News,* v. 50, pp. 38-41, 50-51, Sept. 1951.

GOOSEN, E. C. "David Smith." *Arts,* v. 30, no. 6, pp. 23-27, Mar. 1956.

GREENBERG, CLEMENT. "David Smith." *Art in America,* v. 44, pp. 30-33, Winter 1956.

HUNTER, SAM. "David Smith." New York, Museum of Modern Art, 1957.

Includes exhibition catalog and bibliography.

MELTZOFF, STANLEY. "David Smith and Social Realism." *Magazine of Art,* v. 39, pp. 98-101, Mar. 1946.

SMITH, DAVID. "Thoughts on Sculpture." *College Art Journal,* v. 13, no. 2, pp. 96-100, 1954.

—— "Second thoughts on sculpture," no. 3, pp. 203-207, 1954.

YOUNG

ADDISON GALLERY OF ART. "Mahonri M. Young: Retrospective Exhibition." Andover, Mass., Phillips Academy, 1940.

ZORACH

WINGERT, PAUL S. *The Sculpture of William Zorach.* New York and Chicago, Pitman, 1938.

Index